The Courier-Journal
The Louisville Times

Hunting & Fishing in Kentucky

by Earl Ruby

Hunting & Fishing in Kentucky

by Earl Ruby

This book is dedicated most sincerely to all of the gracious landowners who have allowed good sportsmen to hunt and fish on their property.

Author
Earl Ruby

Book Design
Eilers/Hewett, Louisville, Kentucky
Steve Eilers and Ainslie Hewett

Illustrator
Derek Grinnell

Library of Congress Catalog Number: 78-69674

Book Printer
Pinaire Lithographing Corporation
Louisville, Kentucky

First Printing
November, 1978

Contents

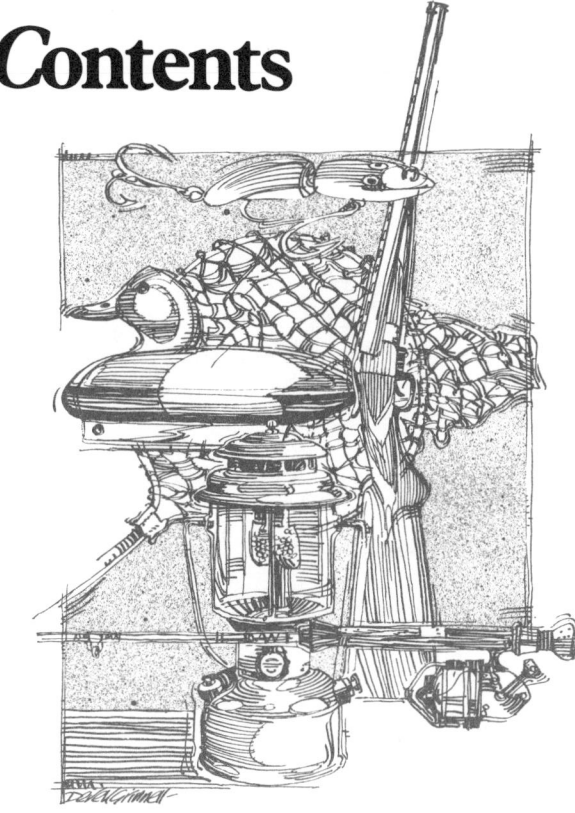

Introduction

Nowhere in all the country is there an enchanted place that has the lush green fields, cool virgin forests, and crystal clear water with which Kentucky is blessed. It is a land where more than a million sportsmen can find the rewarding pleasure of hunting in nearby fields and good fishing as close as the next pond. Kentucky—a land so abundantly gifted with so many forms of wildlife that Indians appropriately called it their Happy Hunting Grounds.

From the bottomlands of Ballard County through the plains of the Pennyrile and the Bluegrass to the mountains of Daniel Boone National Forest and the folding hills beyond, good hunting and fishing attract sportsmen from many states. Yet very little has been written to help the nimrod and the angler enjoy these bounties. That is one reason for this book.

The haunting call of the mourning dove lures countless camouflaged hunters to the field, yet the little gray streak continues to blaze across Kentucky's skies. It may not be the smartest bird in the world, but its crazy antics when under fire make the dove one of the most difficult of all game targets and the favorite of thousands. During the early fall days when corn, soybeans, sorghum, wheat and millet ripen, doves zoom in by the thousands to the small grain belt of Southern and Southwestern Kentucky, where hunts by more than 50 men and women are not uncommon.

The ruffed grouse, so impressive with its faintly barred brown and white breast and fan tail, is a majestic creation found mostly in the mountains of Eastern Kentucky. But hunters occasionally encounter it as far west as Mammoth Cave, and to do so is a great thrill. This feathered bolt of lightning for generations has fired the imagination and admiration of countless mountain marksmen for its perfection in camouflage and maneuverability.

The bobwhite quail, lends its kingly presence to any area where small grain, water and a bit of cover permit. Despite an ever-spreading urbanization, the little fellow—hardly nine inches in length from tip of tail to tip of beak—has managed to thrive in most localities, especially in Southwestern Kentucky.

The wild turkey is, of course, Kentucky's largest game bird and its least plentiful. Founding fathers enjoyed this regal bird in abundance. Sadly, it was all but wiped out. Now, thanks to a continuing scientific restocking program, this bird with the polished bronze sheen, small head, and powerful legs and wings is hunted in selected areas of far Western and Eastern Kentucky counties.

The whitetail deer is another native that almost disappeared, only to return strongly through persistent restocking. Because the whitetail loves brushy, wooded country uncluttered with people, it has thrived best on expansive military reservations, the Land Between the Lakes, and in Mammoth Cave National Park (off limits) and Daniel Boone National Forest.

While not overly blessed with waterfowl, Kentucky is slowly building large concentrations of ducks and geese in and near Ballard County in the far western portion of the state and in the sloughs around Henderson. A high number of popular mallard ducks and Canada geese can be found in the state, and with them such favorites as the canvasback, wood duck, redhead, ring-neck, goldeneye, ruddy duck, bufflehead and hooded merganser.

But the wildlife on Kentucky's surface should not cloud the fact that the state's waters are filled with aquatic life. The 15 major lakes, a large number of state-owned impoundments, and more fishable streams than any other state except Alaska provide anglers with virtually every type of action.

Black bass abound in all of the state's lakes and in most ponds and streams. The world record smallmouth came out of Dale Hollow Lake, and near-record croppie (Kentucky spelling for the slabs usually known elsewhere as crappie), monster muskellunge, rockfish and catfish are taken every month of the year.

A put-and-take program of stocking rainbow trout has brought an interesting new sport to youngsters as well as to fly rod enthusiasts. And stocking of rockfish has been so very successful that many fish weighing 30 pounds and up have been taken from Lake Herrington, Lake Barkley and Lake Cumberland.

No matter where a person travels within Kentucky's borders, he or she will find good fishing, good hunting, pleasant surroundings and affable companions—just the perfect ingredients to make it a hunter's and fisherman's paradise.

I don't profess to be an expert in all fields, or any field, for that matter. But in these pages I try to present the best possible means of taking fish and wildlife within our border, much of it gleaned from the experiences of other Kentucky and Hoosier hunters.

Earl Ruby

Hunting *in* Kentucky

Quail

The Bobwhite quail gets it's name from the male bird (above) which utters the cry of "bob-bob-white" through nesting seasons and early on bright mornings, in quail season.

There was a time before urban expansion when the bobwhite quail was plentiful and the most popular bird hunted in Kentucky. The dove since has moved in front in terms of annual kill, but there are still thousands of Kentuckians who wouldn't trade one hour spent in quest of quail for a lifetime of sniping at doves. Most of these fellows hunt the small grain belt of Southern Kentucky from Scottsville west past Hopkinsville, but plump bobwhites are also found in lesser numbers throughout the rest of the state's areas of truck farming. Kentuckians love quail hunting for reasons too numerous to mention but primarily for the sporting targets, the companionship of good dogs, and the supreme table fare.

The quail is called a bobwhite because of its distinctive call that makes that sound. You usually find quail in open fields where small grain and weed seeds are plentiful yet close enough to woods and fencerows where they may find safety when hunted.

Most of Kentucky's quail are found on private property. You'll discover that Kentucky farmers generally will give you permission to hunt if you are considerate enough to ask and have a good track record. When you are allowed to hunt, remember that you have been entrusted to not disturb farm animals, not leave gates open, and not damage fences or any other property. Although farms producing regular crops offer the best quail hunting, there are numerous public hunting areas where quail can be found. The limit on this bird may change, so always check with Fish and Wildlife authorities before the season opens.

In warmer weather, quail feed early and late and rest during the middle of the day. But on very cold and blustery days they usually sit tight under honeysuckle and in woods, venturing out late in the day and feeding until dusk. Don't bother to hunt in the rain. You may not mind being soaked to the bone, but you won't see any birds.

Quail usually will be in the same place day after day and even year after year. An experienced hunter might have from one to a dozen coveys spotted before the hunting season opens on the third Thursday in November.

Because the quail's beige, white and buff color helps the bird to conceal itself in fields and brush, a bird dog is necessary to locate the coveys by scent. A good bird dog not only will point the coveys but also will retrieve dead birds. A downed quail is almost impossible to find, even in light cover, without the help of a good retriever.

When your dog flushes a covey of quail, don't let yourself be shocked into a premature shot by the noise of the wings. Quail are not fast fliers, and you'll have time to shoot twice before the birds are out of range.

Quail may be hunted successfully with any shotgun from a .410 to a 12-gauge. Before you select a heavy gun, remember that you'll be doing a lot of walking and that your gun will get heavier before the hunt is over. Best shot sizes are No. 8 and No. 9, with No. 7 ½ held for late season hunting. I like a skeet barrel for quail and doves alike. For the hunter with only one gun, I recommend a variable choke attachment.

Hunting for quail can be hazardous, as all hands in the party circle around the dogs on point and all guns explode almost as quickly as the birds flush. I like the admonition Dick Watkins of Leitchfield gave several of us before starting into a field near his home one year. "I have three rules to go by," he said. "Don't drink, don't shoot my dogs, and" — he paused and laughed — "don't shoot me!"

Watkins and his two excellent bird dogs — one called Old Sue was especially active — joined former Gov. Bert Combs and Bob Patterson, two Louisville sportsmen, and me for a hunt one November day. Our day got off to a shaky start when, at Patterson's insistence, we awoke at 5 a.m. so that we would be at our rendezvous in Grayson County at 7:30 a.m. There was only one problem: He had forgotten the difference in time zones (Kentucky is divided). We had to wait an hour before it was light enough to shoot.

After we finally got into the field, we quickly discovered that the two inches of snow that hung on the field of corn stubs and alfalfa sprigs was going to be a problem. A light snow usually forces quail to come out and feed, but the cold night had held this snow and it was too heavy. The birds hadn't moved from their roosts. In characteristic circular formation with heads out and bodies pressed close together, any where from six to 30 birds covey up together for mutual protection and warmth. On cold wet mornings they peck the snow and wait for the sun to make the world more comfortable before spreading out and creating a scent the dogs can pick up.

Twice the dogs ran through large coveys and scattered them in all directions without getting scents. We picked up a few singles but never saw a covey hold until midmorning. Combs was walking into the edge of the woods when he came to a sudden halt and cried, "Hey! Here are some birds!" The dogs were working a considerable distance away. We all walked up, thinking he had spotted a single.

"Walk on in," he said. "This is a covey!" Sure enough, as we moved quietly toward him, we could see the birds in a circle in a dry area under an evergreen. When we were all set, Combs stamped a foot, and the birds exploded in all directions. The dogs were still running around like crazy while we were retrieving dead quail.

Although on that hunt we were at the field a little too early, usually on opening day you can't afford to be late. Like the time in November 1970 when I went back to Grayson County to hunt with Bill Vincent, Wales Montgomery and Patterson. We had a marvelous hunt; we saw more than 100 quail. But we made one big mistake: We tarried too long over breakfast, an opening day ritual. Two groups of hunters had been in our fields first and scattered the birds. Vincent and Montgomery managed to get their limits, in spite of this.

That hunt was probably the most convenient one I ever went on. All we did was walk out Vincent's back door, untie three of his dogs, and start hunting. "There's one big covey just down this hollow," Vincent said. Well, sir, we hadn't gone 150 yards when the dogs came on point. A covey of about 15 birds flushed, and we managed to get three of them.

"There's a bigger covey down this hill," Vincent said. We were headed in that direction when we heard so many shots fired it sounded for a moment as if we were in Ft. Knox on the opening day of the deer season. "Well, there goes that one," said Vincent. "Let's cut down to the left where I know there's another." From then on we were in birds, mostly singles, most of the morning. Unfortunately most of the birds flushed in rough timber, and we couldn't get clear shots.

There was a time, before the early 1960s and the growth of suburban Louisville, when there was good quail hunting close to my home in eastern Jefferson County. Over a period of time I charted at least 40 coveys in the vicinity.

One memorable hunt was with former Gov. Lawrence Wetherby of Frankfort and Joe Stamper. We beat the bunny hunters into the field less than a mile from Stamper's Anchorage home. It wasn't much past daylight when we arrived. I broke the ice in an old heel print. The sky was clear. A light wind was blowing. And not another hunter in sight. The perfect conditions for quail hunting.

In spite of the fact that we were within 100 feet of residential property when we let the dogs out, we were in deep cover almost immediately. We climbed two fences and were in a stubble field where Stamper had spotted a covey the week before. The

Lawrence Wetherby, former governor, holds a limit of quail. Joe Stamper of Middletown, holds his setter.

dogs found nothing. "It's too early," said Wetherby. "The birds haven't moved yet."

About then he discovered a circle of droppings at the far end of the field. "Hey," he cried. "Here's a fresh roost! They've moved out." One of the dogs wriggled through the fence and raced across an alfalfa field.

"Call him back," I said. "No birds would be in alfalfa this early." Just as I finished, the setter froze on point, and we all scrambled over the fence behind the dogs.

We walked a half circle to keep the early sun out of our eyes, but we saw no birds. The dogs started circling. Suddenly quail flew up all around us. From then on it was a matter of hunting singles and exploring new fields. There were more relaxing places to hunt than in Jefferson County in those days, but on that early outing we all managed to bag our limits.

On opening day a hunter usually must choose between quail and rabbits, as both seasons open the same day. Most bird dog owners would rather disown a pup than have it point a rabbit, much less pick one up. Any guest who would shoot a rabbit anywhere near a dog would be strung up in the nearest tree. And that makes Jerry and Frank Ikerd, William Marcum and Dr. Robert McLeod, all of Somerset, different.

Bert Combs and I hunted birds with them on their farms near Somerset one opening day. Several rabbits jumped up in front of us, but neither Combs nor I fired. "If you want a rabbit or two, go ahead and shoot," said Frank Ikerd. "It won't bother these dogs a bit."

So, about midmorning when a bunny jumped up almost at my feet, I shot it as it disappeared in the brush. Clipper, one of Marcum's setters, immediately dashed into the brush, found the rabbit, brought it to me, then went back to scenting birds with the others. Quite unusual, as any hunter will tell you.

Clipper is unusual in another way. It is the only dog I ever knew that couldn't swim. Marcum thinks it's because the dog carries a few bird shot in one hind leg; yet somehow it can run with the best of the other dogs. One day Clipper gallantly jumped into a lake to retrieve a quail. It got the bird in its mouth, then floundered. Frank Ikerd quickly jumped into the water and rescued the dog. No wonder Marcum grabs Clipper's collar and lets another dog retrieve whenever a dead bird falls into a lake.

During part of that morning I hunted with McLeod, and that was a mistake. The doctor from Somerset, who once pitched for Connie Mack's Athletics when in college, has stayed in perfect physical shape and can outwalk and outwork even the dogs. Also in our group were Bill Curlin, Dick Barbour and Buddy Combs, all of Frankfort. Curlin and Barbour moved up on a pointing dog during the afternoon, fired simultaneously, and were surprised to see that the bird wasn't a quail but a king-sized pheasant, one that remained from some the Ikerds had stocked the previous year.

We were a long time finding the birds. After two fruitless walks we climbed into a truck to go to another field, and from then on we were in birds most of the day. We flushed 10 coveys, but unfortunately all of them were in the woods. About 4 p.m. the birds began moving out to feed again, but darkness fell like a blanket as the sun set, and we gravitated homeward. As we walked back we could hear the bobwhites whistling all around us, going about their task of coveying up before dark.

The area over which we hunted near Somerset was reclaimed strip-mined land, now overgrown in lush quail and rabbit food. At the other end of the state, in Western Kentucky, an increase of at least 5,000 acres of good wildlife habitat is the ambitious goal of a cooperative effort spearheaded by the Department of Fish and Wildlife Resources and the Kentucky Reclamation Association, a nonprofit conservation service organization for coal and other mineral producers. All of the acres will be land reclaimed from mining. The purchase of the 5,000 acres by the Department of Fish and Wildlife was finalized in 1978.

A pilot reclamation project also got underway in Ohio County. It consists of a watershed of 95 acres around a seven-acre lake, which forms the focal point for the wildlife habitat planning. Food plots and cover lanes lead to and from the water. The seven plots and lanes have been seeded in buckwheat, lespedeza, millet, ragweed, sorghum, sunflowers and such. Lining each lane are rows of such woody plants as autumn olive, bicolor lespedeza, crab apple, elderberry, honeysuckle, silky dogwood, sumac and wild plum. The rest of the land will be planted on conforming ground cover. All of this reclaimed land holds the possibility of providing even more excellent quail hunting in Western Kentucky.

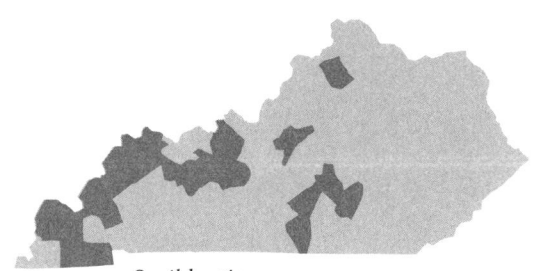

Quail hunting areas

A perfect point brings Peck Walker and Earl Gordon of Lawrenceburg up to a covey.

Dove

the mourning dove is a bird for the good shooters, up to five shells may be fired sometimes to bag one bird.

while an abundant gamebird in kentucky some states protect the mourning dove as a "songbird."

One of the most challenging targets on the Kentucky hunting calendar is the dove. By far the nation's No. 1 game bird, the dove is faster than the grouse or the quail.

If you can hit doves consistently, you can bag any other bird. But being a good quail shot doesn't mean you can do equally well with doves. With its long, trim wings and spear-like tail, the dove is the most streamlined of all game birds. It cruises at about 40 miles an hour and can accelerate to speeds of 60 miles per hour. Coupled with its terrific speed is the dove's ability to change its direction within the blink of an eye when peppered with shot or when spooked. Because of this erratic flight, a second shot often is difficult, if not impossible.

The mourning dove with its sad voice is the species of dove found in Kentucky. It is dusty gray with a pinkish throat and has two white feathers on either side of the tail. The smallest of all game birds, a dressed dove will average only about three ounces.

Of all wing-shooting, the dove permits the hunter the greatest comfort. You can carry a stool and just sit in the shade and fire away, with a cooler of soft drinks on one side and your shell case on the other. You should wear drab or camouflage clothing, however, and have plenty of shells handy. Anything from 7 ½ to 9, skeet, field, or express loads will do. And you can use any kind of gun from .410 to a 12-gauge, preferably with a skeet barrel. If you average one dove every six shells, you'll have a lot of company.

Best shooting usually is found over milo, foxtail, millet, wheat and cut silage. Doves also will congregate in hogged-down corn and in newly plowed areas. In Kentucky you can expect good hunting during the first few days of the season wherever truck farming is done. But the biggest and most successful hunts are found in the small-grain belt of southern Kentucky. More about that later.

The season usually opens in Kentucky on Sept. 1. During the first week, when cut silage fields are small and scattered, you're likely to find doves swarming all over them. As the season progresses, and cut fields become more numerous, the birds begin to scatter and grow wary. They begin coming in high and circling to spot trouble before drifting down to feed. This is what they were doing during one hunt I was on near Frankfort not long ago.

I sat on a camp stool under a lean pin oak on a hillside slanting away from the field. Just down the hill was a dense grove of trees and brush. Former Gov. Lawrence Wetherby of Frankfort, known to the bunch as "Guv'mint," was under a tree to my right, also facing downhill. Beyond him and around the field was Shelby Kincaid of Lexington, Wetherby's son, Larry, and his 5-year-old grandson, Christopher, whose nickname is Pasquale. The excited little fellow, outfitted in a camouflage suit made by his mother, gleefully ran to retrieve his father's downed doves. Our group was small for a dove hunt. The field of millet wasn't much bigger than a building lot, and we had it covered.

The birds came in over the trees going like the wind, circled, and came back lower. Occasionally one put on the brakes as if to light in a nearby tree, but for the most part they came high and fast. Being so few in number and closely bunched, the hunters kept up a running banter for two hours or more.

Near the end of the shoot Wetherby downed a dove that fell about 25 yards in front of him. "I'll get it," cried the boy, running through grass almost as tall as he was.

It's a little to your left, Pasquale," said Wetherby. "Right there."

The boy reached down, picked up the bird, and took a long look at it. Then he yelled at the top of his voice, after the fashion of the bantering: "Granddad, you bust hell out of this one!" A great end to a pleasant dove hunt.

Less than 20 years ago, Kentucky hunters were limited to eight doves a day during a short season. Fifteen years ago the limit was raised to 10 and the season extended as an experiment. To the surprise of virtually everybody, the dove population continued to increase. Well, if the limit of 10 wasn't denting the supply, why not try 12? And so the federal biologists raised the limit to a dozen. Amazingly, the birds continued to thrive and multiply.

The biologists studied their records, examined the remains of killed birds, and made counts in areas where no hunting was allowed. They came to the conclusion that the number of doves still was increasing and that 77 percent of the young doves died from disease and other factors even when not hunted. So in 1970 they raised the daily bag limit to 18 as an experiment in the Eastern Management Unit, which includes Kentucky. The trial lasted only two years, and the limit was reduced to 12.

It is amazing how quickly doves grow to maturity. Most of the birds killed any year in Kentucky were hatched that summer. Most of the birds I've downed were less than two years old. The average longevity of a dove is less than 12 months.

On one September hunt in Hardin County I sat on my stool comfortably cool under a large tree and moved out just long enough to get my shots. While sitting there I "aged" the birds I had downed. Two had been hatched just one month earlier, nine came in July, and one appeared to be a survivor from the previous year.

You can easily tell the age of your doves if you follow a few simple guidelines laid down by the three leading biologists and explained by Dan Russell in his book, *The Dove Shooter's Handbook*. Count off the first 10 large wing feathers from the tip back. These are the primaries. The doves molt these feathers from the 10th up to the top, in that order. Beginning when the dove is 35 days old,

these primaries are replaced one at a time every 10 days. In about five months the doves will have completed this juvenile molt and will be considered an adult.

To determine your young dove's age, see which one of the 10 feathers was the last primary to molt, then count back. You can tell the newly molted feathers by their silky appearance. Frequently the newest will be shorter than the others, not having fully grown.

If you downed a fully molted dove, you can tell whether it was hatched that year or the previous one by examining the condition of the primaries. If they are new and shiny, the bird is a hatch of that year. If they show signs of wear, it probably is a holdover.

I was with a group of sharpshooters on that trip to Hardin County. The field was small, and we had just enough hunters to keep the birds circling. At one end of the field were Frank Phipps, a Frankfort sportsman who can outshoot almost everybody, and Jerry Simcoe, now living in Hardin County.

I was halfway down a row of trees bordering the field. On one side of me was Richard Simcoe of Louisville. Below me were Pap Glenn of Louisville and Sam Garnett of Danville. Garnett, a former wildlife commissioner, had his grandson, James Edward Garnett, along to retrieve for him. At the upper end of the field was Wetherby, Ed Rogers of Frankfort and Joe Stamper of Middletown. Dennis Nall of Elizabethtown took a stand on a hillside behind the trees. The birds were a bit late flying, but once they started they came in bunches, flying high over the trees. This meant that most of us had a lot of difficult shots, but we all got our limits. Oddly all of mine were holdovers.

Some of the most enjoyable hunts I've ever had were around Franklin in the 1960s and early 1970s because of the gracious hospitality extended by J. M. "Blick" Smith, one of the best sportsmen I have ever known, and former president of the League of Kentucky Sportsmen; Redmon Payne, former league secretary, Owen Mullins, and Noble Lanier. Smith and his friends spent the entire week before the opening scouting Simpson and Logan counties for farms where silage was being cut. They asked for permission to bring vistors to hunt and, in at least one case, paid a farmer $50 for the privilege.

After the opening day's hunt under a blazing sun, 40 to 50 blistered visitors were invited to the cooling shade of the sportsmen's club grounds and were served a barbecued pig with all the trimmings and plenty of cold suds and soft drinks. Some of the visitors, such as Judge Lester Mullins of Williamstown, were extended the privilege of pitching camp on the club grounds. Others were put up at home by Smith, Payne and others.

On one opening day I drove to Smith's house, and the yard was crowded with so many fellows in camouflage suits it looked like a convention of creatures from another planet. Smith had located a 25-acre field where silage had been cut. We decided to try it first, and if the birds didn't come we'd look elsewhere. The truth is, however, that if you don't find doves in a cut-silage field, you might as well give up until farmers begin cutting milo.

We reached our field about a half-hour after legal hunting had begun. With me were Smith, Bob Wilson, Howell Patton, Buck Newbold and Henry Bogan, all of Franklin. Al Bridges, a state trooper, was under a telephone pole in the center of the field having a field day with doves headed for the wires. Tom Norwood, also of Franklin, had taken up a station farther along the wires at the end of uncut corn. Others from nearby, including J.B. Dobbs, T.C. Willis and James Clouse, were up at the far end, also near uncut corn.

We scattered through the center of the field and waited. The wait wasn't long. Wilson killed five doves on his first five shots; I didn't get a feather on my first five. The wind was so high it seemed to make the birds fly faster, but that was just my excuse. I had opening-day jitters. Four of the hunters limited out with 12 each before I had two doves. I moved over to where the successful Norwood had been. It seemed the doves slowed along there because of the wires. It was either my imagination or I had shaken the buck fever, but the birds began to drop.

Smith had a voice that carried three counties and let every hunter around the 25-acre field know each time a dove was coming even remotely near him. He yelled at me so loudly a couple of times I fell off my stool trying to turn around quickly. That scared the oncoming doves into banking at right angles and out of range. They weren't any more shaken that I was, however.

Our group hadn't been in the field more than half an hour before most of the earlier arrivals had left with their limits. We moved to the better spots, but the reduction in the number of hunters allowed many birds to settle without interference into patches on the field. Smith and Wilson put their kills and guns down and did a bit of "bird dogging," or retrieving, for the rest of us. By 3 p.m., all of us were ready to go. I still needed one bird to complete the day and got plenty of help and advice. "There goes one!" "Hey, what's a'matter with that one?" "Get him before he flies over the corn!" But it was a beautiful, cool, sunny afternoon; I hated to have it end. Finally a dove came floating over so invitingly I had to call it a day.

On another memorable opening day, this one in the early 1970s, I should have known something unusual would happen when Smith said we were going to hunt at Schochoh. When Smith told the hunters where we were going, Buck Newbold said, "You mean Chocktaw?"

"No, he means 'Shock-oh,' " said Redmon. "That's a historic place. Andrew Jackson fought a duel down that way once. That's the heart of the Red River Valley on the Tennessee border."

"All I know is it's right near the field were we're going," said Smith. "Now you fellows follow me so nobody gets lost."

We left Simpson County and entered neighboring Logan. After a long stretch of narrow, winding roads, we turned onto a gravel road and flushed more than 50 doves that had been graveling. A few hundred yards farther, we flushed some more. "What did I tell you," Smith cried. "Doves are thicker here than flies on a wet mule."

The long, slim, newly cut silage field had considerable grain left. It was flanked on two sides by ripe milo, and more than 100 doves got up as we arrived. We scattered eagerly to points along the milo on both sides on the field. The time was 12:45 p.m. Shooting started before most of us had our places. A light rain started falling as I took my stand. I had fired only twice when T.C. Willis of Franklin walked by. "I've got my limit," he said. "Go take my place. It's red hot." I moved and had fired only twice more when Edgar Paul of Louisville killed his 12th bird. His two shaggy retrievers were so worn out from chasing everybody's kills that he had to get that last bird himself. We all had our limits in less than three hours.

In the 1971 season, William T. Roark, president of the Franklin Rotary Club, opened his large Simpson County farm to controlled hunts for the benefit of the Rotary Club scholarship fund. Hunters came from many surrounding counties,

John Claypool of Lebanon takes aim with his antique 42-inch muzzleloader, and his aim is true.

You know it was a bad day for Pap Glenn, the old Male High athletic director. The rain just wouldn't quit.

Sam Garnett of Danville eyes a dove.

Miss Bonnie Babcock was on her first dove hunt when she went with the boys in 1964.

Richard McQuillan of Louisville, picks up a dove. George Grayer of Albany holds three he has bagged as Crissy McQuillan looks on.

paid $5 each into the scholarship kitty, and enjoyed Roark's hospitality. Roark's plan has been tried in other parts of the state with some success.

William J. Daniels, who had come all the way from Paintsville for the hunt, got to his stand at noon—the minute the season opened—and limited out at 3:30 p.m. Barry Bingham Jr. of Louisville, J. B. Dobbs and Newbold of Franklin, and I got our 18 (the limit that year) with only minutes remaining until sundown. Most of the other 60 or more hunters averaged between eight and 12. Had the limit of one dozen prevailed, the hunters in the best spots would have moved out early and given the others a chance, and probably all would have gone home with a better average. The 18-bird limit made for unequal distribution of the kill.

Probably the craziest kill of all time was made by Blick Smith. Dr. R. J. Vermillion of Franklin took a shot at a high flier, and the injured dove made one of those crazy dives toward the ground. It then leveled out and flew about four feet off the ground directly toward the corn row where Smith was camouflaged as a scarecrow. Smith had no time to draw his gun. Being an old baseball player, he swung his gun like Babe Ruth swung his bat and caught the bird head-on. It fell dead at his feet. And true to baseball tradition, Smith whooped and hollered like a Yankee fan following a home-run swat. If he had missed the dove it doubtless would have died far back in the corn.

I generally use a skeet barrel, but on one hunt near Lexington with John Farra of Lexington, it wasn't enough. The birds were coming over high on a strong wind. I was lucky to get four. Farra, stationed under a small oak, did a masterful job of picking off a limit. The ideal gun for doves, Farra thinks, is a double with one barrel full choke. His reasoning is that near water holes you get many shots of less than 30 yards, but some pass shooting calls for shots up to 50 yards, which is true. I simply don't try for long ones.

Kentucky opened one of its most unusual dove seasons in 1970 with unprecedented waves of doves zeroing in on stamp-sized fields of cut silage, millet, wheat, milo and corn. Virtually every first-day hunter who could hit a barn door at 20 paces bagged near his limit of 18 birds between noon and sunset.

The corn blight that year caused early silage cutting on a farm about eight miles from Muldraugh. I got there about 2 p.m. with Maj. Gen.

Richard V. Irby, commanding general at Ft. Knox at the time; Fred Bramblett, a retired Army man who at the time was manager of the Ft. Knox Rod and Gun Club, and eight others. The 30-acre field was too big for our group to hunt properly, but a light early rain caused the doves to feed late near a large pond. We were able to converge on one end of the stubble field and get more than our share of exciting shooting as the birds came in like dive bombers over a blight-ravaged cornfield.

Irby and I stood talking under some sycamore trees when we first got there, and no birds were flying. Suddenly two doves quietly passed overhead. The general banged at one and I at the other. His kept right on flying; mine dropped dead. "Wow!" I thought. "I outshot a general!" A short time later we walked out to the end of a large cornfield. Two more doves came like jets directly toward us. I raised my gun, but before I could swing into position the general fired twice and both birds fell at our feet.

"Great shots!" I said. "That's a beautiful double-barrel gun you've got there. What is it?"

He smiled. "It's a little 20-gauge I gave my wife a long time ago. She didn't like it. I use it for doves because it's so light and you don't need much of a charge to kill a dove".

Near the end of the hunt, about an hour before sundown, the general had a stand at the corner of the cornfield. A wave of doves barreled in, and he hit three in succession for his limit. He placed them in a nylon net game bag on his back and headed out. A game bag like that lets air get to the game and no doubt keeps it in much better condition than a canvas bag, or a brown paper bag so many Kentuckians use.

The envy of the crowd was Col. Charles Krampitz. He brought a beautiful black Labrador with him. While the rest of us tramped endlessly up and down corn rows looking for dead birds, this four-legged fellow pounced on the colonel's birds almost before they touched the ground.

Ret. Col. D. L. Cool probably did less moving and scored a higher rate of kill than anybody. He clocked maybe 100 feet of walking, used less than one box of shells, and had his limit while some of the rest of us were still scrambling. As our group prepared to leave, I plucked most of my doves. A dove is easy to clean in the field while it is warm and that sure saves a lot of fuss and feathers at home.

Two years ago I passed up the certainty of a quick limit in Southern Kentucky to try an area not usually considered great for dove hunting—Jefferson and Shelby counties. While 60 or more hunters are needed to keep birds flying over very large cut silage fields in Southern Kentucky, only 12 or so are needed, or wanted, at the much smaller fields in the Louisville area.

Our group met at the Middletown home of Joe Stamper and took off in a caravan to a field he had gained permission for us to hunt. In the parade were Ed Seabolt, Carroll Burchett, Bud Waits, Bobby Hayden, Pap Glenn and Jim Claiborne, all of Jefferson County, and Sam Garnett of Danville. We turned off the road after a long drive and pulled into the shadow of a barn to hide the cars from the birds as much as possible. The L-shaped field had been sowed in millet, and it wasn't long before everybody was getting action. There proved to be just enough birds to allow us all to limit out minutes before quitting time.

One day I was fortunate enough to be counted in on a typical Kentucky opening-day party at Dr. Charles Caldwell's farm near Danville. For me Danville has so many pleasant memories—Old Centre, Norris Armstrong, Ben Cregor, Rice Mountjoy, Sterling Towles, fishing at Lake Herrington—and after that hunt, I could add dove hunting to the list.

There were 34 of us, almost all from Danville and the surrounding area. Our rallying point was a newly cut cornfield along the ancient Wilderness Trail. The field was big enough to absorb us at about 30-yard intervals. We got located comfortably at 3 p.m., and the firing began immediately along a line of trees uphill from me. My station along an adjoining field of uncut corn was poor. I hadn't had a shot when one of the boys on the hill moved, and I took his place. In less than an hour most of the hot guns had their limits, and a number of hunters walked jauntily back to their cars. The tailgates came down, refreshments appeared, and the stragglers were razzed by the early finishers.

Sam Garnett, city manager of Danville, was among the first in, along with Judge Henry Pennington, former president of the League of Kentucky Sportsmen, who had his two young sons to retrieve for him. Also finishing early were Joe Stamper, Perry Hall, Marshall Ishom, Van Woodrow, Leonard Eubank, W. C. McConnell, Jim Begley, Dean Rice, Tom Ross and Oliver Payne.

Then came Sammy Hays Jr., Sam Hays III, J. M. Frank, James Lee Murphy Jr., Judge Darren Peckler, David Gonder, Bill Irvin, Scott Duncan, Gene Harmon, Harold Martin, W. J. Hoskins Jr., John King, Pat McDonald, Manley McBeath, Julian Hardaway and Nelson Rhodes, all of Boyle County and nearby. All of us had to move several times to vacated hot spots before we could take our limits.

Mountjoy is a favorite with everybody in and near Danville. The Danville Board of Education named the Danville School stadium after the former football coach. "I got confused," said Mountjoy about his shooting. "Most every time I drew down on what I thought was a dove, it turned out to be one of those monarch butterflies."

"Funny thing about this cornfield and doves," said Begley. "There's plenty of corn spilled by the picker, and doves kept coming in to it, yet every bird I killed has a craw full of ragweed seeds." I was plucking my doves downwind from the tailgaters. There wasn't more than one kernel of corn in any craw, but plenty of ragweed seed. Cutting the corn exposed the low-growing weeds and that apparently had drawn the birds.

One of the most avid dove hunters I know is Mrs. Doris Claiborne of Louisville. No one is more eager for opening day than she is, except maybe her English setter, Pepper. She hunted near me one day and missed her limit by only two birds, the wide-ranging Pepper, trembling with excitement, retrieved two limits downed by others. Mrs. Claiborne spent a part of her afternoon returning birds to their rightful owners.

Mrs. Claiborne and her husband, Jim, were among the first to arrive at a Shelby County farm for that hunt. They settled down in the shade of a tree to await action. But not Pepper. He did two quick laps around the field just to be sure there were no birds lurking in the stubble. The day was very hot, and the birds came in late. It was more than an hour before a lone dove crossed one end of the field. Ray Holton, a major league baseball scout from Jeffersonville, Ind., knocked it out, and Pepper raced over and took it to Mrs. Claiborne. The Claibornes couldn't seem to get in the right spot at the right time and shifted positions several times. But jubilant Pepper continued to bring them doves.

"If we had shot every bird Pepper brought us, we would have limited out ahead of everybody," Mrs. Claiborne said, laughing. Mrs. Claiborne comes

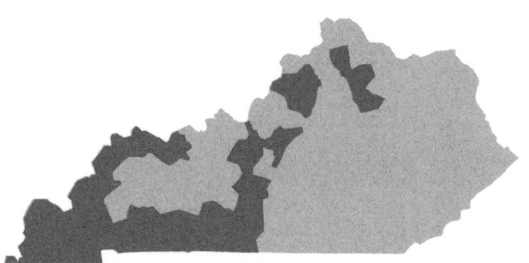

Dove hunting areas

Dove hunters Wes Strader, left, and Chuck
Shuffett with their Brittanies Buffy and
Chad

from a long line of sports enthusiasts and has kept
in shooting form by skeet shooting with her husband
and son, Hobson. In the old days she and her
brothers used a hand-thrower and clay targets in a
field on the old homestead. Her dove hunting dates
back 20 or more years to the days of the Cave Dove
Shooters, who gathered annually on opening day on
a Simcoe Lane farm owned by Bert Finzer. Bert
provided refreshments and food for some 60
hunters.

Locating a large shoot isn't difficult, if you are a
careful hunter and know who to ask. Melvin Tabb
of Russellville has helped many a friend obtain
permission to hunt. On one typical bright day he
took a few of his friends to shoot a 58-acre field in
Logan County. I was to meet Al Blum of Murray
near the site, but our signals got crossed and we
went to the wrong field. We didn't see a bird but did
hear a tremendous amount of gunfire not too far
away. Following the noise, we traveled about a mile,
turned down a lane, and finally came upon the
action. We unpacked and walked toward the racket,
which by now was deafening. The first person we
saw was Blum. "I forgot to tell you guys where the
hunt was," he said, laughing, "but I knew you'd
follow your ears. How come it took you so long?"

Just then Joe Taylor, wildlife officer from
Auburn, crawled through a wire fence and asked for
licenses. After we had shown our bits of yellow
paper, Blum handed the officer an old, well-worn
badge. "Guess you never saw a hunting license like
that before," he said.

"Never," said Taylor. What's more, he'll never
see another one. It was a lifetime hunting license
given to Blum by the Jefferson County Sportsmen's
Club in 1941, one of the years he led that
group. It was the first and only such license issued
and cost $50.

Many hunters often ask if doves fly and feed
when it's raining. Well, I'll tell you. Several years
ago a light drizzle became a steady rain as a bunch
of us splashed and slid up a steep gravel and mud
road to an elevated field of millet in Oldham
County. We saw no birds when we arrived. I put on
a rain suit, pulled my cap down as far as possible,
and carried my sitting bucket, a five-gallon,
driveway sealer can in which I carried shells and
snacks, to a small tree halfway down the edge of the
field. Sam Garnett was along again, and he took a
spot off to my right and blended into the scenery
with his camouflage suit covered with a transparent

rain coat. But still no doves.

Pap Glenn of Louisville, Gene Holmes of
Middletown, George Davis of Danville, Bud Waits
of Eastwood, Eddie Seabolt, Ralph Tingle of
Middletown and Buzz Caye of Pewee Valley, and
Floyd Gullett of Oldham County found spots
affording a bit of cover around the field. Ray
Holton, followed by his pointer, took a position near
a dead tree over a fence from the rest of us. Nearby
was the sorriest sight in the world—Bob Hayden of
Middletown, who had forgotten to bring his rain
gear. Everybody was miserable, but Bob was
pathetic.

But after about an hour the doves started coming
in. They arrived in batches of up to six and eight,
some too high to try for, some too low for a safe
shot, causing Joe Stamper, in the line of flight, to
yell, "Low bird! Low bird!" Holton and Stamper,
whose dogs keep them from losing time by
looking for downed birds, limited out in no more
than an hour. Davis and Hayden, who moved into
Holton's spot, straggled in next, followed gradually
by the others. I finally grew tired of the rain fogging
my glasses and walked in with less than my limit.
We all left the field by 4 p.m., more than three
hours before the legal quitting time of a half-hour
before sundown.

Yes, doves do feed in the rain. But it's no fun to
hunt them then.

A word or two on how, when and where: Never
go dove hunting in pairs, threes, or fours, as you
would in quail hunting. You need several guns
surrounding a field to keep the doves from lighting
as they come to feed.

You will find your best shooting near a dead tree
at the edge of a field, usually along a row of trees
bordering the field, or sometimes right in the center
of the field if it is large enough to make such a stand
safe and you are wearing camouflage clothing.

While you usually get a free swinging shot first,
your second shot can be unbelievable. You've never
seen a kite do more dips and turns than a scared
dove. Keep your gun on the bird and hope it doesn't
dip too low for a safe second shot.

Almost all good dove hunts are on private land. In
Kentucky the best hunting, as I said, is in the small-
grain belt that stretches from Scottsville west
through Barren, Warren, Logan, Todd, Christian
and Trigg counties. There are also several state-
owned hunting areas that occasionally offer one or
two good dove hunts a year.

Turkey

wild turkey

The wild turkey's sharp eyesion and ears make it virtually impossible to sneak upon.

the gobbler's mating plumage.

The wild turkey has gained its reputation as a prize catch not only because of its regal bearing but also because taking a turkey requires more hunting ability than accurate shooting skill.

The turkey is the biggest, wildest, smartest and most succulent game bird in the world. The majestic gobbler has a blue head, sometimes accented with red, a black breast and a beard that occasionally grows to nearly a foot long. It will measure up to four feet in length and weigh 18 or more pounds. Hens are brown or gray and have little color on their heads.

Through indiscriminate killing, this traditional Thanksgiving bird had become extinct in Kentucky except for a small native flock in Land Between the Lakes. In 1938 a restocking program was begun, and some of the Western Kentucky gobblers were transplanted in the Eastern Kentucky mountains. Also, as part of the program, seven big fellows were obtained from Missouri in exchange for grouse, and a few were donated by Ohio. Ft. Knox obtained a

starting flock from Ft. Leonard Wood, and it now has more than 400 birds on its reservation. In 1978 Kentucky swapped Mississippi some deer for turkeys. Kentucky's total flock numbers between 1,600 and 1,900, which is very small in comparison with neighboring mountain states but is slowly growing and spreading.

Hunting is permitted in Land Between the Lakes, at Ft. Knox, and in several Eastern Kentucky counties, subject to yearly change. Kentucky has only a spring turkey hunting season, usually in April. Hours for hunting generally are from a half hour before sunrise to noon, except in Land Between the Lakes, where hunting normally is permitted from one-half hour before sunrise to a half hour after sunset. Because the hours may change from one year to the next, hunters should check the legal hours before starting after turkey.

The spring turkey season can be one of the most exhilarating—and frustrating—challenges a small game hunter can face, as mere man is pitted against

Ricky and Frank Henson look over a
17-pound gobbler.

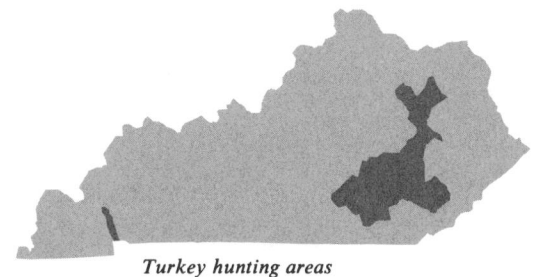

Turkey hunting areas

the wisest and wariest of Kentucky's game birds.

Here are a few tips on how to see, if not necessarily bag, a turkey, gleaned from hunters more expert than I:

First, be sure to wear camouflage clothing, including gloves; even a head mask will help.

Scout the woods a week or so before the opening. Look for tracks and scratchings around creeks and ponds and edges of open areas. Try out your calls (this is legal before the season opens as long as you carry no weapon); you usually can hear an answering call as far away as half a mile. After not too many miles and hours you should locate a roost, usually on high ground, as well as a feeding area and perhaps a watering hole.

Scout around for a good natural stand, much as you would before a deer hunt. Make sure that it is in an area where a hen might likely be—not in a swag or dense thicket, for instance.

Get out before daybreak, find your stand and wait.

Harold Knight of Cadiz, a champion turkey caller and maker of several excellent wild bird calls, believes you don't have to be an expert to call a turkey, but it helps. "The most important part of the call is timing and rhythm," he says. Also, calling is only 25 percent of the hunt. Having a thorough knowledge of the woods and turkeys is most of it. "Calling," he says, "is just icing on the cake." Knight says he likes to challenge a gobbler a bit, but relies mostly on seductive hen calls:

"A soft seductive call of a hen will make most any lazy old gobbler come to do a little courting."

Knight says that while the calls aren't all that important, he thinks every newcomer to the sport should improve his calling by listening to a turkey hen in the chicken yard, or listen to good records of turkey calls.

Use of the rifle has been permitted in Eastern Kentucky (this may be subject to change), but at Ft. Knox and in Land Between the Lakes only shotguns are allowed. Most hunters prefer a 12-

gauge shotgun with No. 4, 5 or 6 shot. The No. 6, being far smaller and more numerous in the shell than No. 4 and No. 5, is best for head and neck shots.

If and when you get a shot at a bird, it is best to aim at its neck and head. Body shots usually just wound the turkey, and a bird with an injured wing can still outrun almost any hunter.

For every person who bags one brilliantly colored gobbler, there are dozens more hunters who wait out the season without even seeing a bird, so don't be disappointed if you don't score on your first six or eight hunts.

Land Between the Lakes turkey permits may be obtained at the Information Office at Golden Pond or at the Center or North Information Station. For information on the Ft. Knox turkey hunts, write to: Turkey Hunt, Recreation Services, Directorate of Personnel and Community Activities, P.O. Box 1052, Ft. Knox, Ky. 40121.

Grouse

A male grouse greets the Spring by beating the air with his wings above a hollow log.

Courtship (male)

Ruffed Grouse and display tactics above

The first time I went grouse hunting—it was with Al Blum of Murray, president emeritus of the League of Kentucky Sportsmen—I thought it was the worst sport in existence. We climbed miles of mountain paths, saw only three birds, got two shots, and went home with empty bags.

Since that time I have changed my mind. It's one of Kentucky's great sports. But I'll leave it to the younger men. You not only have to have legs of iron and the endurance of a mule, but a quick eye and instant reflexes as well. When you come upon a grouse, you can't just stand there and get your breath, like I'd have to do. Generally, you have only a split second to aim and fire before this bit of lightning disappears through the trees.

Because of this need to swing and fire quickly, Al recommends a light gun and open barrel. Hope Carleton, a veteran of the woods, recommends a modified barrel. Some great hunters prefer a double barrel for short and long shots, and it will work quite well. My problem was I rarely, if ever, got a second shot.

Blum, Carleton and others say to stick to areas near bubbling creeks, wild grapes, strawberries, flowering buds and, above all, apples. An abandoned apple orchard is a natural place for grouse. Some hunters insist they should be red apples.

Bill Hall and his Brittany Spaniel, Rust, with a grouse

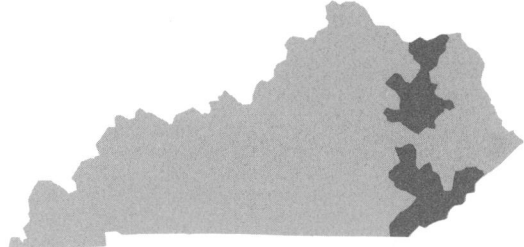

Grouse hunting areas

Like the mourning dove, the grouse, when flushed, will demonstrate surprising evasive tactics. Also if flushed in low ground cover, it might run until safely out of range.

The grouse is beautifully marked in shades of brown for camouflage in the woods. This forest bird generally is found in and east of the Daniel Boone National Forest, and around Mammoth Cave.

It is a very tough bird to kill. Just when you think you have it on the ground, it may suddenly come to life. Beware especially of a wing hit. The grouse has sturdy legs, and might outrun your dog. Speaking of dogs, a good grouse dog will freeze maybe 100 yards away from the bird, then move up slowly with you. At such a time, there's no chance to call on friends to move up. You go ahead and hope the grouse will hold long enough to get a shot.

When setting out on a day's hunt, try to keep the sun to your back, but of course this isn't always possible. As Hope says, one thing's for sure: If you try the ridges the birds will be in the hollow, and if you're in the hollow they will be on the ridges.

The Kentucky grouse season usually opens on the third Thursday in November and runs through February. Check current rules for dates and daily bag limit, as they are subject to change.

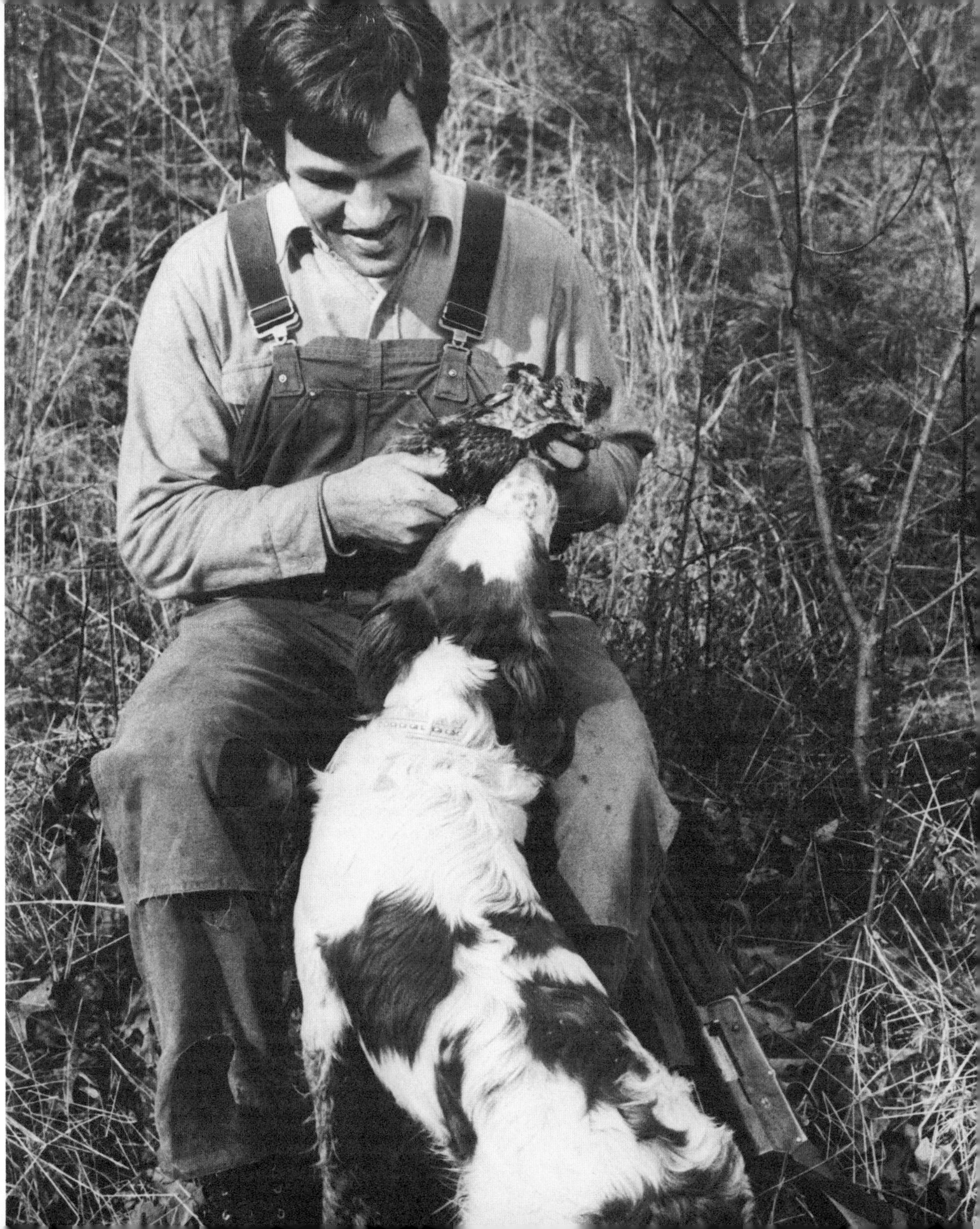

Waterfowl

purple speculum
(male)
green head
white collar~ruddy breast
white tail
(female)
whitish tail   Mallard

Hunting geese and hunting ducks have one thing in common. You don't go after the birds; you just sit quietly without moving and let the birds come to you. But don't think that these are sports designed for loafers. Being in your blind and setting your decoys before dawn on a bitterly cold, windy day is not an easy task.

Both puddle ducks and diving ducks are hunted in Kentucky. The green-headed male mallard, with its plain hen, is the most popular puddle duck, it feeds on shallow-water plants and grain and, therefore, makes a delicious meal for the hunter. Diving ducks feed on plants in deep water. The canvasback is the most familiar diver in Kentucky.

The intelligent black-necked Canada goose is the most popular goose in Kentucky. Also found in the state during the winter migration period are the blue goose and the snow goose.

Kentucky, for years the poor boy among goose-hunting states in the Mississippi Flyway, one of four migration routes over the country, soon may be the envy of its neighbors. Thanks to the tremendous Ballard County Wildlife Management Area near Bandana developed several years ago, geese have flocked into Kentucky in increasing numbers.

There was no quota harvest on geese in the commonwealth until 1977, when the Mississippi Flyway Council set a limit of 15,000 for the Ballard County district. In the rest of the state only the limits on individuals apply. Other states along the Mississippi Flyway have had quotas for years. The council ordered Kentucky Fish and Wildlife officers to keep an accurate count on the Ballard district goose harvest in the winter of 1976-77. From that study, the quota was set. The count, conducted by Jim Moynahan, manager of the

Ballard County Wildlife Management Area, exceeded 12,400.

The 8,000-acre Wildlife Management Area is beautifully organized with strict rules for safety. There is transportation to and from the action, plenty of game, and a thrill a minute. Hunters draw for pits before going out. If one pit gets no early shooting, trucks often come along to move the occupant to a shooting site vacated by hunters who have their limits.

A sportsman obtains the privilege of hunting in the management area by making early application and spending $8 for each day he wishes to hunt. The limit is four days a season. A total of 170 shooting pits, placed 200 yards apart, surround a 1,400-acre refuge where no hunting is permitted. Inside the refuge, farmers grow corn, wheat and soybeans. They harvest half the crop and leave the rest standing as food for migrating geese and ducks.

I hunted Ballard County one opening day with Arnold Mitchell, then commissioner of fish and wildlife, and Hope Carleton, star of the television program "Kentucky Afield." We toured the restricted area the evening before the opening with Jim Moynahan. Geese flew up all around us as we slowly moved along. Their cackle and soaring rafts are something not easily forgotten. (Late in January 1978, the official count showed 125,000 geese feeding in the refuge).

For those hunters who haven't been fortunate enough to hunt Ballard County yet, let me tell you what to expect. When you arrive, you give up your license and the required federal duck stamp (insurance that you won't try anything funny like shooting too many geese) and draw for your pit. Only 37 of the 170 pits are opened each day, to keep the geese guessing and to leave some for later days.

By 5:30 a.m. all pits are assigned and Moynahan mounts a bench in the headquarters building and lays down the law: Only eight shells per man. Only three hunters to a pit. Daily bag limit is five, and only two Canadas per hunter. (He points to a picture of a Canada, a blue and a snow goose, to show the difference between the three birds and explains the bag limits for each.) Keep guns in cases until you're in the pit. No alcoholic beverages. No fires in the pit. Shooting stops at noon to give geese a chance to regroup and feed in the fields.

On the day we hunted, eight large trucks outfitted with canvas tops and wooden benches lined up near the door. Drivers called out the pit numbers for their trucks as the hunters, dressed in

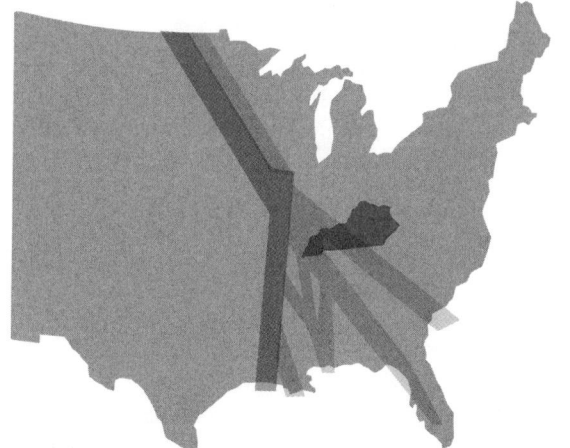

The Mississippi Flyway

the camouflaged clothing that waterfowl hunting requires, poured out of the building.

"Everybody here for pits 80, 81, . . ." one of the drivers called. We had drawn pit No. 80 and scrambled aboard. So did six others. After bumping along about 10 minutes we stopped and three hunters got out. "Your pit is about 30 yards over there," the driver said. The men disappeared in the darkness, their small flashlight indicating their progress.

We found pit No. 80 with no trouble. The concrete pit, sunk in a patch of Johnson grass stalks 10-feet tall, was about eight-feet long with a slanting concrete top covering half of it. "Watch your head when you jump up to shoot," Carleton cautioned. I didn't bump my head, as things turned out, because I had no reason to jump. We hadn't seen or heard a goose when, about 8:15 a.m., a truck drove up.

"Get out," the driver said. "We're taking you to a pit where three guys limited out." The men were waiting with two Canadas each when we drove up. We dropped in the pit and loaded up as the truck pulled away. Geese were flying all around us. Five swished close enough for us to hear the silky sound of their wings, and Mitchell knocked one down. By 9:50 a.m. we had five geese in the blind and one shell left—in Carleton's gun. He waited for an easy shot, then we vacated the pit and three others moved in. After retrieving three of our geese from a pond covered with a thin sheet of ice, we returned to the check station at the building we had left earlier, where our geese were tagged and our licenses returned. ·

When the Department of Fish and Wildlife Resources bought those 8,000 acres of bottomland in Ballard County in the 1950s for the wildlife refuge and waterfowl shooting preserve, Archie Renfrow owned an adjoining farm of 120 acres. When duck and goose hunting was opened on the preserve, Renfrow built two blinds and advertised for hunters. They weren't long in coming. He had 15 hunters his first year, and business has increased annually.

Four of Renfrow's five sons—Ivan, Hugh, Harvey and Jerry—grew up enjoying the hunts. They soon learned to serve as guides and callers. Gradually they acquired more land until now they have 400 acres in the heart of the state's goose and duck country. With their father, they operate five of 16 licensed commercial hunting perserves

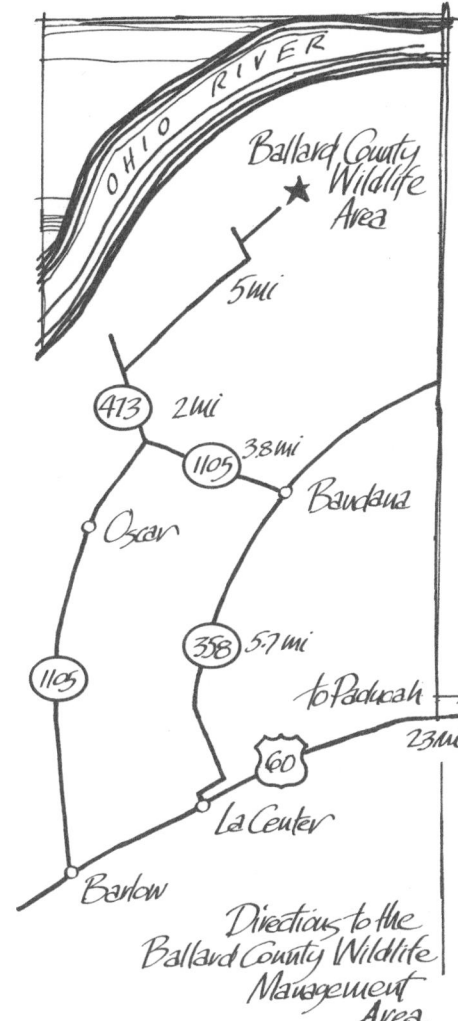

Directions to the Ballard County Wildlife Management Area

Waterfowl hunting areas

Smith Broadbent, Cadiz, right, and Gardner Spicer his duck and goose guide of 50 years, an unforgettable team.

bordering the refuge. (See list of commercial preserves in back of book). All together, the commercial outfits can accommodate 375 or more hunters a day. Customers enjoy two advantages over those taking state-owned pits: They are not restricted to shooting hours short of the federal regulation, which allows hunting to continue until one-half hour before sunset, or in the number of shells that can be taken into the pit.

Most of the preserve operators pump water into sections of their land to attract more geese and ducks. They also plant corn, soybeans and wheat, as Jim Moynahan does on the state preserve. And they scatter decoys in large numbers out from their pits on water and in fields. "We also encourage duck shooting from the same blinds we use for geese," said Ivan Renfrow. They don't do that on the refuge.

The price for hunting on the commercial ranges begins at $15 a day. Most encourage advance reservations.

Good duck and goose hunting is not limited to Ballard County. The sloughs around Henderson are well known for waterfowl hunting. The Department of Fish and Wildlife Resources owns 3,400 acres there, and much of the land is open to hunters. There are no permanent pits, but temporary blinds are permitted. Also in that region the state leased 4,000 acres on the Henderson County-Union County line from the Army Corps of Engineers in 1977. It is known locally as Powell's Lake Grassy Slough. Temporary blinds are to be permitted there.

Building a temporary blind can be a problem. What you use to build it will depend greatly on the material available. It is best to use local reeds and brush to make it as inconspicuous as possible. Of course, what you are wearing may make all the difference. The blind doesn't have to cover you completely if your cap and jacket match the ground cover and you don't move about.

The creek bottoms in Fulton, Hickman and Carlisle counties are ideal for ducks and geese, and nearby Kentucky Lake and Lake Barkley attract many ducks and geese. Temporary blinds are permitted, but at Barkley hunters must draw for locations in a drawing conducted by the Army Corps of Engineers.

Three islands totaling 997 acres near the Smithland Lock on the Ohio River were obtained for hunting by the state in 1977.

There was a time, not too many years ago, when duck and goose hunters in Louisville had good hunting at their door. They could sit at the head of 18-Mile Island on the Ohio River and watch rafts of ducks so thick they formed a solid mass from shore to shore. Gradually the thousands of acres of bottomland corn have given way to Johnson grass and subdivisions. Ducks and geese don't flock to that part of the Ohio in such numbers anymore. But some waterfowl do land there, and some hunters still manage to pick off their limits of mallards occasionally, especially when the weather is its worst and near zero. During the hard winter of 1977-78 many ducks and some geese flocked to the river; more than 2,000 birds were counted at one time for brief rests on their trips south.

In the days of big rafts of ducks, almost all hunting on the Ohio River around Louisville was done in sneak boats, which could be tilted so high to either side that the paddler and hunter would not be seen by the ducks until the boat was upon them. Just when I was beginning to think the old sneak boats were of another era, the unique craft seems to be making a comeback. Ian Henderson of Louisville helped design one made of fiber glass with a flange along the side to keep him from kneeling in too much ice water as he paddles. Other Louisville hunters using sneak boats now include John Barr III, Jim Hardy, Neville Blakemore Jr., Terrell Dickey, Bob Ferguson, Bob Martin, Gene Dorval and Rusty Broaddus.

Duck and geese also are attracted to Reelfoot Lake and the Obion River bottoms, which are so close to Kentucky that many hunters think of those areas as home grounds and some even forget to buy Tennessee licenses.

Clyde Reeves, then executive director of the Kentucky Fairgrounds; Smith Broadbent, then chairman of the Kentucky State Fair Board, and I were among several hundred hunters who spent the last two days of one duck season on Reelfoot Lake, that picturesque nether world of cypress, stumps and shallow water formed by an earthquake. We had Theodore Spicer as one of our guides. For that reason we returned with limit kills both days while other hunters in the same area were coming in with only stiff necks from watching the flocks winging by.

There was a biting wind out of the north, and the temperature dropped into the teens both mornings. We had to break ice to get through a channel across Nix Towhead Island into Lost Pond, which lies a

snow goose — (white body and black wing tips)

blue goose (white head with dark body)

the blue and snow goose are really different colour phases of the same species and can be seen in flocks of thousands at migration. Snow geese are very much less organised than the "V" formations of the Canada geese

Canada's in "V" formation

Canada goose

little south of the deep water of the lake and is the center of the best duck shooting area. When we got to our blind, we found that ice had formed around each decoy. Naturally this had to be knocked off before we placed them.

When hunting in open areas, the more decoys the better, but for average hunting six to nine should be ample. Be sure to place the decoys so that they look natural. You might even tie a line to one or two and pull it occasionally to give the make-believe duck a semblance of life. Remember that ducks usually will come in heading into the wind, so, if possible, set out the decoys in such a manner that the ducks will come in from left to right, for easier shooting. Mallard decoys are best for all hunting, since they will decoy all other species.

The first morning we had just cleaned the decoys and started a charcoal fire in a small potbelly stove when 100 mallards pitched in. Spicer and I grabbed our guns only to realize spray had frozen on the guns, and we couldn't release the safety. We thawed them over the fire and then sat for an hour before our next visitors arrived.

Reeves is a rifleman. He loves to hunt squirrels and varmints with a .22 rifle and bear and antelope with something slightly more powerful. He even has killed ducks with a rifle. Shotguns were a new twist in hunting for him, as were jump and pass shooting. When five fat canvasbacks came over, Reeves was the first to knock one down, a really brilliant shot. Sitting back and grinning restfully, Reeves said, "That's the first shotgun I've killed with a duck!"

There is a daily kill limit on ducks. The limit is calculated on points, which puts a premium on the hunter's ability to distinguish one duck from another in flight. You have reached your bag limit for the day when the point value of the last duck killed added to the sum of the ducks already taken during that day reaches or exceeds 100. These points vary from year to year, and a chart showing the species of ducks and their point vaue should be studied before your first hunt of the year.

The points, through the season of 1978-79 follow: Canvasback 100; hen mallard, wood duck, black duck, redhead, hooded merganser, 70; pintail, blue wing teal, cinnamon teal, green wing teal, widgeon, gadwall, shoveler, scaup, 10; drake mallard and all others not listed here, 35.

Before you go duck hunting you might study the markings enough to distinguish one from another

27

Hidden in this blind were three Louisvillians; Ralph Day, Wayne Richardson and Brack Ferrill.

Arnold Mitchell, former fish and wildlife commissioner for Kentucky takes a peek out of this Ballard County pit.

The unique sneak boat once was popular on the Ohio River. By tipping it to one side it hid the hunters from the ducks.

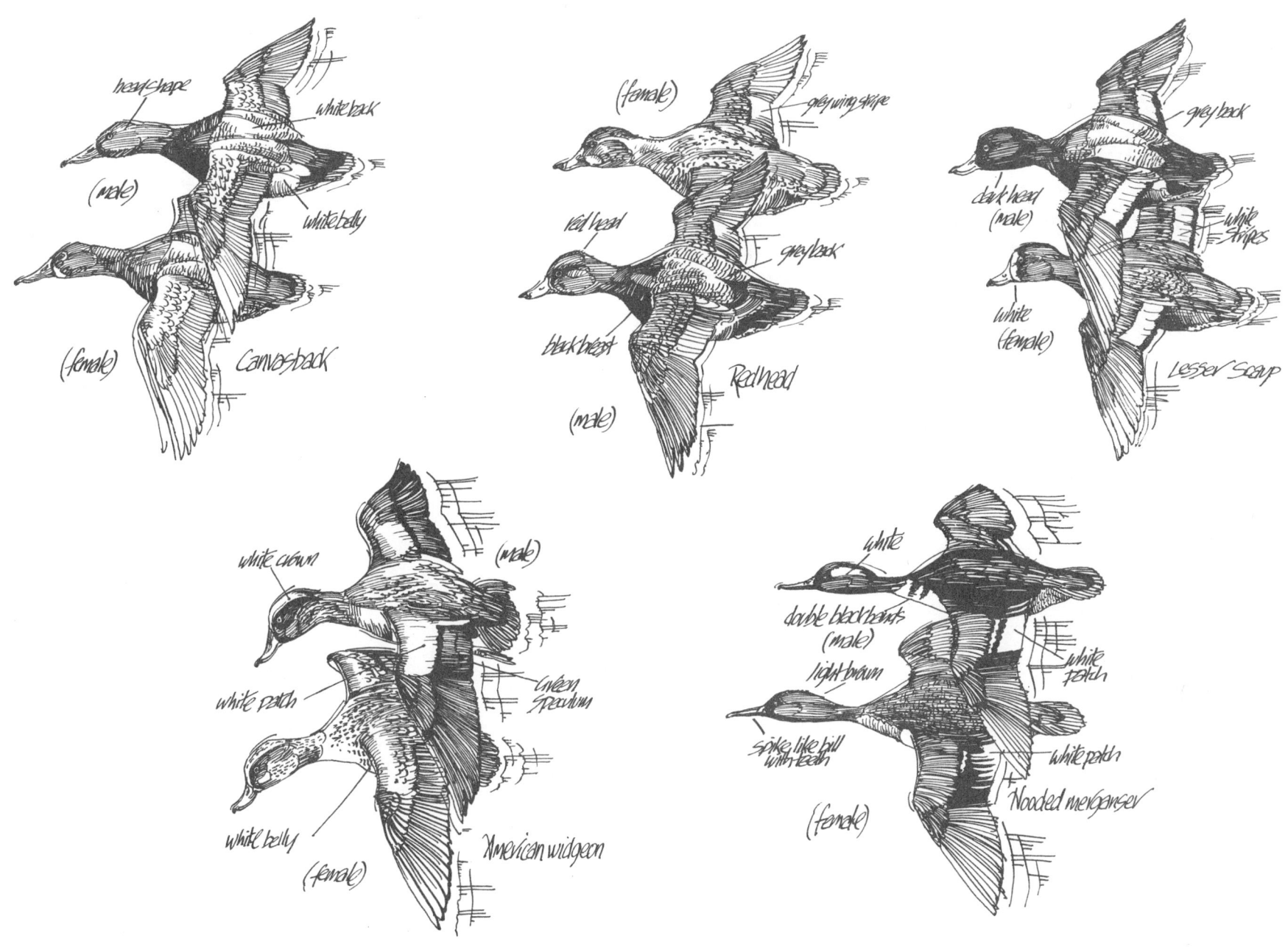

head shape • *white back* • (male) • *white belly* • (female) • Canvasback

(female) • *grey wing stripe* • *red head* • *grey back* • *black breast* • Redhead • (male)

grey back • *dark head (male)* • *white stripe* • *white (female)* • Lesser Scaup

white crown • (male) • *white patch* • *green Speculum* • *white belly* • (female) • American widgeon

white • *double black bands (male)* • *white patch* • *light brown* • *spike like bill with teeth* • *white patch* • Hooded merganser • (female)

in flight.

As you prepare for the duck hunting season each fall, you will probably engage in the same argument—how much of a lead do you take on a duck? The average hunter blames most of his misses on his inability to judge the lead required since

mallards wing past at 40 miles an hour. But old-timers argue that more often than not, their failure to bring down the quarry is due to the bird's being out of shot range.

On shots up to 40 yards, the velocity of the charge will put you on the duck if you are swinging with it

as you fire. On long-range shots, you should swing past and learn by trial and error just how far to lead.

I rarely try a shot longer than 50 yards, using a 12-gauge shotgun with full choke and No. 2 to No. 4 shot, heavy load, for geese, and No. 6 shot,

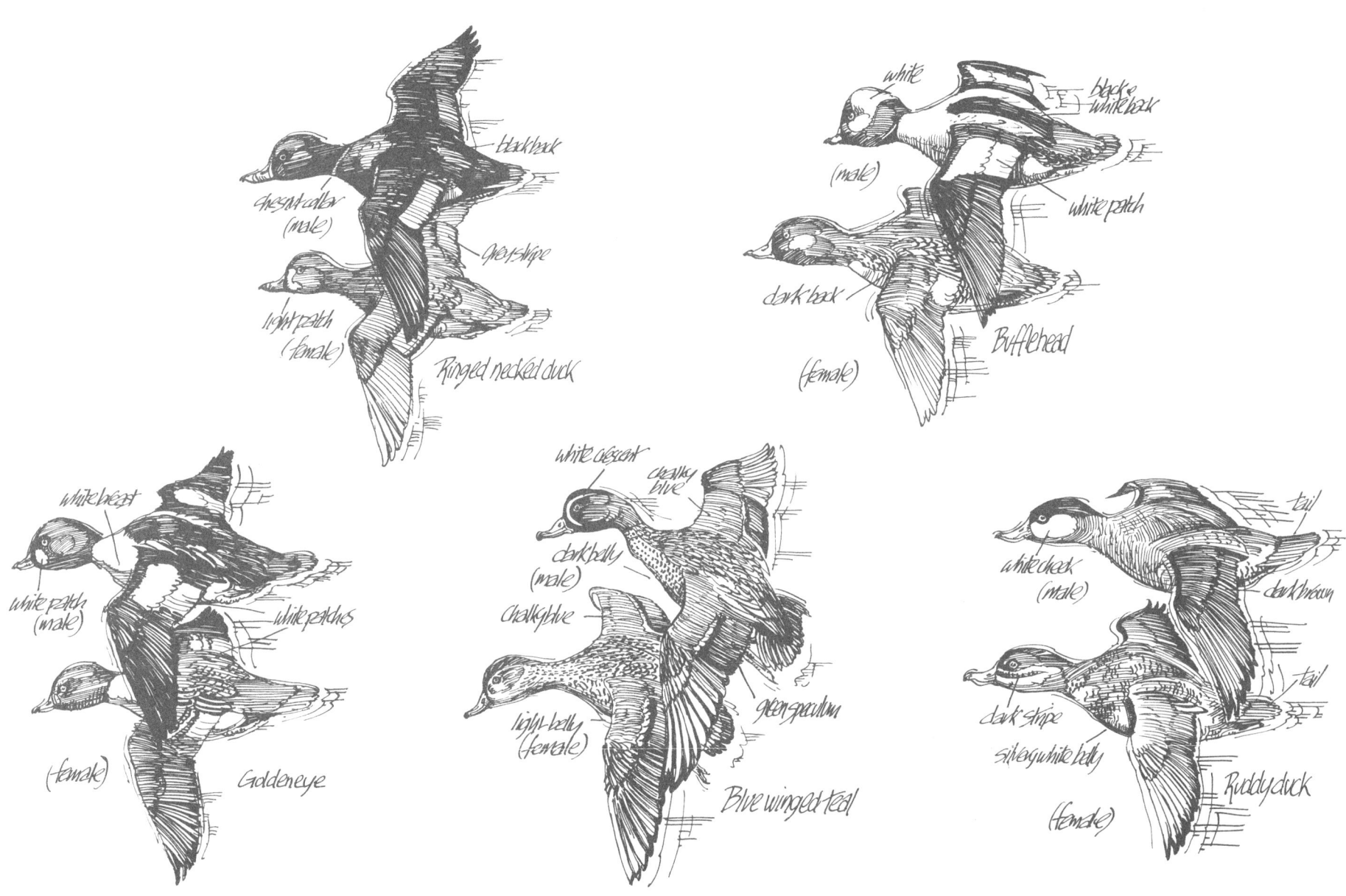

Ringed necked duck — black back, chesnut collar (male), green stripe, light patch (female)

Bufflehead — white (male), black & white back, white patch, dark back (female)

Goldeneye — white breast, white patch (male), white patches, (female)

Blue winged teal — white crescent, chalky blue, dark belly (male), chalky blue, light belly (female), green speculum

Ruddy duck — tail, white cheek (male), dark brown, dark stripe, silvery white belly, tail, (female)

heavy load, for most ducks. I recommend the 12-gauge for all waterfowl shooting to reduce the chance of losing cripples.

Barrel length is another argument-producer. The 30-inch barrel used to be standard, and I still use this length. The trend, however, is toward shorter barrels, usually a 28-inch, that swing faster. There simply is no truth in the claim that long barrels shoot farther. The powder in shotgun loads is burned long before the shot travels 26 or 28 inches of barrel.

When the freezing and the waiting are over, and you have brought down a duck or a goose, there is real work ahead, and the sooner you do it the better. It is easier to pluck the bird while it is still warm. And after you remove the feathers, the downy fuzz and pinfeathers remain a problem.

Some rugged fellows say they can rub the down

Black duck

tail pin (male) brown white (female) Pintail

black rump (male) white speculum light rump white speculum (female) Gadwall

green patch white (male) green speculum (female) Green winged teal

dark wing edge light white belly white chin (female) red & white bill white chin (male) white belly dark Wood duck

off with their bare hands or a gum eraser and then burn off the pinfeathers over a flame. I've never had any luck with that method, maybe because I don't have a gas range to provide a steady flame. I suggest that after you get the big feathers off, out in the field, you try hot paraffin on the down and pin- feathers.

To do this, bring a bucket of water almost to a boiling point. Melt two or more cakes of paraffin and pour into the water. Being lighter than water, the paraffin will float. Dip the duck or goose into the bucket and withdraw it slowly, allowing the paraffin to adhere to the bird. Let the wax dry hard and then peel it off, taking fuzz, pinfeathers and all with it. Then complete the cleaning job and get on with the cooking.

Squirrel

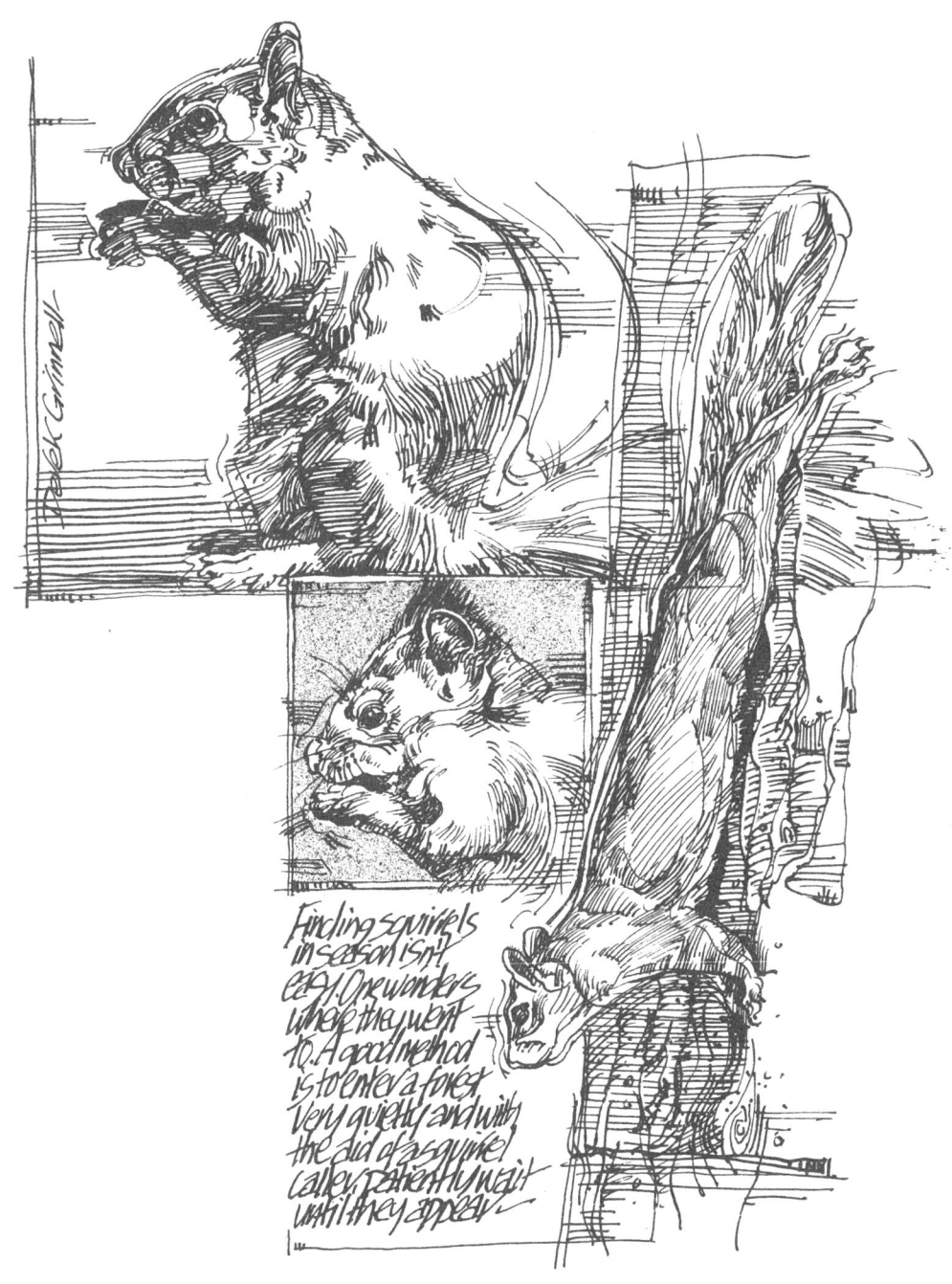

Finding squirrels
in season isn't
easy. One wonders
where they went
to. A good method
is to enter a forest
very quietly and with
the aid of a squirrel
caller patiently wait
until they appear.

From pioneer days until the last decade when doves became so plentiful, squirrels were rated the most sought wild game in America.

There was a time in earlier days when squirrels were far and away too numerous in Kentucky. In 1795, for instance, the state legislature passed an act obliging every white male over 16 to kill a certain number of squirrels each year. The *Kentucky Gazette* of May 17, 1796, said: "A hunting party at Irvine's Lick killed 7,941 squirrels in one day, and high men were rewarded with choice quarters of beef."

Squirrels are found in every county in the state, in virtually every speck of woodland that includes nut trees, including most of the state-controlled public hunting areas. The gray squirrel is the most popular and most populous. The adult will weigh up to one pound and will measure up to two-feet long, including the tail. Its color is silver gray. The fox squirrel, sometimes called the red squirrel, is larger than the gray, frequently weighing up to two pounds. It is gray on the top of its back with reddish underparts and face.

The mid-August start of the squirrel season in Kentucky can be a blessing in many ways. With such an early opening, the hunter has the opportunity to get out into the woods with his gun and case the area for big hickories for use when the nuts ripen (and also to locate deer trails). Meanwhile he can knock off an occasional squirrel by adopting the walk-look-listen technique which has been successful since Daniel Boone's time. Wear soft shoes and subdued clothing and enter the woods quietly. Travel very light. The woods can get hot and muggy after the sun comes up, and the warmer you get the more you will be bothered by mosquitoes. It's a must to have a bottle of repellent along.

"Watch ahead and on both sides for ground activity and scan the upper branches of trees on the possibility of mealtime there", says Ray Ashcraft of Elizabethtown, the best squirrel hunter I know. "Stop every few steps and listen for the unmistakable rustle of leaves caused by a squirrel or the patter of cuttings falling through foliage and onto the dry carpet of leaves on the floor of the forest. Frequently in the early morning, dew dropping from the trees will give you a start, but if you listen closely you can note a distinct difference between the sounds. The dew falls all around you; the cuttings will be heard only from one direction".

As the fall progresses, the nuts on the big hickories and walnuts will ripen, and squirrels will begin to concentrate in these trees. That is when the early explorations pay off. Many hunters go for squirrels only during the first days of the season then turn their attention to the dove season, which usually opens on Sept. 1. These fellows miss the best of the squirrel season.

I guess the toughest squirrel hunting is in oak trees. The oaks are so tall and so numerous that you never will find more than one or two squirrels to a tree, and those usually are almost out of shotgun range. The best early shooting you can get is in gum trees. The squirrels seem to congregate on one tree at a time and stay with it until it is bare. Sometimes you'll find six to eight in a single tree. But the best all-around shooting is in hickory trees. The hickory cuttings are so heavy they make a noise you can hear from a great distance, if the wind isn't blowing and if the floor of the woods is relatively dry.

As the squirrels concentrate, you will be able to pick out the best trees during the afternoon before the hunt by observing the new cuttings on the ground. If you are wise to the woods you can find these trees the next morning. Sit down near one or two before daylight, and wait for the little fellows to arrive for breakfast. It is not unusual during this period for a hunter to kill his limit without moving from one spot. The bag limit on squirrels is subject to annual change, so check with your conservation officer or outdoor writer before your first hunt.

Hunting squirrels with the help of a dog can be great sport. Many a farm pooch is a natural squirrel chaser. It usually hunts by sight, which makes it a big help during the late season. When leaves are off the trees it will quickly give chase when it sees a squirrel and will bark up the tree where the squirrel has taken refuge. As it continues to yip on one side of the tree, the hunter may move quietly to the other side and get a clean shot. Often, however, the barking dog will cause the squirrel to hole up.

I use No. 6 shot because both the grays and the foxes have tough skins and are harder to stop than the beginning hunter might think. I have used 7 ½ with fair success, but I believe No. 6 is better.

Hunting squirrels with a rifle is a Kentucky tradition. Our pioneering fathers used the internationally famous old long rifle, known as the Kentucky Rifle. Many men still living in the state's rural sections recall happy and productive hunts with this muzzle-loader.

While roaming Hardin County one August day in quest of information on the squirrel supply, I met "Uncle Jack" Moore, a farmer who lived near Colesburg. "Did all my early hunting with a muzzle-loader," he said. "Later I got a double-barrel 12-gauge and still later a .410, but for squirrels I never had anything to equal that muzzle-loader. Knocked off 25 with 25 shots one morning. Had to have a boy follow me and carry 'em."

"How far would it kill a squirrel?" I asked.

With a farmer's typical distaste for figures, he replied, "Aw, a fur piece." Pressed for more definite measurement, he offered, "Well, as fur as that gate." I judged the gate to be about 90 yards away.

"How long ago was it that you got 25 on 25 shots?"

"That was a right smart ago."

"How far from the farmhouse did you have to go for your squirrels in those days?"

"No distance a'tall."

Moore said he liked a rifle because it made less noise than the shotgun and didn't scare the squirrels for miles around. He said he'd heard of fellows "barking" squirrels—stunning them by hitting the bark beneath them—but that he never had done much of it. "If you got a ball in your gun and you got the squirrel in your sight, there's no sense to missing it, just to see if you can," he philosophized.

Fifty or so years ago, hunters trying for near-silence in winter squirrel hunting would equip their .22 rifles with mufflers. One of these old-time weapons came into my possession in 1965. Several friends tried it over the years and reported only slightly better success with it than with a regular .22. Using it for target practice, I found that what the muffler gained in silence it lost in accuracy on long shots. It may be that a small dent—made when the government stamped my permit number on it—on one side threw it out of balance. At any rate, I use the muffler—it is easily removed—as a conversation piece and get my squirrels without it. I might add that it is now unlawful to buy, possess, or use an unregistered gadget like that.

Early winter, when most trees in the woods have lost their leaves, is the time of year men who hunt squirrels with rifles like best. Bare branches stand out starkly against the gray winter sky, and any little ball of fur becomes a tempting mark. The second half of the split season on squirrels was designed for this. There is no more chance of a hunter hiding from a squirrel in a naked forest, however, than there is for a squirrel to hide for long from a hunter.

Like virtually all fellows who hunt squirrels with a rifle, I like to find a likely looking tree, sit with my back against a nearby tree for comfort and to conceal my body as much as possible, and rest my elbows on my knees to steady my rifle. Then all I have to do is sit and wait. I become a part of the general scenery if I don't move. Before long the squirrels, if there are any, will resume their daily chores. A quick aim and—ping!—it's down. It's not only down, but it's also dead when it's hit with shot from a rifle.

I continue to sit, knowing that, unlike many hit by a shotgun, this squirrel won't be going anywhere. Pretty soon the wildlife activity in the woods begins again, and I get another shot. If I miss, it's usually a clean miss, and the object of my attention usually will reappear in a few minutes and give me a second try.

In August, squirrels spend much of their time on the ground, digging up nuts they have buried or burying others. Those in the trees usually are there just to take a nap. If you see one and shoot and miss, it won't be long before it'll be itching to go down. It'll watch you warily, finally decide you are just another stump, and slowly come around the tree and down, head first, giving you an easy shot.

Going after a fallen squirrel might spoil your hunt by spooking the other ones but it may be necessary, early in the season, unless you are a dead shot. Hunters like Ashcraft might have their limit on the ground before moving to pick up any—I've seen him do it many times and he's never lost one— but the next time Tom Fowler kills a squirrel, he'll pick it up immediately. There's hardly a squirrel hunter alive who hasn't lost a squirrel he knew he had killed yet couldn't find, but I'll venture that nobody has lost one in the way Fowler, a Louisville hunter, was denied his prize.

Fowler was hunting one day in a Russell County woods with John Linkous and Dan Cubbage. He found a good spot at the edge of the woods next to a cornfield where squirrels had been stealing corn as far as five rows back. Fowler sat down and waited. His patience was rewarded with five squirrels, but he carried home only four.

Fowler had spotted that fifth squirrel high in a poplar tree. He aimed carefully and fired, and the squirrel hit the ground and bounced. "I'll just let him lie," thought Fowler. "He's surely dead." Then it happened. As Fowler started to reload, there came the noisy swish of big wings. A bolt of brown and red feathers in the form of a red-tailed hawk zoomed in on the kicking squirrel, grabbed it in it's claws, and rocketed off through the woods. All in the space of seconds. "I was dumbfounded," Fowler said later. "It happened so fast. That hawk must have been watching the squirrel from a nearby tree and started after him the second he fell."

What are the best hours for squirrels? Early and late, but don't overlook peak periods in the Solunar Calendar, carried in various newspapers. While hunting a woods south of Elizabethtown one morning with Ray Ashcraft, I had unusually good luck at daybreak, the time noted in the calendar as most active. Action came to a dead end about 9 o'clock, and we stopped for a rest. The Solunar Calendar showed the next best period to be 1:15 p.m. I'd never found a squirrel feeding or moving much between 9 a.m. and 5 p.m., but we decided to

test the calendar.

We went to different woods close by and separated. The air was still, and the woods quiet. Gradually birds began to call. Fifty or more doves winged overhead. Bees buzzed, gnats nibbled and woodpeckers pecked. There was activity all around. The closeness of the air fogged my glasses, but not so much that I couldn't see a plump gray squirrel come bobbing through the tops of the trees in my direction. That outing proved to me that the Solunar Calendar sometimes works for game as well as fish.

Do squirrels migrate? No doubts about it remained after the fall of 1968—the year of a ruined nut crop in Tennessee and the great squirrel migration out of that state and into Kentucky.

A boatman on Old Hickory Lake near Nashville saw a squirrel swimming far out in the lake. He was so surprised to see the little varmint fighting the water that he threw it a life preserver. Not being one to refuse a helping hand, the squirrel hung on while the fisherman towed the preserver to shore. The squirrel jumped off, shook itself, and quickly disappeared into the trees.

The angler's gesture was an act of kindness, but it was not necessary. A squirrel doesn't like to swim, but it can if it must. In 1968 squirrels were forced to swim, and they did.

During that year, one hunter reported using a fish dip net to pick 15 squirrels out of Chilhowee Lake, and at Dale Hollow several fishermen reported seeing 30 to 50 squirrels at a time crossing the narrows from Tennessee into new feeding grounds in Kentucky.

So desperate was the situation in Tennessee that the state's Department of Fish and Wildlife doubled the daily bag limit from six to 12. "We never before had experienced a combination of such a shortage of food and an abundance of squirrels," a spokesman in Nashville said. "We doubled our limits and continued the double limit through the close of the season. We felt it was much better that the squirrels be harvested than left to die."

Speaking of water, some of the most enjoyable squirrel hunting I've experienced has been on float trips down such pleasant streams as the Green, Barren and Kentucky rivers. There's nothing like such an excursion for relaxation and fun. Next best, I guess, is taking a gun along on an early morning fishing trip on one of the big lakes. It is easy to spot squirrels in the top of hickories near the water and

not hard to get out and walk up on them.

It is legal to hunt from a boat on any Kentucky stream. If you haven't combined squirreling and fishing on one of our rivers where the trees in many places form a canopy over the water, you've missed some mighty interesting hours. If you wish to hunt from a boat on any of the lakes, you'll need to know that on the Army Corps of Engineers lakes (Cumberland, Rough, Nolin, Dewey and Dale Hollow, to mention a few), hunting is restricted to shotguns (no rifles). And don't ever forget, it's illegal to hunt along state parks, game preserves and many other state and federal restricted areas.

Hunting squirrels from a boat can have its problems, of course. I'll never forget one trip I took on the Nolin River with Ray Ashcraft. Ashcraft is an expert with a little 20-gauge automatic shotgun he has used for more than 40 years. I guess he has killed more than 2,000 squirrels with that gun, and he prizes it highly. You can imagine the situation when, while on that float trip, I accidently knocked the gun into the water. It was October, and that water was cold. I tried to snag the gun with a fishing line, but before I coud do any good, Ashcraft had stripped to the skin and dropped silently over the side. He waded in that cold water above his waist until his toe touched the gun. He raised the tip of the barrel with one foot, then lifted it into the boat.

One of my most memorable squirrel openings I shared with that unpredictable man of many sports interests, Bernard "Big Six" Henderson, then a United States government revenue agent who made his home in Bowling Green. Because of the early opening, we didn't know exactly where to look for the squirrels, but we did know that since all animals need water, we had to locate a stream. Fortunately in the woods of our choice a winding creek still bubbled along, if somewhat weakly. I settled down in lazy contentment beside a black oak on the edge of a promising grove of giant beeches and waited. Henderson prowled deeper into the timber.

My eyes glued to the beeches, I had sat for more than an hour when suddenly a piece of acorn shell fell at my feet. I leaned back to look straight up and got an awful scolding from a breakfasting youngster. It was almost too close for my 12-gauge, but luckily from my awkard position I shot high and got it with two pellets through the head. If I hadn't ducked it would have got me in the head, too, as it tumbled down.

So that's what they were cutting—black oak

Squirrel hunting areas

Joe Fay Britt of Madisonville carries two squirrels and looks for more.

acorns. I lazed around a bit until I found a little clearing bordered by several oaks. After 20 minutes or so a young fellow streaked along a spreading white oak branch extending in tortuous form off toward the early sun. A shot was impossible, but higher in the same tree another member of the family was ringing the dinner bell, and I banged away at it. So they were going after white oak acorns too, I thought. (Oaks in Kentucky are mostly white, which have pale gray bark, and the black, red and scarlet oaks. The bark of this latter group of trees is heavier and darker and rougher than the bark of the white oak. All of the oaks look very much alike until autumn, when the brilliant foliage of the scarlet oak sets it apart from the rest).

Later that afternoon, I picked off another young squirrel which was swinging along toward the creek, and in retrieving it I found a couch-like formation of moss-covered rock too cool and comfortable to resist. A rapping woodpecker awakened me just in time to spot a gray piece of fur picking its way across the treetops high above the creek. It reached the other side and dropped into a cornfield. So they were feeding on corn as well, not uncommon for squirrels. I quit with a bag of five, all young. The old animals were either too wary or had been cleaned out by those quaint backwoods fellows who honestly don't know there is a game law and probably wouldn't obey it if they did.

While in the neighborhood I made a quick trip to Glasgow for a three-hour late afternoon hunt with Bernie Matthews. As we turned off the highway down a dirt lane flanked by deep woods on one side and cornfields on the other, seven fat and sassy squirrels dashed across our path. I resolved to hunt the stalks and let Matthews keep to the woods. I tried walking along the edge of the woods, keeping an eye on the top of the stalks, but the underfooting was so dry that every step was as loud as a cannon cracker. Every squirrel in Barren County knew I was on hand. I wound up with one scrawny little fellow, and Matthews, who sat quietly on a log about 200 yards off the road, bagged the limit.

Sometimes the woods can get a bit crowded, especially on opening days, as Bert Combs, can testify. On one opening day Combs and I were guests of Tom Cubbage of Leitchfield in a nearby woods. Combs sighted a number of squirrels and was just about to draw a bead on one when a boy in overalls came ambling through the trees carrying a rifle in one hand and a shotgun in the other.

Gov. Julian Carroll congratulates son Kenny on his squirrel hunting as son Brad looks on.

Tom Turner, Brad Fable and Gene Knight of Madisonville eye the trees for more bushtails.

Cy Layson of Frankfort likes to hunt squirrels from his boat.

"Having any luck?" he asked, loud enough to scare ducks in Barlow Bottoms.

"I'm just naturally lucky," Combs said, relaxing as he saw his quarry sneak away through the treetops. "I've had a redheaded woodpecker follow me for an hour, and now I get to meet the only fellow I ever saw who could hunt with two guns at a time."

"Most of the time I lay one down when I use the other," explained the young man seriously as he moved on out of sight.

Combs tagged up later with Cubbage, and they cornered two fox squirrels that didn't get away. When a breeze blew up about 9 o'clock, it became impossible to see squirrel action in the swaying treetops, and the hunt was over.

The afternoon before I was to hunt near Cynthiana with Louie Nunn, then governor, I scouted the woods with Jim Keeton, the area wildlife officer. The floor of the forest was dry and crackled under our feet. "If we could just get some rain tonight we would have a better hunt," said Keeton. He lived to regret his remark. It rained. Oh, how it rained. The governor managed somehow to bag four squirrels in spite of the weather. When he returned to the car with them in hand, somebody yelled, "Did you shoot 'em or drown 'em?"

Nunn smiled as the water ran off his nose. "I shot one," he said. "The other three were so wet I just picked them up off the ground."

Another governor, Julian Carroll, is one of the most avid and able sportsmen I've seen, but one opening morning of the squirrel season he lost the honors of the day to his young executive assistant, Don McCormick. Taking a week's vacation, Carroll fished Kentucky Lake for bass one day with his son, Brad, flew to Tampa to boat more than 100 fish in the Gulf of Mexico with another son, Kenny, and the final day joined up with friends at a woods near Cadiz for the opening of the squirrel season. Very few squirrels were seen and even fewer shot, but the trip set a new mark for comfortable camping, since our group settled into two well-equipped mobile homes.

The day before the opening we scoured the woods in search of good spots. Joe Fay Britt of Madisonville and I walked an area close to our quarters. I chose a hickory where there were new cuttings. Britt picked out trees for himself and Carroll. To find my way back to my tree before daylight the next day, I broke a small twig every 15 or so feet. This worked fine; my small flashlight picked them up instantly.

Carroll and I were using Model 1100 Remingtons. I had only my skeet barrel, which seems to do a fair job on squirrels, as it does on quail, rabbits and doves. Everybody else had a similar gun, except McCormick. He hauled out an old single-shot with full choke and long barrel. "Where on earth did you find that blunderbuss?" somebody asked.

"It's the best squirrel gun you'll ever see," he said, "and it cost me only $10 about 15 years ago."

One by one we picked up our guns and flashlights and disappeared quietly into the woods. The less said about the rest of the morning the better. The cuttings under Carroll's tree appeared very fresh, but not even one squirrel returned for a second helping. After an hour or so he slowly walked three miles back through the woods and saw only one squirrel, which he bagged as it moved down the trunk of a beech tree.

Along about 10 o'clock the men began drifting back into camp. Most of them, like me, had nothing to show for their efforts. Jack Brooks and Britt had one each. Britt's had an enormous tail which he thought might win a contest in Madisonville for the longest tail on a squirrel killed that season. The tail measured a full 14 inches, but the contest was won that year by Rudy Jones of Louisville with a 16 ½-inch squirrel tail.

Eleven o'clock, the time set for breakfast, came and went, and no McCormick or Carroll. Finally, about 20 minutes after the hour, they walked out of the woods. Carroll held McCormick's arm high in the air. "Here's our champion," he said. "He's got three, and I know nobody can match that because I heard only six shots fired all morning." McCormick beat all of us. He said he found all three on the ground, and that those were all he saw. Our trouble, we decided later, was the noise made the night before when two boys in the group drove motorcycles through the woods, probably scaring all the squirrels in the area.

Care of squirrels after the kill is important. If the day is hot, carry them hanging from your belt rather than in your jacket or a pouch, and clean them as soon as possible. To clean a squirrel, make a cut across the body under the tail. Step on the tail and pull up on the hind legs. The skin should peel off if you made the proper cut. Save the head; the tiny brain is a real delicacy.

Rabbit

The cottontail rabbit an important small game

Rabbit hunting, the favorite of young sportsmen, seems to be improving in Kentucky. The statewide kill has been averaging at least one a day, even for the youngest hunter. There is no minimum age for hunters, but youngsters under 17 years old should go with an adult.

Most older hunters use beagles to chase cottontails around to them, but beagles are a luxury most kids know nothing about. Young hunters are able to do so much more walking through briars and tall brush than their elders that they jump just as many if not more rabbits than the dogs.

When a freeze comes, a young hunter will do well to stomp through draws with a friend stationed at the far end. He should look for action in the edge of woods and on·sunny banks between the draw and the woods. On hot days, cottontails will feed at night and hide in cool cover during daylight hours.

Most boys, having so much youthful energy, usually have a common fault: they hunt too fast. In walking up rabbits without beagles, it is necessary to walk slowly, kicking at every clump, bush, pile of trash and fence row. If this isn't done, a smart rabbit will sit tight and beat a quick retreat out the back after the hunter has passed.

Also remember to stop dead still every 100 or so feet. If you are near a bunny in its squat, chances are it will get panicky and make a run for the rear where you might have a good, clean shot at it.

The rabbit's coat blends perfectly with autumn brush, and it is almost impossible to spot a cottontail in its squat in deep cover. But out on a sunny hillside of clover, small cedars, scrub trees and clumps of brush, it can be done. You have to keep your wits about you and look closely at every inch of ground—don't look too far ahead or you may miss a cottontail—watching for a slight difference in coloration or the bright sparkle of a wary eye.

The best and safest gun for a beginner is a 12-gauge, single barrel shotgun with an open bore. Many insist that a beginner should carry only a 20-gauge or a .410, but those smaller guns only discourage a beginner and leave a lot of injured rabbits. The 12-gauge carries a maximum number of pellets, and the open barrel allows a wide pattern, giving the hunter every chance to bring down his prey. Shot can be No. 6 to 7 ½, depending on the country. It's tricky shooting, yet plenty of rabbits have been killed with .22 rifles. Just don't use this gun in settled areas. If a beginning hunter uses an automatic-ejection gun, it's a good idea to give him only one shell at a time.

With an experienced hunter, the 20-gauge is probably enough. I frequently hunt in Nelson County with Walton Jones and Joe Thieneman of Louisville. Jones and Thieneman carry 20s and I use my 12-gauge. Our luck averages just about the same.

Hunters are a happy lot by nature, but the happiest—it has been my good fortune to hunt with—are those two companions. They are content to let a rabbit take a turn or two around the field, their beagles in wild and noisy pursuit, before bringing it down. That several of the cottontails elect to dive for a hole before coming around doesn't bother them a bit. (Cottontails do not dig holes but often use those of other animals as hiding places.)

For some reason known only to them, rabbits prefer to run uphill when pursued. A group from Louisville hunted at Paul Moore's farm near Glasgow one December day in 1965. In the group were Cecil Moore, Reed Moore, George McAleese and James G. Stewart. Along about 11 a.m. Stewart picked out a smooth bit of ground in a flat field and stretch out on his back to rest. Soon he was snoring. The others watched while their nine beagles yelping and yapping got up a bunny and trailed it, into the open field.

The rabbit saw a mound ahead, gave one leap, and was on top of it. It took one look back at the hounds and bounded on again. Before the hounds arrived, the "mound" rolled over and grabbed a gun. It was Stewart, scratching his belly where the bunny had sat. The rabbit hopped merrily away while the beagles sniffed Stewart. But other rabbits weren't so lucky that day, and the fellows went home with six each.

W. K. Davidson of Lexington takes issue with a statement I once made that only a greyhound is fast enough to overtake a scared, healthy rabbit. "I have a dog that's done it, and I feel that others have had dogs capable of doing it," he wrote. "As a boy I grew up on a fairly large farm in Virginia. For a number of years our stock dog was a large collie-shepherd mixed breed. Since he was a constant companion when we were in the fields, I saw him down and catch dozens of full-grown rabbits. In fact, any rabbit that was jumped a considerable distance from one of the stone fences, for which they always made a beeline, was a sure goner with old Todd in pursuit. And since those were the days before rabbit fever was ever heard of, I am sure that all, or at least most, of the rabbits were healthy and mature."

I wish I could have seen old Todd on the job. I can't help feeling, however, that the old stone fence proved more of a downfall than the speed of the dog. A rabbit just can't resist trying to take a short rest when it reaches cover like that.

Even though rabbits are extremely quick, I have seen more than one old-timer so adept at spotting rabbits and so schooled in the ways of the rabbit that he could pick cottontails up by hand. Not so many years ago I was hunting in Grayson County with Murrel Carter of Leitchfield. Sleet began peppering us in the face. The sleet turned to snow, and the snow turned to a light rain. The dogs weren't finding any quail, which we were after.

"We're wasting our time," Carter said. "The birds are here, because I saw them as late as yesterday. But the weather or something just isn't right. I say let's head for the house for lunch." I certainly didn't need any urging.

"No need to hurry," Carter said. "You've been writing about boys and their dogs hunting rabbits. Let me show you how they can be caught by hand, without a dog or a gun."

I would have thought he was kidding if I hadn't heard about him from Robert South, also of Leitchfield, one of his long-time hunting companions. South, Carter and C. E. Glasscock, another Leitchfield resident, were coming in from a quail hunt. Carter was out of shells, and Glasscock said he wished Carter had saved one shell for a rabbit.

Carter said, "You really want a rabbit?" Glasscock said that he sure did.

Well, Carter saw one sitting about 30 yards in front of us. The other two didn't know it and kept right on talking and walking. Carter just walked along at his normal gait then suddenly reached down and grabbed the rabbit by the neck and held it up in the air yelling, "You wanted a rabbit! How's this one for size?"

I was pondering that story as we moved along toward our car. We hadn't walked more than another 100 yards when Carter stopped and held up his hand. He was below me in a rather deep creek bed. "Look straight this way," he said, "and you'll see a rabbit in his squat." I studied the bank carefully and finally spotted the rabbit. It was flattened out like a mother hen over a nest of chicks and was watching me sharply.

"You just stand there and hold his attention," Carter said. Quickly he moved up the steep bank behind the rabbit until his hand was within six inches of the cottontail's back. Suddenly he grabbed. The rabbit gave a terrific kick, twisted loose from Carter's grasp, and aired out of there. Almost too spellbound to shoot, I finally brought the bunny down just as it was about to disappear into a briar patch.

"Well, you see what I mean," Carter said. "I was a little slow. Besides, I didn't have a glove on, and they can scratch like mad with those big hind feet." I saw what he meant. I'm convinced he could pick one up with either hand. His secret is being able to spot a rabbit in its squat and having a natural-born hunter's instinct about what to expect from wild game.

That brings up a talk I had with an old-timer in Mount Sterling.

"I see where you tell the young'uns it's hard to find a rabbit without a beagle these days," he said

"You're almost right, but not exactly. If everybody would wait till the season opens to kill rabbits, we'd have enough for a boy to knock down one or two without a dog, like we used to. But food is food, summer or fall, and they's nothin' better'n a rabbit. I used to feel it was my right to knock one down any time of year me and my old lady needed a dinner. Buy my thinkin's changed. I know we all better stick to the law or we won't have nuthin' to hunt before long.

"The only reason rabbits ain't extinct is their

Rabbit hunting areas

Howard Nethery, Jerome and Vincent Weis, Louisville, head for the fields.

39

Ed Wiegand of Louisvile heads home with two fat bunnies.

Some of Ruby's hunting buddies. From left, Ed Burckle, Bobby Cooper, Walton Jones and Jim Augustus

J.B. Long, one of the state's most successful cottontail hunters, gives his beagles a whiff of their prey

smartness. You know, a rabbit is plum clever. I've seen 'em hop right up into trees. I've seen 'em swim, too. But their greatest trick, which fools man and beagle alike, is 'afreezin' up when caught in an open field.

"If I was tellin' a kid how to hunt rabbits, in almost any kind of weather, I'd say look right under yore nose. It takes a bit of practice to detect a rabbit in his squat, but if you keep a sharp eye on the ground around you, you might notice a grayish brown spot in a green and brown clump of grass and briars. Take your time and look real close. You'll soon find a smart ole rabbit trying to fool you. If you pass him, he'll light out like lightning behind you, and you may not even get a shot. But if you see him, you've got him. Just move in on him, then stand there and wait. He can't stand that. He'll make a break and then you shoot.

"Now, another thing to remember is that rabbits like company. Where you find one, you'll find more. Comb a field real good, stopping every now and again. A rabbit will hold tight if you keep walking, but if you stop close by him he just can't stand it. He'll take off.

"Don't pass a single bit of cover. Even a clump of grass a foot tall in an open field. Rabbits like to bed down in such places during the day. Especially on the sunny side of a hillside on a windy afternoon.

"Another thing—walk the woods if the weather is bad. If you don't see a rabbit, don't give up. Just make your next sashay around the outside of the woods. Ten to one, you'll walk one or two that sneaked around the outside of the woods ahead of you and was just waitin' for you to pass so they could get back.

"Now about them beagles. I like a smart dog as much as anybody. And the smartest thing a beagle can do for you is help you find injured rabbits. If a beagle didn't do anything more than that he would be worth his feed and keep.

"One last word—tell a boy he ain't ever gonna be a good hunter if he ain't willing to stay with any injured game until he finds it, even if it takes him the rest of his afternoon. Beagle or no beagle."

The cottontail population thrives wherever it has the two necessities—food and cover. The rolling countryside around Scottsville seems to have several concentrations of rabbits in uncultivated lowlands. The Red River Valley in the border country around Guthrie is fairly thick with cottontails. Other wonderfully productive areas are in the vicinity of West Liberty, Lawrenceburg, Hopkinsville and the bottomlands of Ballard County.

It was my good fortune to be rabbit hunting near Scottsville a number of years ago with Charley Lambert of that town. Lambert had a whole shed filled with the littlest, speediest beagles I had ever seen, and he liked to take four or six of them along. He enjoyed walking the woods by day and listening to the excited yelps of his scurrying beagles in the same way a fox hunter delights in sitting atop a hill by night listening to the baying of his bounding hounds.

With us were Bob Coleman of Bowling Green and Ed Ferris and Lawrence Wetherby of Frankfort. We let the pups out in a honeysuckle thicket along a draw, and we took up positions in a meadow that ran uphill from the draw to a woods. We hadn't been in the field five minutes before one little beagle threw his nose in the air and howled lustily. The others joined the chorus, and a cottontail came bobbing through the grass directly at me. I fired three times and missed all three. But from then on it was a picnic. The beagles were barking, the rabbits were bobbing up everywhere, and the guns were firing.

Rabbits have a great power of reproduction and, given enough food and safe place to hide, are almost impossible to exterminate. Yet Kentucky has had its problems with the rabbit population in the state. A few years ago Fish and Wildlife officers set up two roadblocks on highways leading out of the state, one near Cincinnati and one near Ashland. More than 600 hunters were checked. Nobody had even the limit of bunnies. The average kill was found to be just under one rabbit per person. Similar roadblocks had been set up in 1952. During a 3 ½-hour period that year, officers counted 5,000 rabbits and made 81 arrests for game law violations.

What caused this cottontail decrease? Hunters or natural predators? Lack of food?

Some biologists say that insecticides have killed more rabbits than all other factors combined. Another theory is that increased use of Kentucky fescue grass for pasturage has played a large part in killing off the rabbit population.

Dr. Malcolm L. Barnes of Louisville said he had been distressed over his inability to find good rabbit country where his young son could learn the joy and exercise of hunting. He said he is sure that foxes kill their share of rabbits but that he has been told that Kentucky fescue is one of the real culprits. Examinations of the intestinal tracts of many young rabbits found dead show multiple tiny perforations, Dr. Barnes said. Biologists attributed the perforations to fescue, which has sharp spines on every blade. These spines are so sharp that sheep and cattle grazing on fescue frequently turn up with what farmers call "fescue foot," a soreness caused by rubbing against the grain of fescue blades.

Arnold Mitchell, then state commissioner of Fish and Wildlife, said he had not been informed of any recent examinations for damage caused by fescue but that such a danger no doubt exists. He said it was his belief, however, that rabbits eat fescue only when forced to as a last resort—that better food and better cover are prime requisites to bringing the bunnies back.

When you do kill a rabbit, the animal should be eviscerated while still in the field. It should take you very little time to behead the rabbit and pull out the innards. During all steps of preparation, it is best to wear rubber gloves. Tularemia, better known as rabbit fever, has been cut way down, but not erased completely. If the liver of a rabbit you are cleaning is full of white or yellow specks, it may have the fever and should be buried. But there is no reason to panic about tularemia. Any germs that might be present in a rabbit are killed by below freezing temperatures and cooking.

The rabbit season in Kentucky traditionally opens on the third Thursday in November. Rabbits thrive on the state's farmland, and most farmers will give you permission to hunt the cottontails if you are known to be a careful hunter. In addition, there are at least 45 state-controlled public hunting areas throughout the state.

Deer

the whitetail deer has ears that are finely attuned to high pitched sounds.

The beautiful and graceful whitetail deer is the only big game species in Kentucky, and it wouldn't be here except for an ambitious restocking program undertaken by the Department of Fish and Wildlife Resources.

Deer thrive in every county of the state and are hunted legally in all but a few. Counties closed to hunting as late as 1978 were Jackson, Owsley, Clay, Harlan, Powell, Clark, Leslie, Wolfe, Perry, Johnson, Knott, Martin, Floyd, Estill and Magoffin, but deer from such populous areas as the Ballard County Wildlife Management Area are being trapped regularly and dropped into these counties. Deer hunting also is prohibited in Mammoth Cave National Park and in certain wildlife management areas.

Teddy Grant of Louisville once asked if we have two species of whitetail deer in Kentucky, one gray and the other brownish. The Department of Fish and Wildlife Resources has stocked only northern whitetail, which are brownish with variations in coloring that might be misleading. However, a few whitetails from an unknown source were stocked in Pulaski County many years ago, and it is possible that these have survived and multiplied.

Land Between the Lakes not only has a large herd of whitetails but also a number of fallow deer, a stocky European import. These highly prized fellows were stocked in that area in the early 1920s by the Hillman Land and Iron Co. which owned much of the land there at that time.

Kentucky's whitetail herd now numbers more than 80,000 and is increasing rapidly. Poachers, however, remain a big problem.

About 8,000 deer were killed legally by hunters in 1978. Given the size of the state's herd, this number was very high, but the harvest is far below that of our neighbors.

Kentucky's statewide deer season usually runs five or six days in November and December for gunners, and two months or more for archers. Most deer kills are made in areas where hunting is controlled (Land Between the Lakes, Ballard County Wildlife Management Area, Ft. Campbell and Ft. Knox), and the Mammoth Cave region of Barren, Hart and Edmonson counties, outside the park proper.

When deer hunting, I much prefer a 12-gauge shotgun and slug to any rifle. A slug will kill at distances up to 75 yards and isn't likely to carry far enough to strike another hunter out of view. In some areas of high hunter concentration, the use of rifles is prohibited.

Here is what a hunter cannot use legally:

buckshot, except on Pioneer Weapons Area, or any type shells; fully automatic rifles, since holding down the trigger will fire all remaining shells; full-jacketed, military-type ammunition; tracer bullets; any rifle smaller than .240-caliber; any .256-caliber rifle; any M-1, .30-caliber rifle, either military issue or commercial; muzzle-loading shotguns, except on Pioneer Weapons Area and a portion of Land Between the Lakes; some types of handguns; archery equipment during the gun season; shotguns larger than 10-gauge or smaller than 20-gauge; muzzle-loading rifles smaller than .38 caliber. In some management areas, only shotguns with slugs are allowed.

Bow hunters also have some restrictions. The legal archer's equipment consists of a longbow or compound bow and barbless arrows with broadhead points at least 7/8-inch wide. Chemically treated arrows or arrow attachments containing chemicals are forbidden. And archers cannot carry firearms of any kind.

Along with his bow and arrow or a gun, there are several items every deer hunter should carry. These include a flashlight to locate a stand in the dark, a sharp knife and swabbing cloth for field dressing, a rope with which to elevate the deer's carcass for easier cleaning, and a can of pine, apple, or musk scent to mask the human odor. Also, according to state law, some article of wearing apparel must be hunter's orange.

I was on one hunt at Ft. Knox during the 1971 season when a hunter failed to wear the bright orange clothing. The man died shortly after he was rushed to the base hospital with a slug in his right shoulder. That's a large price to pay for failing to heed the clothing warning that's printed on every deer tag.

There are three standard methods for hunting whitetails—still hunting, stalking and driving. I prefer to still hunt, but have encountered several groups of drivers. In some states hunters are allowed to use dogs to drive deer, but not in Kentucky. However there's nothing in the book that says a hunter can't bark like a dog, and the result in some cases can be almost as fruitful.

On one opening day, I got out before daylight to take up a stand at Camp Breckinridge, a controlled area in Western Kentucky. With a flashlight, I found crossing deer trails near a large tree and made myself comfortable for the wait until daylight.

According to carefully laid plans, each hunter was to have several acres of woods to himself. But I hadn't been settled long when another car rolled down the dirt lane and stopped just beyond where I was parked. Then came another and still another. I heard several voices and the metallic clicking of shells being loaded into shotguns.

With dawn still a full half-hour away, two of the fellows stomped into the woods in front of me, both barking and howling and sounding like a cross between sick beagles and tenor coonhounds. Neither breed would have claimed them, I'm sure, but they accomplished their purpose. A deer in a thicket about 50 yards to my left staggered to its feet and took off down the hill away from me with the barkers in noisy pursuit. They turned the deer directly toward their friends waiting at the roadside where a crossing into the restricted impact area (that area where live shells hit the ground during practice) was marked plainly. A minute or so later three or four shots shook the forest, and the first deer of the day had been killed.

Later in the morning a deer crossed the little road behind me, about 70 yards uphill from my stand. Two hunters in a car spotted it, gunned their motor, roared to where they had seen it cross, stopped, and jumped out. One ran in my direction, barking loudly. The other walked quietly uphill. The deer circled away from the barking, and shortly a shot from the barker's buddy brought down the deer—a large doe. Me? I just sat there and cussed.

I prefer to still hunt for several reasons, not the least of which is that it's easier on the legs. Deer have rather poor vision, have a habit of remaining within a relatively small area, and use well-defined trails, ridges and crossings where a hunter may take his stand. Of course, the hunter first must figure the direction from which he expects the deer to appear and choose a spot toward which the deer will approach downwind. Above all, the still hunter must remain absolutely quiet and not smoke.

Stalking can't be done on controlled hunts where each hunter is allotted a limited area, but in the mountains it can be a must because of the vast areas to be covered. The stalker walks slowly and quietly, moves behind trees and shrubs rather than in the open and just inside the fringe of a thicket rather than outside it, trying always to keep moving against the wind.

Deer are hunted best in cold weather, but there is such a thing as too cold, even for deer. They bed

down just as a human might and refuse to budge all day unless walked up. Such a day—two days, really—came in December 1974. I was one of 16 men who hunted a promising hillside, covered with fresh deer tracks, near Brandenburg. No one got a shot.

A light snow fell, which should have helped, but a sudden drop in temperature and a wind of gale velocity plunged the chill factor to 8 below. Some of the others on that hunt were Walton Jones, Joe Thieneman and Arnold Robinson, all of Louisville.

I put on everything I had with me—regular and thermal underwear, then light hunting pants and shirt, then heavy hunting pants, a thermal jacket, my heavy hunting coat, rain boots, rain pants, rain coat, and my hunter's orange cap with the flaps down. I was so heavy that Jones had to give me a hand to bring me upright. Climbing to my tree stand was a physical impossibility, so I sat beneath it. Not a deer moved all day.

On that unsuccessful outing I saw another hunter who was bundled up and who wore a large red placard on his back: "Don't Shoot—I'm A Man."

Deer hunters will do well to combine their sport with squirrel hunting. While stalking squirrels watch for signs of deer tracks and trails. Once found, mark them well and even build a tree stand to which you return when the deer season opens. A tree stand can consist of one plank across two limbs or can be a more elaborate platform of enough planks to form a comfortable seat. Of course, in some areas permanent tree stands are forbidden, and this should be checked before your hunt.

Ed Shields of Frankfort is just one of the hunters who has successfully combined squirrel and deer hunting. As a native of Franklin County, Shields returned to old hunting haunts in the Bald Knob area when the squirrel season opened in August of 1968. He went toward Carrollton, turned off near the Bald Knob School, and soon was in country he had known as a boy. Before the morning was over, he had killed his limit of squirrels, which he expected, and counted a total of 20 deer roaming the woods, something he certainly did not expect. So when the deer season opened, Shields got out before daybreak with an old 30-06 rifle and made his way back to the deer trail in those squirrel woods. He hadn't been on his stand quite an hour when he spotted a large buck about 300 yards away.

Shields had no scope on his gun, but his long experience in the Army told him almost as much as a scope would have. He steadied himself against a tree and fired. The deer fell crippled, then got up. Shields ran as fast as he could for a closer shot. His second effort hit the head for a clean kill.

Once a deer is killed, the hunter must attach the locking tag portion of the deer permit to the animal. This tag must remain attached to the deer until it is processed and packaged. As soon as a gun hunter kills a deer and tags it, he must take the animal to the nearest check station or conservation officer.

Attaching the tag is no problem, but hauling the deer out of the woods can be quite difficult. Three of the happiest hunters I met in 1976 were Earl Parr, Herb Vernon and Bill Stiner of Okolona. They knew from Parr's earlier experiences how to prepare for a hunt, how best to take a deer, how to get their deer out with no back-breaking drag, and how to enjoy all the comforts of home while "roughing it" outdoors.

I first met this trio early the night before the Saturday opening at Ft. Knox when I checked into a bunkhouse at Camp Carleton, named for R. W. Carleton, former chief of staff at Ft. Knox. It can accommodate up to 180 people. Deer hunters are allotted stripped-down Army cots at only $2 a night on a first-come, first-served basis. Hot breakfast may be bought there at 4 a.m. on the morning of the hunt.

If you want to bunk nearby when you go for deer at the fort and Camp Carleton is filled, try Otter Creek Park, the 3,000-acre spread adjacent to the post, owned by the City of Louisville. An ideal place for hunters to camp, Otter Creek has two lodges accommodating up to 30 persons each, four cabins that hold up to six hunters each, and a large area for campers.

Nowhere is deer hunting safer and more closely controlled than at Ft. Knox. Advance registration must be made, and the 2,000 or more hunters allowed to hunt each Saturday and Sunday of the season are divided into groups of 25 and dispersed over 112 designated areas in the 96,000 acres. Each group has a leader and two assistants. Each hunter is checked into and out of the woods by his leader. No one is allowed to roam from his stand into another hunter's territory.

After an early breakfast at Camp Carelton, Parr, Vernon, Stiner and I were assigned to Area 27, presided over by party leader Don Torrance, post forester; who knows every inch of the woods. Our caravan of cars followed Torrance and his son, Ted,

over incredibly rough dirt roads for about 10 miles. We arrived at our area and were dropped out of range of each other well in advance of daylight.

Stiner found honeysuckle so thick that he had to climb up to the fork of a big tree for a clear view. He hadn't been there more than three hours when a 150-pound buck ambled beneath him. Stiner dropped it with one shot. Did Stiner have to drag it out like everybody else? No. Parr appeared with their four-wheel-drive Jeep and carried the deer and Stiner out comfortably.

Parr returned to his stand about 75 yards from Otter Creek. He saw several deer but didn't get a good shot until just before dark. He made an accurate shot at 50 yards and once more went for his Jeep.

The next morning Vernon, feeling a bit abused at not even having sighted a deer, took a stand on a ridge above his previous day's location. Three deer moved within earshot but not within gunshot. Then, around 3:30 p.m., a small buck came right at him, and Vernon felled him with one slug. Once more the Jeep did the hauling job, and the three buddies happily pulled out for Okolona.

Another hunter who likes Ft. Knox for deer is Gov. Julian Carroll. Although he had hunted whitetails before, it wasn't until the winter of 1972, when he was lieutenant governor, that Carroll first got one.

Having been told about the big herd at the post, he gathered a group of friends and went there for the opening day of the season. With him were his son, Kenneth, Bill Short of Louisville, Bill Cox of Madisonville, Roy Rubel of Frankfort, Ted Hottel of Louisville, Doc Moore, wildlife officer from Frankfort, and Ralph Penn of Frankfort. They arrived at the old Rod and Gun Club at 5 a.m. (across from Camp Carleton on Highway 60). Carroll was wearing a lightweight plastic jacket of brilliant Chinese red, a marvelous piece of apparel for deer hunting in moderate weather. Again, Torrance was the party leader.

Carroll hunted about a mile east of me along a high ridge overlooking Salt River. After sighting two big bucks ambling along about 200 yards away, he decided to move in that direction, intent on bagging a trophy buck. He hadn't much more than settled when a large doe browsed past. He held his fire, waiting for that buck. Four more does appeared, and still he waited.

At one point there seemed to be as many hunters

Arnold French's 16-pointer was a near-perfect rack.

traveling that area as deer. Carroll thought he heard another hunter walking up behind him and didn't bother to look around until the walking stopped. When he looked, there was a young two-point buck not more than 25 feet away. By the time he could raise his gun and fire, a bouncing white tail disappeared in the woods. There's no tougher shot than at a deer going at top speed. A deer doesn't run like a horse; he bounds like a rabbit. Your gun invariably seems to zig when the deer zags.

Having had an unsuccessful first day, Carroll decided to get a deer regardless of sex the next day. He took a stand overlooking a well traveled deer trail. About 10:30 a.m. he detected a slight movement off to his right. He slowly brought up his gun and soon recognized a large doe as she came closer. The deer kept moving at a fairly fast gait. When it was about 60 feet away it scented Carroll and turned abruptly to its right. Carroll fired. The deer stumbled, got up, and went 75 feet before dropping.

Youngsters as well as governors have had good luck at Ft. Knox. In 1972 when Robert G. Liberty Jr. of Jeffersontown was 11 years old and weighed only 86 pounds, he shot a doe that weighed 85 pounds. His father, a group leader at Ft. Knox, fell asleep on his stand and didn't even see a deer. You know who kidded whom at dinner that night.

And then there was Timmie Distler of Louisville, who bagged a deer when he was 15 years old. Hunting near the fort in 1973, Distler watched an eight-point buck amble his way about 9 a.m. He fired, but for some unknown reason the end of the barrel of the gun exploded and a piece of the metal flew back and cut the boy's head. The slug stayed on target, however, and the deer fell.

Not realizing that he was hurt, Timmie yelled, "I've got a buck!" When his father, Don Distler, raced up, there was his son sitting on the deer and holding it by the horns. Distler saw immediately that the animal wasn't dead and shouted for his son to run. Timmie jumped away just as the deer, which was shot only in the jaw, sprang away.

Father and son trailed the deer more than 2 ½ miles before overtaking it. The buck dressed out at 192 pounds. Distler believes that the explosion, which could have been deadly, was caused by a faulty shell or that his son got some mud in the tip of the barrel while waiting on his stand—a warning to those hunters who would lean on their guns.

But without doubt the youngest hunter ever to get

a deer was Stephen Chilton when he was 9 years old in 1972. With his father, Forrest Chilton, and cousin, William Chilton, all of Louisville, Stephen headed for a spot they knew near West Point. As Stephen took a stand near a deer trail, the other two walked a long way around and began a drive, slowly moving back toward Stephen and making noise as they went. In just 28 minutes they heard a shot. They hurried to the place where Stephen had been left and found him sitting on a log, the eight-point deer beside him.

St. Hubert, patron saint of hunters, must have smiled on this young hunter:

I pulled out of an assigned area at Ft. Knox on opening day '77 to join friends in another area for lunch. As our four-wheel-drive buggy lurched onto a feeder road a boy and man flagged us down.

They had a large doe and needed a lift to the check station. "My," I said, "that's a large deer. Who got it?"

"I did," said the boy.

"What's your name, son?"

"Mike Brown."

"How old are you?"

"He's only 13," said the man as they heaved the deer onto our tailgate. "I'm his stepfather. Name's Col. Rex Turner. He saved up for that gun and bought it himself. It's a 20-gauge. How many men have you ever seen kill a deer with a 20?" (It may have been the only 20 on the hunt.)

"We were late getting into the woods," he said. "Mike hadn't been on his stand 20 minutes when the big doe came along about 7:30. He bagged it with one shot, the first shot he ever made at a live target."

"I'm not surprised," I said. "Kentuckians learn to handle a gun early in life. You from Louisville, son?"

"No sir. Ft. Knox."

"I mean, where is your home. Like where were you born?"

"France."

"Oh, and then you moved here?"

"No. We moved to Korea."

"Then you came to Kentucky?"

"No. To Thailand."

"Then where, for heaven's sake?"

"To Wyoming."

"Then here?"

"Yes. In July. That's when I got my gun."

"So now Kentucky is your home."

Deer hunting areas

Boone and Crocket Club scoring sheet

"I guess so, but maybe it's Indianapolis. My grandparents live there."

A true Army offspring, Mike went with his stepfather on several hunts in Wyoming, but had never carried a gun until this day.

"I saw this big deer coming toward me," he said. "It was just ambling along. When it got about 25 yards away, I fired. I really wanted a buck, but I'm happy."

Deer hunting, however, is not limited to young boys and men. Many Kentucky women also find it an exciting and challenging sport. One of the largest deer ever killed in the state by a woman was a 10-point, 225-pound buck bagged by Wilma Snyder of Prospect several years ago. Miss Snyder usually hunted with a bow, but one time she took a gun on a trip to Henry County and in less than a half-hour after sunrise had her buck.

Mrs. Helen Sawyers of Louisville killed one of the biggest deer reported by a bow hunter that same season when she took a 177-pounder at Ft. Knox. And a real veteran deer hunter is Mrs. David (Nancy) Thomas of Fern Creek, who managed to bag a deer every time she went to the post.

If you're having trouble locating deer, try a stand near water. Frank Gnau of Louisville bagged an 11-pointer in 1975 that dressed out at 183 pounds. His stand was in an area called Hog Waller near Fort Knox, a site few hunters choose because of the steep climb.

"I was sitting there in the rain with my poncho covering me and my gun when this big deer ambled to a small stream in front of me for a drink," he said. "I got out of my poncho fast. The deer still didn't see me. It didn't move. I nailed him with my first slug."

Ray Moss of Louisville had a similar experience. Moss was stooping down to get a drink from a clear spring when a 193-pound buck quietly walked in to quench its thirst. Neither got a drink.

If you do search for deer near water, remember that there is a law forbidding hunters from taking an animal when it is swimming or in water up to its neck. Also, a deer cannot be shot from a boat or from any kind of land vehicle.

If you're really serious about still hunting for deer, you'll need to learn one lesson: Be very quiet. This was driven home to me again on a camper-trailer outing, a relatively new form of sport that has grown so fast a hunter who beds down early beside a remote logging road can't be sure he won't wake up the next morning to find himself in the middle of a community of campers.

Needless to say, all this motorized movement in the deer's domain doesn't add to the hunter's chance of seeing a deer, but it is good fun. Two hunters who enjoy these outings are Jerry Stine and Louis Hamilton of Lebanon. They set up their camper near New Hope early the night before the opening day of a recent season, gathered firewood for breakfast cooking, unfolded camp chairs, and turned on a portable radio for news and music. I joined them at 5 a.m., and a large pot of coffee was waiting. That was one of the most relaxing deer expeditions I've ever been on, but the day's hunt was doomed from the start. You just can't build fires, cook and clatter near where you hope to hunt. None of us saw a deer. We calmed down the next three days, and each made a kill.

One of the most prized deer ever taken in Kentucky was killed by C. W. Shelton of Bowling Green. And he has the rack to prove it. The Boone and Crockett Club at its biennial awards presentation in Pittsburgh announced that Shelton's trophy, bagged in 1964, had the widest spread found on any species of deer killed in the period. Generally mule deer, found west of the Mississippi River, have bigger racks than whitetails, but there was no mule deer, Pacific Coast deer, blacktail, or any other species registered that could equal the inside spread of 30 ¼ inches recorded by Shelton's kill. His trophy undoubtedly will rank among the 10 largest ever registered in the United States.

Deerhunters who bag trophy racks can use the chart and table reproduced here to determine just how great the trophies are. The chart and table are used officially in the North American Big Game Awards program and reproduced here by special permission of the Boone and Crockett Club. The minimum score for a typical whitetail deer accepted by the club is 170 points.

You can make a preliminary measurement by use of a score chart and a quarter-inch-wide flexible steel measuring tape. Should such a measurement show that your trophy is above or very near the minimum score, you should contact an official North American Big Game Awards measurer to have a measurement performed for trophy entry.

There are ten such qualified measurers in Kentucky. To obtain the one nearest you contact the Department of Fish and Wildlife in Frankfort.

A state-wide program for determining the largest deer and the most-prized rack was initiated in Kentucky during the 1978 season.

Only trophies taken in fair chase are eligible for awards. You may be asked to document such circumstances if your trophy qualifies for the program. Therefore, you should retain copies of your hunting license, special deer tags and other related papers.

(Official score charts with scoring instructions are available at a cost of 20 cents each. Address orders for score charts and other correspondence to: North American Big Game Awards Program, c/o Hunting Activities Department, National Rifle Association of America, 1600 Rhode Island Ave., N.W., Washington, D.C. 20036.)

Bow hunting deer is a sport in itself, completely separate and apart from target and field archery.

Bow hunters are encouraged to maintain a tradition of fair chase and good sportsmanship by their own Pope and Young Club, honoring the memory of two great bow hunters, Saxton Pope and Arthur Young. This club's awards program is patterned after that of Boone and Crockett. Minimum scores are set lower for this group than those required by Boone and Crockett, because bow hunters cannot be quite so selective as gun hunters. Official scoring charts, very similar to those used by gunners, and a list of nearby scorers may be obtained by writing Scott Showalter, Records Committee Chairman, Box 1001, Garden City, Kan. 67840.

Bow hunting for deer is legal in every state where deer hunting is allowed. October is the favorite month, probably because of the beauty of the season, freshness of the air and good stalking conditions. In Kentucky the bow season usually starts the first of October, ends in mid-November, and opens again for two weeks in December.

While the normal killing range with bow and arrow is about 45 yards, there have been cases recorded where game has been taken at far greater ranges: A Pennsylvania hunter took a running mountain lion at 100 yards; in South Dakota, a running antelope was hit at 130 yards. The average 50-yard bow will drive a sharp broadhead completely through a deer at 40 yards.

Kentucky's bow hunters number more than 7,500. Many are members of the Kentucky Bowhunters Association, which owns a 500-acre shooting preserve close to Ft. Knox. It was there

R.L. Wright of Louisville bagged a deer that had lost part of his rack in a fight.

Bob Neely of Owensboro, draws a bead on a venison dinner.

that Dennis Spalding set something of a record for archers at the start of the 1975 deer season. A newcomer to archery, Spalding decided to go competitive. On his first recorded shot he killed the biggest woodchuck to win the club's annual chuck contest, and his second shot dropped a deer.

How does a bow hunter go about bagging a deer? Garry Rau, assistant superintendent at Otter Creek Park in 1976, was one bow hunter who had a definite plan. Rau took what was perhaps the largest deer felled by a Kentucky bow hunter that year at Ft. Knox on the last day of the bow season. It weighed 195 pounds field-dressed and had a magnificent 11-point rack.

His work actually began during the small game season when he hunted squirrels and scouted the area where he later would hunt deer. Selecting a spot near the crossing of two deer trails, Rau nailed a temporary stand in the fork of a large tree, just high enough to be above the vision of a browsing deer. With binoculars, camera, pen and pad, and a little snack, he got into his stand before daylight on opening day, remained until noon, got back into it at 1:30 p.m., and stayed until dark. He repeated this every other weekend until closing day.

Each day Rau charted a pattern of deer action. He noted the movement of each deer he saw, how close it came, and from which direction. He saw between 10 and 15 animals each day and had several opportunities to bag a doe or small buck but held his arrow for a trophy rack.

On the final morning Rau climbed into his stand just before daylight. Here is the log he kept of the morning activity:

8:05—Doe ambled into view and disappeared off the left, followed by an amorous young buck.

8:10—An eight-point buck came from the same direction and also followed the doe. She must be in heat.

8:25—Saw young buck come back from direction the doe had gone. He was acting spooky. The bigger buck must have driven him off. Doe and two yearlings appear from up ahead and remain fully 15 minutes before going off to the right.

9:10—Saw eight-point buck. Took shot at him too soon. He jumped as the arrow approached, and the arrow went under him.

9:55—Eleven-point buck followed big doe directly in front of me, down a gully, and up. He stopped about 30 yards away. I waited. He made a motion to cut off to the left and I let go. Got him

right in the chest. He ran about 120 paces and fell dead.

How did this charting help? "Mostly," he said, "it showed me that deer move all day long on good days, not just very early and late, as I had been told. Also direction of travel and browsing habits." Rau's record: He spent 53½ hours on his stand; saw 34 deer, 13 of which were bucks; shot at four, missed three.

Another very patient bow hunter is Ed Johnson of Anchorage. He also is a glutton for punishment, but on one occasion he received a well-deserved award. Nine days he drove to Ft. Knox in the dark of the night with his bows and arrows. He clamped pole-climbing spikes on his feet and climbed eight feet up into an oak tree. He fastened a homemade seat of iron and wood—a portable tree stand—to the tree trunk and made himself as comfortable as possible, which wasn't too comfortable at all. And there he sat.

Eight times the sun came up and occasionally a deer came near but not near enough. Then came the ninth morning. It was 8:45 a.m., and Johnson noted quiet action below. A truly magnificent buck followed a doe along a deer trail. It stopped directly under Johnson, who held his breath for fear of spooking his prize. The buck moved on about 15 yards and stopped again. Johnson took careful aim and let go. The arrow hit the mark, and the deer traveled less than 200 feet before falling dead. Dressed out, the buck weighed 210 pounds and had a rack of 10 points.

Allan Thewes and Jim Carter of Louisville also had a plan for hunting deer. They had been bow hunting for three years, but all they had to show for their efforts were unused deer tags and sad memories—until one autumn day in 1971.

Their plan revolved around daily practice sessions that began two months before the season opened. When the day finally arrived, they packed up food and equipment for a four-day hunt in Land Between the Lakes, determined they would live in the woods until they bagged a whitetail. The next morning they were up before dawn. They took their stands and waited silently, not smoking, not moving.

The sun was hardly up when a young buck appeared about 20 yards from Carter, who took careful aim and let his arrow fly. The deer fell less than 50 yards away. Thewes and Carter carried it back to camp, dressed it out, ate lunch, and returned to their stands that afternoon. Some

shooting nearby galvanized two young deer into action, and they loped past Thewes's stand. He drew down on the larger of the two and dropped it almost in its tracks.

How's that? Two deer in one day for hunting pals on their first hunt of the year—and the first deer either had killed with a bow and arrow. Thewes's deer dressed out at 105 pounds, and Carter's at 96, the perfect size for table use.

While usually the hunter surprises the deer, on one occasion it was the other way around. Leon Williams of Fairdale had been bow hunting with his neighbor, Woody Henson. Henson felled a large buck in 1975 to become the first hunter to bag a deer in the Yellowbank Wildlife Management Area, which opened that year. (It since has been closed to deer hunters.) Williams was somewhat disappointed that he hadn't seen a whitetail but got over his disappointment long enough to go fishing in the area. He was on one side of a small lake, and Henson and John Hilkey, wildlife officer, were on the other. "Wouldn't it be funny," said Henson, "if a deer showed up now and nibbled Leon's ear?"

"Don't be too sure one won't," said Hilkey, nodding in the direction of Williams. A large doe and fawn had just ambled out of deep cover and were heading toward the water. Williams was watching his bobber so intently he neither saw nor heard the animals until they were almost on him. At the crack of a twig he jumped, and the deer, almost as startled as Williams, bounced back into the woods.

A year later John Boggs, Ken Hoff and Bob VanArsdale of Louisville hunted Yellowbank one morning with no luck. They were resting by a bank of the river when three young bucks quietly wandered up for a drink. Boggs and Hoff each bagged one; the third got away.

The 4,200-acre wildlife area, less than 60 miles from Louisville, includes a colorful expanse of deer woods and rippling fields of millet, clover and soybeans, all dotted with cool, clean pools of water. Yellowbank gets its name from a fishable creek by that name that flows leisurely through it. The wildlife management area was purchased in 1974 by the Department of Fish and Wildlife Resources especially for use by sportsmen in the Louisville metropolitan area.

Yellowbank stretches several miles along the Ohio River, starting about 18 miles west of Brandenburg. There are several routes to the area.

At Brandenburg, take KY 1692, turn right on KY 144 through Payneville and Andyville, then turn right again on KY 259, and the entrance is right there. It has been closed to deer hunting temporarily.

Taking the deer to the table can be as challenging as the hunt. What you do immediately after you shoot your deer, and before you freeze it, will have much to do with your future enjoyment of venison on the table. The following tips, gleaned from many sources, should be followed in detail if the meat is to retain its full flavor and quality. Read these carefully before you go on your next hunt.

Field dress the deer immediately. Drag it to a spot where you will have plenty of working space and prop it up on its back with logs, stones, or anything you can find. Open the deer on the underside from the breast to the tail.

Make the first opening through the skin and thin muscles of the upper abdomen just behind the breastbone. Lift the skin around the cut enough to insert two fingers of your free hand into the body cavity. Then, keeping the cutting edge of the knife up and between the fingers, slit the skin down to and around the anal openings. The two-finger guide assures that the stomach and intestines are not cut.

When this is done, cut the upper leg muscles between the hind legs down to the soft bone of the pelvis. Then cut through this aitchbone, as it is called, and spread the two rounds. This exposes the canal through which the large intestine passes.

Some hunters prefer not to cut the aitchbone until the deer is butchered. Instead, they cut around the anus and tie it off. This way you draw the part of the intestine between the rounds up through the canal into the body cavity and out to remove it.

Now that the abdominal cavity is opened and ready for cleaning, cut the diaphragm (the membrane separating the upper and lower body cavity) away from the ribs. Splitting the breastbone part of the way makes it easier to finish the job. However, if you have to drag the deer very far or over snowless ground, it's best not to cut the breastbone immediately. With the smaller body opening, you will collect less dirt and debris as the deer is pulled along the ground.

Next, cut the liver and heart from their attachments and put them in a sack to take back to camp. Pull the remaining innards down and backward. Be sure you don't rupture the bladder in pulling the intestines free from the body. The deer doesn't have a gallbladder, however, so you can handle the liver without fear of contamination.

The kidneys usually adhere to the upper body wall and may be removed during field dressing or left until the animal is butchered. To finish the field dressing, wipe the inside of the body to get rid of excess blood or loose tissue.

The deer is now ready to be taken to camp or to your car for transportation home. If you want to mount the head, be careful not to injure it as the carcass is dragged from the woods.

Once you get the deer home it should be hung, outside if the air is cold, or in a cooler, head down or head up. To hang it head up use a rope around the antlers. The best device for hanging with the head down is a gambrel or stout stick between the tendon and the hocks with the legs spread well apart. Tie the rope to the center of the stick to suspend the animal. A short stick placed crosswise in the body cavity will keep it open and help keep it aired to prevent spoiling. (See Figure 1.)

A deer in this condition is "hog dressed." If you want your venison aged like prime beef, leave the skin on and hang the animal up to two weeks at just above freezing temperatures. The hide prevents excessive moisture loss during this period.

If you want the head mounted for your trophy room, special care is needed. Start skinning with a cut along the back of the neck (not the underside) from the shoulders to between the ears. (See Figure 2.) Remove the hide by working forward until the skull is exposed. Then cut the flesh where the skull joins the neck and twist off the head.

At this point take the tongue out. It's edible. Now give the hide and exposed part of the skull a generous salting and take it to a taxidermist immediately.

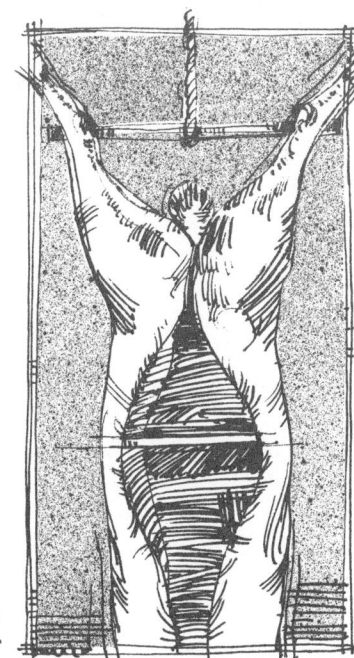

Fig. 1

Fig. 2

Fox

The Red fox of North America is a close relative of the European, Asian, and African Species. They are the closest to man and known by him for their sly and cunning ability to outwit their adversaries.

When I retired as sports editor of The Courier-Journal in 1969 to become outdoor editor, I had in mind tramping the fields in the autumn with a gun and writing about men with guns. Then one day I found myself out with a bunch of fellows who didn't even carry slingshots—foxhunters.

Foxhunters are the only sportsmen who get up before dawn and hunt all day, hoping all the while that they won't kill anything. Their chief concerns are that they see a fox or two and that nobody gets hurt, including the fox. Although red foxes are becoming scarce in some areas, a sufficient number remain to ensure exciting hunts.

In October 1969 I went on a typical fox hunt (my first) in Lancaster. C. E. "Bud" Waits, former president of the Kentucky State Foxhunters Association, and I shared a room at the Hotel Walker, the only hotel I know that was named after a foxhound, or at least after a family which developed a foxhound.

Up at 5 a.m., we bundled up for the 34-degree weather and found our way to a little restaurant that had opened two hours earlier than usual to serve the fox hunters who had come from 10 states for the annual state event. After a long car ride following trucks, station wagons and jeeps filled with noisy hounds, we turned off a winding dirt path to a flat meadow.

A blazing hot fire quickly drew a circle of characters ranging from a gnarled old-timer, who talked about the days when moonshine was the only thing that drew people out in those hills, to nattily attired girls who had their horses vanned in for the chase.

"Where are they gonna make the cast?" somebody shouted, referring to the place where the hounds would be turned loose to find the fox.

"Up on the ridge to the right," came an answer. Hounds, handlers and rattling chains moved continously in that direction.

Finally the first crimson and yellow streaks of day began showing in the east. I left the fire. Generally I could make out the skyline. What had seemed to be a row of bushes or trees became a row of hunters on horseback, all dimly silhouetted against the dark gray sky.

Buck Allison of Nashville, master of the hounds, was calling out numbers. Owners of the hounds painted with the corresponding numbers yelled back, "Here." Usually the master of the hounds wears colorful clothing, but Allison was bundled up in the heaviest coat he could find, and it was anything but colorful.

Finally the last of the 255 hounds was checked and in line. Allison looked at his watch. At the official hour of sunrise he gave the signal, and the hounds were off with a deafening chorus of deep-throated barking that is beautiful music to the ears of proud owners. Ten minutes later the hunters on horseback were allowed to start following.

I walked to a bluff overlooking a broad valley. The hounds had picked up a warm trail almost immediately on reaching a woods far down to the right. As I watched, a beautiful red fox streaked out of the woods, ran across a wide open field, across a narrow brush-filled ditch, and diagonally across another large field. Then came the hounds. What an unforgettable sight.

No wonder more than 7,000 Kentuckians follow this ancient sport. No wonder the Walker family of Lancaster has been revered for generations as developers of a leading (the Walker) strain of foxhounds. And no wonder that Everett Mackey of Nicholasville and many others have joined the International Sportsmen's Committee pledged to improve and protect their sport.

Fox hunters are a breed unto themselves, like the hounds they own, and little is understood by "outsiders" about their wonderful world. Here's a list of questions and answers I picked up from Bud (where he got it I don't know) that may help you understand their sport.

Q. Does a foxhound hunt by scent or sight?

A. By scent, like beagles, bassets and coonhounds.

Q. In hound-man talk you hear the word "strike". What does it mean?

A. A strike occurs when a hound hits a scent trail and gives voice.

Q. What do they mean when they say a hound is a "babbler"?

A. A babbler is a hound that gives voice when it doesn't have a scent.

Q. What do they mean when they say a hound "opens"?

A. When a hound first picks up a scent and gives tongue, it is opening — a big moment because it means the hunt is on.

Q. What does "tallyho" mean?

A. It means that somebody has spotted a fox.

Q. What do fox hunters mean when they say a hound is "skirting"?

A. They mean a hound is running alongside the pack and letting the others do the work. Sometimes cutting ahead is called skirting also.

Q. How can so many hounds perform in one field trial?

A. It takes a lot of wide-open country. The hounds are lined up together, then they are let go to strike a trail and form into packs of up to 100 hounds each, hot in pursuit of the fox. Mounted judges and judges in cars, jeeps and trucks range the countryside to catch sight of the packs as they go by and score the outstanding hounds.

Q. What are the main strains of foxhounds?

A. The strains include the Walker, July, Goodman and Trigg. The July strain got its name from a famous Georgia hound of that name; the others got their names from the men who did most to establish them.

Q. What is meant by "hilltopping"?

A. Hilltopping is what hardy fox hunters call their sport of running foxhounds just to hear the music. Hilltoppers usually meet at dusk, cast their hounds, wait for the music of a strike, then settle back — usually by a warm fire — and listen for their hounds' voices, argue whose dogs are ahead, and swap endless stories throughout the night.

Q. What is a field trial derby?

A. A field trial derby is a dog young enough to run in special trials called the derby stakes.

Q. What do they mean when they say a dog is a "front-end hound"?

A. A front-end hound is one that stays up in the front of the pack and does more than its share. It gives its owner something to really brag about.

Varmint

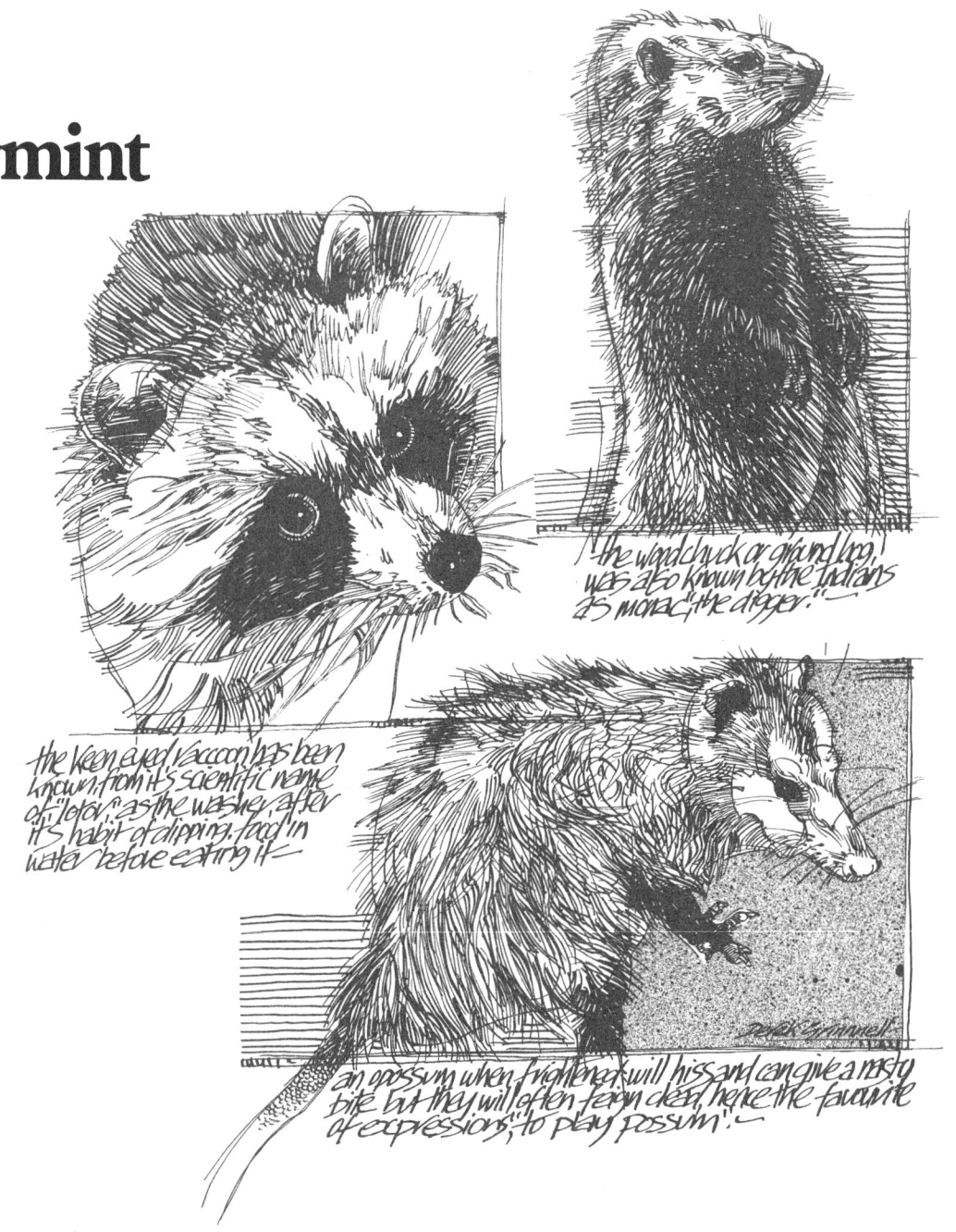

the woodchuck or ground hog was also known by the Indians as monac the digger.

the keen eyed raccoon has been known from it's scientific name of "lotor" as the washer, after it's habit of dipping food in water before eating it.

an opossum when frightened will hiss and can give a nasty bite but they will often feign death, hence the favourite of expressions "to play possum".

When you speak of a varmint dinner in Kentucky, you are talking about a combination of raccoon, opossum and woodchuck, which are found in abundance in Kentucky. When properly prepared, these furbearers can provide a rich feast.

Raccoon

The raccoon, or coon, is a tree-living small game animal that averages up to 20 pounds in weight. It has a stocky body and short legs. The raccoon bears a black band across its face, giving it the look of a masked bandit. It has a long bushy tail with rings of dark hair running the length of it.

A clean animal, the coon washes almost everything it plans to eat. And the coon eats almost anything—corn, vegetables, berries, eggs, frogs, fish, even garbage. Almost totally nocturnal, the coon does its feeding after dark, and that is when hunters go forth.

With specially bred and trained farm hounds, hunters go after these tricky and intelligent animals in areas well known for their coons. I have been regaled by many a tale of exciting hunts told by Joe Stamper of Middletown, Jesse Harp of Simpsonville and Floyd Gaines of Pewee Valley.

They go in groups of four or five. They try to park near a creek and turn their hounds loose along the bank, because coons dearly love crawfish, and usually can be found there.

The hounds hunt silently, like beagles, until they strike a track. Then they open up with their running bark and race pell-mell in pursuit. They might run 10 minutes or two hours before they tree the coon and their "tree bark" is heard. The coon may remain in the first tree it elects to climb. In that case the hunters have a choice—to shake it out and watch one of the dangdest fights ever. (Nothing fights a dog like a coon at bay)—or to take aim with a shotgun at its shining eyes and bring it down.

If the coon taps the tree—takes a mighty leap as

far out as it can—it will quickly run for another tree, or hole up. A good coon hound will circle the tree in widening circles until it takes up the trail.

Only 7 to 10 percent of coon dogs develop into top-grade hunters. For this reason they may cost up to $2,000.

Opossum

The opossum weighs up to eight and as many as nine pounds. Instead of the beautiful tail of the coon, the opossum has a scaly, naked tail. Not a very popular animal, the opossum is hunted much like the coon, but the sport is far less exciting.

Woodchuck

The woodchuck, or groundhog, is pursued by day, usually in open fields in Eastern or Central Kentucky, by men and boys carrying rifles with scopes. This rodent measures about two feet in length, weighs about nine pounds, is stocky and generally is brown with some gray in color. It uses its short legs and long claws to dig dens and burrows and thrives on garden vegetables, grains and alfalfa.

Using binoculars, you can survey a great distance without having to walk a lot or even leave your car. Once you have located a chuck, you must approach as close as possible without arousing its attention. When within range of your rifle and scope, usually about 200 yards, lie prone and fire at will.

The best time to go looking for woodchucks is in early mornings and evenings from spring through summer. Chucks will take a break from their digging and sit outside their dens. When they sit, chucks are easy targets because they hold their bodies erect.

If a woodchuck sees you, it will dive into its hole. For this reason the hunter must stay low and be quiet. But the chuck is a curious animal. Even if it knows you are watching, it eventually will come out to take a look.

For hunting woodchucks, find appropriate farmland and ask the owner's permission. Because of this varmint's reputation as a destructive pest to farmers, you should get the permission easily. Woodchucks may be hunted throughout the year except during the period preceding the opening of the small game season. A hunting license is required.

Woodchuck holes are lifesavers at times for other wildlife. Rabbits, opossum and even quail find them safe havens in extremely bad weather.

Hope Carleton, Jr. draws a bead on a groundhog

There's a coon up that tree, yessiree.

Tips for the *Hunter*

Selecting and Training a Bird Dog

Most every Kentucky boy whose father does a lot of hunting dreams of the day when he will have a gun and a dog of his own and go into the fields and woods after rabbits or perhaps quail.

The dog for such a youngster must be a specialist, one which knows about birds, or coons, or squirrels, or rabbits. The day when a young fellow could kick up a rabbit without a dog soon may be gone. And of course, nobody ever could do much good with quail without a bird dog—one that can retrieve as well as point.

The time for a boy and his dog to get together is just about any old time, so long as it is at least a full year before the boy gets his first gun. The hunter should be allowed to grow up with his first dog. The best kind of dog for him is one that he can keep around the house as a pet during the off-season, yet one that will serve as a competent hunting companion and helper in the field when the season is on.

Tom Dunlevy of Jeffersonville, Ind., is a rabbit hunter. He rates a beagle as a hunter's best friend. "In no time at all the kid and pup will become inseparable," Dunlevy said one day when we were hunting rabbits in Indiana. "And when the rabbit season opens, it won't take the average beagle more than a few romps through the fields to pick up all his natural traits of scenting and chasing rabbits, barking and yipping his head off, giving the boy the time of his life." The beagle, the smallest of the hounds, has been used to chase rabbits and hares as far back as the year 1300. It is a good-natured dog, easy to keep clean, and a lover of the hunt.

Alvin Ruxer of Jasper, Ind., is a quail hunter. He naturally leans toward a pup that has a nose for birds and whose zest for the chase is not dulled by pampering. "I say give the boy a Brittany spaniel," he said.

Brittany spaniels, orange or tan and white short-haired dogs, point and retrieve birds as instinctively as beagles hunt rabbits. They are, I believe, the only spaniel that naturally points birds. But all spaniels cotton to kids, and, if not too spoiled by overfeeding at home, they will make good retrievers, as well as great pointers, without much coaching or coaxing.

Most natural retrievers, such as the Labrador, make wonderful companions for young people, but I know from my own experience that they can be spoiled beyond use in the field. A magnificent black

Labrador lived so closely with my children that I think he looked upon himself as a person. I tried several times to teach him to retrieve ducks. He refused to go near the water. He wouldn't even walk through high grass if it was wet.

Of course, there are many wonderful breeds of bird dogs to choose from, such as:

English setter, the oldest game bird dog in this country. Long-haired. Color varies from black, white and tan to a combination of liver and white, lemon and white, and black and white.

Llewellyn setter, another long-haired beauty, usually black with tan markings.

Irish setter, a magnificent mahogany color, silky hair. A headstrong animal.

English pointer, short-haired, mostly black and white. Can take hot weather better than most and doesn't pick up burrs. An ideal family dog.

Golden, Chesapeake retrievers, great for waterfowl hunting.

Weimaraner, a very popular, large, short-haired dog, silver gray to dark gray. Smart, learns easily, a good pointer.

Once you select your dog, you may have some problems with training it.

The simplest way to teach the pup that he belongs to you and you are his friend is to be sure you are the only one who gives him his food and water.

Don't bathe him unless it is absolutely necessary. Most dogs don't like it and really don't need it much more than a cat does. To make your dog's coat shine, brush it hard and often.

The best information I ever read about training pups I found in the closing chapters of a book called *Bird Dogs* by Ray P. Holland.

Holland said to start your training as soon as the pup is old enough to run in the field. Bear in mind, he said, that there's one thing no man can teach his pup—how to find game. The pup must be born with the instinct to hunt and the desire to find birds. If he doesn't indicate this urge, you can't give it to him. To a lesser degree, pointing is also an instinct. You can teach your dog to point, but you can't teach him to find and point game.

But there's more to be done with your dog at home. Obedience must be taught from the cradle. One stunt Holland insists on has to do with feeding and is quite simple. He puts a pan of food down but doesn't let his pup approach the food until he says, "All right."

The Pointer must have good bird sense—

Discovered by the Irish as a good breed to find and set birds while on a hunt, the Irish Setter soon became the most popular breed in Ireland. Today it ranks high on the top ten list in the U.S.A. for field work or as a family friend.

a friendly quiet natured breed was introduced to the U.S.A. in 1934.

The English Setter raised to the stock as we know today by two Englishmen named Edward Laverick (1797-1877) and Purcell Llewellin.

The Weimaraner bred as a sporting dog in Germany and introduced in U.S.A. 1929.

A good pointer.

The Brittany Spaniel weighs three from France a day of ??? qualities being exported to the U.S.A. in 1931 enjoying a quick popularity.

The Foxhound was developed from a mixture of hound blood. Primarily used for foxhunting the first known pack was developed in England around 1299 by Edward I.

Derek Grinnell

A racoon is "treed."

Coon dogs consist of several full blooded breeds such as the treeing Walker, black-and-tan, redbone and bluetick.

Beagles are one of the oldest British hounds and one of the most popular especially in the U.S.A.

Derek Grinnell

He continues this training every time the pups are fed, changing the command to "All right" and the pup's name. Then gradually he drops the "All right" and simply uses the pup's name. Thus, when the pup is in a run with other dogs, he will wait until his name is called. There is no better way to teach a dog his name. If the pup breaks for the food before you call his name, make him go back. If you let him get by with it once, he will try it again.

Start by placing the food in front of the pup. Hold him and say, "Back," then "All right" when you release him. This training at mealtime also will teach the word "Back," which is important. Later you won't have to hold him but may have to use a small switch to enforce your command to "Back" before allowing him to go eat. It is a lesson that comes quickly when the reward of food is at the end.

When your pup is five- or six-months old, take him on a leash and lead him around. When he tries to pass you, pull him back, switch him lightly on the nose, and order, "Heel," thus teaching him to walk at your rear. Soon you may do this without the leash.

Next, start him retrieving. Place a pad in his mouth and hold it there, saying "Fetch" every time you put it in and "Thank you" every time you take it out. When the pup reaches the point where he will hold the pad until you take it out, start leading him around with the pad in his mouth. When the pup drops it, put it right back in.

The next step is to make him reach out and take the pad from your hand when you say, "Fetch." This may require patience. When he does this, place the pad on the ground in front of him and give the command. Then toss the pad out a short distance and let him bring it back.

This accomplished, it is then important to teach him "Whoa," a very important word. Hold him tight and say, "Whoa," when he returns the pad. Then release him and say, "Fetch." Throw the pad and walk around a bit before you say "Fetch." If he starts, order him to "Whoa" and drop the pup in his tracks with a rope tied to his collar.

Do a thorough job on this lesson, and the pup will be ready for field work. Toss the pad into a brush field and make the pup locate it by scent alone. Order him to "Fetch" and "Hunt dead." When he finds the pad and brings it to you, be sure to show him you appreciate what a smart dog he is. Switch then to a dead bird.

One other thing, to avoid gun shyness try

approaching him closer and closer with a cap pistol. Then switch to a .22 and so on.

When your puppy is big enough to romp in the fields, take him out every chance you get. Let him chase every bird he sees. Let him chase butterflies to his heart's content. Just don't tire him out. That's important.

Naturally you want your pup to learn to go where you want him to go. Call him to the edge of a thicket. Motion him in with your arm, then start in yourself. When he sees you going in he will start and pass you. Keep doing this, and in a short time he will know what you want when you wave your arm toward the brush.

Often you will wish to cast your dog to the left or right when he's out ahead of you. Give a short blast of your whistle to make him look back. When he does, swing your arm to the right and start walking in that direction. Next time turn him left. The pup will swing the way you are walking. In no time all that will be needed is the swing of your arm. Provided, of course, he is watching you.

When your pup is about six-months old try to get him into game. When he flushes a covey of quail and chases, go along with him to rout out the singles. Let him rout and then chase them. By this time you should have a pretty fair idea as to how good a dog he is going to be.

Some pups will go right out and start pointing as soon as they learn the smell of the game. But it's better if they don't. Many good trainers urge a puppy to keep on chasing in order to build up a desire to hunt long after the time when others would be trying to steady him. If he's a good pup he'll come to pointing in good time.

Some start by flash-pointing and jump in on a covey before you can get to them. This poses a problem. Try to get hold of his tail as you come up. Don't talk to him. Lift him gently by the tail until his hind feet leave the ground. Ease him back to the ground and lift him again. Then put your hands under his chest and raise his forelegs and set him back down. Even lift him clear of the ground and put him back down. If he stays stiff-legged your troubles are about over. Never get in front of him to cut off or interfere with the magic smell that has thrown him into this trance. Try to push him gently toward the birds. If he pushes back toward you, you can bet his days of puppy flushing are over.

Of course, many good hunting dogs have been purchased as fully trained adults. My advice is to ask for a week's trial before you accept the dog. A dog may have an excellent pedigree and still not be able to find a quail in a cage. Performance, rather than papers, is the primary consideration.

Protecting Your Dog from Cockleburs

Before leaving for the hunt, some hunters rub Vasoline on their dog's ears, legs and tail. They find they can pull the burrs off with no difficulty when following this simple precaution.

Wearing Safety Glasses

Terry Showers was a 26-year-old teacher at North Hardin High School and an avid bird hunter until he went hunting for quail one Thanksgiving holiday. After that hunt he wasn't sure he'd ever teach again.

"If I had one wish for all hunters, it would be that someone makes sure that they wear safety glasses every time they go after game," Showers said from his hospital bed where he was fighting to retain vision in one eye after having already lost sight in the other.

Showers had hunted since he was a 14-year-old in Hardin County. "I was taught by an old-timer who was a stickler for safety," he said, "but like most everybody else I got to taking safety for granted. When two friends and I took a youngster with us, I knew the kid had been hunting less than a year. We should have had a serious talk on gun safety before we started. But we didn't."

The four were just coming out of a patch of woods and brush, walking about 75 feet apart and not easily seen by each other. A covey of quail flushed wildly ahead of them. Most of the birds went forward, but one whirled around and flew between Showers and the boy. Showers fired as the bird came toward them. If he had hit, this story would not have to be told. But he missed. The bird kept coming, and when it was between the two hunters, the boy fired. More than 70 of the 7 ½-shot pellets struck Showers in the face, arms, and chest.

"I am the victim of one of those tragic accidents you think just couldn't happen to you," he said. "But here I am. If I had been wearing safety glasses I could have taken all those pellets in my face and body and been out of here in two days."

Showers hoped his accident would jar other hunters into taking safety precautions more seriously. "If they asked me I'd say first of all, don't go into the field without safety glasses.

"Next, don't spread out so far you can't see each other. Keep talking so that all have a good idea where everybody is at all times.

"And above all, sit down and go over safety rules one at a time before starting out."

Choosing Shot Size and Choke

Any discussion of shot and choke brings up questions of what constitutes a heavy or light load and how one bore compares with another.

The size of the load depends on the weight of the gunpowder and shot pellets in the shell. A heavy load might have 3 ¾ drams of powder and 1 ¼ ounces of shot pellets. The lightest load might carry as little as three drams of powder and one ounce of shot.

The extent of a choke in a barrel—the constriction in bore size at the muzzle—determines the spread of the shot pattern at a given distance. Chokes range from full to improved-modified to modified to improved-cylinder to straight or skeet cylinder. The criterion for a full choke is that a 12-gauge will put 70 percent of the total number of pellets in a shell into a 30-inch circle at 40 yards. Improved-modified should put 65 percent, modified 60, improved-cylinder 45 and skeet 35.

Most experienced hunters would agree with these recommendations for bird hunting:

Game	Type of Load	Shot Size	Choke
Turkey	Heavy	2, 4	Full
Geese	Heavy	2, 4	Full
Ducks	Heavy	4, 5, 6	Full or Modified
Pheasants	Heavy	6	Modified
Grouse	Medium	6, 7 ½, 8	Modified- or Improved-Cylinder
Quail	Medium	7 ½, 8, 9	Modified-, Improved-Cylinder, or Skeet
Doves	Medium	7½, 8, 9	Modified-, Improved-Cylinder, or Skeet

Determining a Shotgun's Pattern

Have you ever taken the time to pattern your shotgun? You'll never spend your time more fruitfully. You might think that every 12-gauge skeet barrel will throw the same pattern, but this isn't true. Gun experts have proven that one gun may throw a beautiful pattern with No. 8 shot while another may do poorly with No. 8 and great with No. 6.

Before you go hunting in the fall, pattern your gun with three loads. Tack three large pieces of paper on a barn, walk 40 yards away, and fire No. 6, 7½ and 9 shot. Draw 30-inch circles on each sheet and count the holes inside the circles. Then check with figures above the chart.

A good pattern will show even distribution of pellets without bare spots. If your gun happens to pattern poorly with No. 7 ½ but good with No. 8, just don't use the 7 ½. It is very unlikely that a barrel won't throw a good pattern with some shot.

Different barrels are needed for the different varieties of game, but many hunters can't afford to buy more than one. There is an easy solution—a variable choke fitted on the muzzle. Your gun then should be good for anything from geese to doves.

When you test your shotgun, you should test yourself as well to determine which of your eyes is the master. If you shoot right-handed and your right eye is your master eye, you are fortunate. If you find by sighting with both eyes open and then with one eye closed that your left eye is the master, you must make an adjustment. Either squint with your left eye, or place a piece of masking tape over the top half of your left eyeglass.

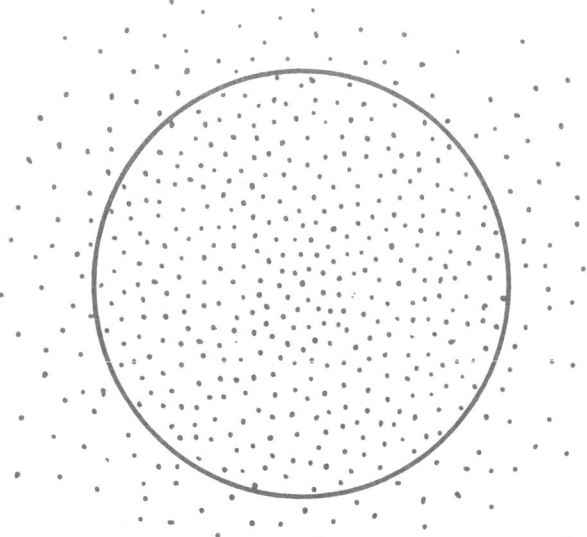

Leading Birds

There are many schools of thought on whether a hunter should lead—shoot ahead of—a bird on the wing. If your own technique works, don't change. But if you have trouble hitting birds in flight, you should consider different methods of leading.

While waiting for the seasons to open, hone up on your knowledge of the relative speed of game birds. Experts say the canvasback is the fastest thing you'll ever shoot in Kentucky. It flies at rates of up to 65 miles an hour. This chart, a composite of several estimates, should start a lot of arguments.

Species	Top Speed	Lead at 40 Yards
Canvasback	65 mph	11 feet
Dove	60 mph	10 feet
Goose	60 mph	10 feet
Mallard	55 mph	9 feet
Quail	40 mph	5 to 6 feet
Grouse	30 mph	3 to 4 feet

Some hunters say you don't aim, you shoot by instinct. Then there's Dr. Keath Hammon of Louisville, a former member of the All-America skeet team, who says, "You MUST aim, and aim very carefully, using both sights on your gun. I even have a center sight on my gun. To become a champion shooter you can't afford to miss more than one percent of your shots, and you can't be that accurate by instinct."

Then there is B. L. "Lucky" McDaniel. This mild-mannered Georgian has convinced fellows like the late President Dwight Eisenhower that you don't need sights on your gun, and you don't have to lead a bird.

I got out before breakfast one morning for a two-hour dove shooting session with McDaniel at the River Valley Club's trap range. Here is what he told me:

"You don't have to lead a dove, or any other bird, at all. You just watch the target (with both eyes open) and forget the sights on your gun. You must keep your eyes above the target—not in front of it.

"When the target (duck, goose, or dove) dives down, don't shoot under it, hoping it will drop into the pattern. Keep your eyes above it, and you'll drive the pattern down into him. You will notice I say the eyes, not the gun sight. If your gun is in position, you hardly will be conscious of it. Your left hand will guide the gun where your eyes direct.

"If you follow this method you may get three

birds—bang, bang, bang—and not know where any fell, because your eyes will not follow any to the ground. Finding birds is dog's work anyway."

You can teach yourself to become more accurate. Use a good BB gun. Toss small objects into the air, look at the top of the target, and fire. Keep at it until you can see the BBs in flight and you can hit the mark regularly. Then switch to a hand trap and have a friend throw clay pigeons for you. Hold the gun in front of you, pointing up, so that when you bring it to firing position you instinctively will lean into it. When the target swings out, bring your gun up with your left hand doing the aiming, and shoot when you get your eyes just above the target.

In this kind of shooting you block out your thinking process and aim strictly by instinct, for lack of a better word. Here's a trick, if you want to call it that, that seems to prove that your eye can do things you can't imagine. McDaniel made a mark with a pencil on a quarter. He said, "I can't explain it any more than you can, but when I toss this coin in the air and you hit it with that BB gun, you'll hit at or near that line." He tossed it, I hit it, and the nick was right on the line.

McDaniel has written a book called *"Instinct Shooting."* I recommend it.

Protecting Against Ticks and Chiggers
Don't ever venture into the woods of Kentucky for squirrels or any other animals before a good freeze without guarding yourself against an attack of chiggers and ticks. Chiggers are bad enough, but seed ticks—or deer ticks, as some hunters call them—are a disaster. More than a hundred of them may get on you from a single contact with an infested leaf or branch.

There are several excellent repellents on the market. Pour some on your hands and rub it into your socks and around your middle and neck. Flower of sulphur also is good, but it must be fresh.

I'll never forget the experience I had on a squirrel hunt at Land Between the Lakes. I used sulphur left over from the year before. By 10 a.m. my legs were covered with little black dots, each smaller than the head of a pin. I quickly jumped into Kentucky Lake and washed myself thoroughly with strong soap. All the little dots disappeared, but unfortunately two or three hundred ticks already had bored under my skin. That night I was one big itch with welts covering both legs and my middle.

Not only that, but my hunting clothes had to be laundered before I could take them into the house.

Several creams are on the market that give some relief to the itching, but an ounce of prevention is better than all the salves on the shelves.

Marking a Trail
Sometimes it is necessary for a hunter to mark his trail in Kentucky's dense woods. Breaking brush, bushes, or small limbs in the direction from which you came is the easiest method. An effective but undesirable technique used by some hunters is to carry a spray can of bright paint and squirt a bit of it on tree trunks, a modernized form of tree blazing that aesthetically damages the forest.

Al Geisser of Radcliff suggests that hunters carry a small roll of fluorescent tape when venturing into an unknown forest. Blaze a trail with it by running strips of tape around small trees to serve as returning markers. This is ideal, as long as you remove the tape on your return trip. It is forbidden in most controlled areas, however.

Waterproofing Hunting Gear
There are several good concoctions on the market for waterproofing hunting jackets and shoes. For the shoes I have used only Vasoline with satisfactory results. As for the clothing, I would recommend a commercial product, but if you are a do-it-yourselfer, you might try one of these recipes, that turned up in my file some years ago:

For cotton gear, dissolve one ounce of beeswax in one quart of white gasoline and brush it on your clothing lightly. For woolens, dissolve one ounce of lanolin in a quart of white gasoline and dip the garment into the solution. While the piece of clothing is hanging to dry, turn it upside down several times to keep the solution evenly distributed.

Preparing a Bird for Mounting
If by great fortune you happen to kill such an unusual specimen that you want to have it mounted, clean out the bird by making a longitudinal cut from the anal vent along the belly line at the sternum. This will allow the taxidermist to sew it up so no seam is visible. And by all means, take your bird to the taxidermist as soon as possible.

Lubricating a Gun
Some oiling is necessary for guns during the winter hunting period. The cold weather tends to stiffen the oil and slow down the action. After each use, simply clean the barrel and mechanism and lightly rub the outer surface with any gun oil to guard against rust.

Make sure that your gun is free of all moisture before returning it to your gun case. If you don't follow this simple precaution, the gun probably will be covered with rust the next time you want to use it.

When the seasons end take your gun apart and clean thoroughly before putting it away.

Using the Distress Signal
Most Kentucky hunters know the standard signal for use when lost—three shots fired in quick succession, a pause, then three more shots. But many hunters do not know the proper reply. If you hear a distress signal, respond by firing two quick shots.

Fishing in Kentucky

Black Bass

Travelling in deep water schools, the Largemouth, Black Bass, can be instantly triggered into feeding as small shoals of bait fish pass over stirring a frenzied excitement at surface.

Three species of black bass—the largest members of the sunfish family—are found in Kentucky. Before we get into the ways and means of taking this fish, let's try to settle here the recurring question of how to distinguish between the average largemouth, smallmouth and Kentucky bass.

First, the largemouth versus the smallmouth. With the mouth of the fish closed, a vertical line running through the pupil of the eye would just nick the inner corner of the smallmouth's mouth but would pass through the mouth of the largemouth. In other words, the mouth of the largemouth extends back behind the eye.

Another big difference is in the body markings. The smallmouth has distinct vertical bars on the sides of its body, while the largemouth has pronounced lateral dark lines running from gill to tail. The markings fade somewhat on older fish.

The Kentucky bass strongly resembles the largemouth but has two easily seen differences— longitudinal lines of small spots on the lower sides, which cause some anglers to call it a spotted bass, and a rough spot formed by teeth on its tongue. The largemouth has a smooth tougue.

Now the smallmouth versus the Kentucky bass. The smallmouth frequently has teeth on its tongue, so there's no help there. But the jagged dark band along the sides resembling the largemouth clearly sets the Kentucky apart from the smallmouth.

One further check for all three: The notch in the spinous dorsal fin is deep on the largemouth, not so deep on the Kentucky, and still shallower on the smallmouth.

Black bass are never as dark as their name implies. The largemouth usually has a dark green back, lighter green sides, and a gray or yellow-white belly. The smallmouth varies in color from pale yellow to dark brown but usually is dull olive-gold. The Kentucky resembles the largemouth in color.

Largemouth Bass

The largemouth bass is unquestionably the most prized fish sought by anglers all over Kentucky. It is a great fighter, wonderful table fare, and found almost everywhere there is life in water. The largemouth is hunted so avidly that more than 100 bass clubs have been formed in the state since 1970.

Because it is such a predator the largemouth bass will take almost any kind of bait—live minnows, live night-crawlers, live red worms, plastic night-crawlers, and any one of several hundred artificial lures made expressly to attract it. No single type of bait will work consistently under all conditions, and most experienced anglers carry large tackle-boxes filled with lures of every description, and switch at will.

In the very early spring when the water is dirty and filled with debris, the largemouth is taken by jigging night-crawlers, even plastic ones, along rocky banks and near stumps and fallen trees. Jig fishing is best in rough weather, and veteran fishermen dress in thermal underwear and heavy woolen togs to brace themselves against cold winds and freezing spray.

The equipment is simple—just a stiff fiber glass or cane pole about 10-feet long, a strong four-foot line, and an ample hook capable of holding from four to six live night-crawlers. Most anglers attach a popping-type bobber about 18 inches above the hook to wake up a bass that might be snoozing. Ease along likely looking banks and jig the squirming morsels around every stump, stickup, bush and rock, letting the bobber pop against the surface of the water.

The art of jigging was developed at Lake Herrington many years ago by two old-timers, Lindsey "Buck" Buchanan of Danville and Nevel "Red" Beasley of Paint Lick.

Buchanan saw some big bass feeding along a shallow bank and tried casting at them. He tossed every kind of lure he had in his box, but with no success. Finally he got out of his boat, walked along the soggy bank, and when he brushed aside the wet matted leaves at the water's edge, Buchanan found night-crawlers. Yanking off his artificial lure, he replaced it with a night-crawler draped on a big hook. Then he jiggled the worm in the muddy water. Almost instantly Buchanan had a vigorous bite and brought in a five-pound bass. Later he tried the same area from his boat using a four-foot line at the end of a 10-foot cane pole. Again he was

successful. Beasley, who was operating the Gwinn Island camp at the time, followed the same procedure. Thus jigging was born.

Since those early days, jigging has been refined until now experienced anglers find they can bring in lunkers by jigging minnows in shallow murky water, by tantalizing bass with a black dollfly-type lure baited with pork rind or a purple worm, or by draping three or four live worms on a treble hook. When the water becomes a little too clear for successful daytime jigging, the more avid jiggers take to the lakes at night, using luminous bobbers to help them hit the right depth (about 18 inches) and the right distance from shore (usually about one or two feet).

Later in the spring the largemouth can be taken on or near a spawning bed by flipping a top-water lure at its nose. The fish may not strike the first time, but if you persist, the largemouth eventually will become angry enough to lunge at the bait.

As the nesting ends and the water temperature rises, the lunkers move out to old feeding spots, on shady sides of rocks, stumps, or fallen trees and wait for food to pass. Surface lures then provide the best action.

As the summer wears on and the lakes clear, bass move into deeper water, near rock outcroppings, and along sloping points and old creek beds. Deep runners and plastic worms played along the bottom are the best producers. Let the lure sink until a slack line tells you it has hit the bottom, then retrieve in slow, short flips. During the night bass will move toward the bank to feed and good catches may be made between midnight and dawn.

The best thing to do during the heat of summer is to go out at sundown and fish on through the night.

Some of the most interesting July and August outings I've been on were with old-timers who long since had given up the daylight hours to skiers and pleasure boaters.

Not too long ago I went fishing with Bob Patterson and Lawrence Wetherby at Shanty Hollow near Bowling Green. We had bets on the biggest and the most. We started fishing at dawn, rested, and then went out again at 4 o'clock, quitting at dark. I was ahead in number and Patterson had the biggest. Looking forward to another round at daybreak, we hit the hay early.

Several hours later Wetherby turned on the light and shouted, "Wake up you guys! Look who beat you!" He was standing in the center of the room

Ralph Dyer with his hefty catch

holding up a string of several largemouth bass. The rascal had sneaked out of bed after we were asleep and had fished by the light of a first-quarter moon. In less than three hours he had caught seven bass, including a four-pounder, and had won both bets.

A Flatwoods fisherman would agree that night fishing is best for catching largemouth bass. Delbert H. Grizzle caught the state record—a 13-pound, eight-ounce largemouth—in August 1966 by casting the shoreline of Greenbo Lake at night with a six-inch purple worm on a weedless hook. His record largemouth was boated a year after he caught an 11-pounder at Greenbo, which he swears by as the place to take lunkers. Grizzle prefers night fishing there because Greenbo Lake is small and somewhat crowded during daylight hours. He chooses plastic worms over any other lure, and his favorite colors are purple, wine and black.

Most anglers say it is futile to fish for bass on a windy day, but a threesome of Kentuckians told a different story after a trip to Lake Barkley.

John Cooper, his son, Johnny, and Bob Blandford planned to fish Alabama's famous bass heaven, Eufaula Lake, but when they phoned ahead the fishermen were told the wind was too strong. They decided to try Lake Barkley, where they thought the weather was calm. They were wrong; it was blowing plenty when they arrived at a small dock near Kuttawa. They tried the backwaters in a creek up from the dock where it was fairly calm, but none of them got a strike. Finally, at about 9 o'clock, they headed for the main lake where the winter draw down had left many stickups far out in the lake. Using a trolling motor to hold them fairly steady in the wind, they began casting deep running lures into the stickups.

Cooper, using a waterdog-type lure that vibrates when retrieved, got a lusty strike at 10 o'clock and brought a five-pound largemouth to the boat. From then until 3 o'clock that afternoon there was activity and excitement for all three. "Almost every time we got our lures on the bottom, about 10-feet down, we got some action," Cooper said. "We didn't land them all, but we got our share." Their share was a string of eight bass averaging five pounds each. Most were caught during the least likely time of day, between 10 a.m. and 3 p.m., and in the wind.

A remarkable thing about their catch was that they didn't get even one strike from a fish weighing much less than five pounds. They did get a hit from one that felt like it weighed twice that, however; the

Derbert Grizzle of Flatwoods holds his state record largemouth.

lunker struck Johnny's bomber-type lure right on the lake bottom.

Nearby Kentucky Lake is another good place to go in search of largemouths. The biggest one reported caught in the state during 1972 was an 11-pound, six-ounce fish taken from Kentucky Lake by Ron Faber of Owensboro. Faber made the catch at high noon with a frog-green surface lure, which one admirer of his catch took as a souvenir.

Robert Metts of Louisville probably set some kind of record for catching largemouths at Kentucky Lake that same year. His unbelievable series of catches started in May, when he boated three fish weighing between 6 ½ and 7 ¾ pounds. On June 1 he caught a largemouth that weighed 7 ½ pounds. Then on Oct. 24 he weighed in with four fish—the largest going at 7 ½ pounds—totaling 27.7 pounds.

Craig Fleming and his father-in-law, Jack Wheatley, both of Louisville, boated a prize catch at Kentucky Lake one August day about that same time. They caught six bass, and none weighed less than four pounds; one weighed a bit more than seven pounds, and the other five together tipped the scale at 34 pounds. Fleming and Wheatley used only surface lures early in the morning and deep runners during the heat of the day.

Lake Cumberland is the favorite largemouth bass spot of two Louisville fishermen. Sam Smith and Ralph Denham went there one spring day when there was a lot of drift and trash in the water, as is usual at that time of the year.

After a try at the main lake they headed upstream from the Lake Cumberland State Park dock to the mouth of Caney Creek. The sun was just coming up when Smith made his first cast. "This is the dirtiest lake I've ever fished," he complained. "It's terrible. I don't think I'll ever come back." He pulled some debris from his black bushwacker-type lure and made a second cast. This time the lure lit in some willows. He flipped it out and the lure quietly plopped into the water. When Smith gave it a little flip to impart some action, it wouldn't come loose.

"I guess I've got another one of those snags," he said. Just then the snag moved. Smith quickly set his hook and began the biggest fight of his spring outing. He finally got his fish to the boat, and Denham slipped a net under it.

When they returned to the dock, they weighed the fish, which had been on ice during a morning of fishing. Smith watched the dial turn to a fraction

more than 12 pounds but short of the 13-pound, eight-ounce record.

A. Mingus of Axtel caught a 12-pound bass in Rough River Reservoir and thought he had a world record smallmouth, but after a careful study state biologists identified it as a largemouth. The lunker shared the state largemouth record prior to Drizzle's 1965 catch.

Another never-to-be-forgotten catch was made by Tubby Taylor of Louisville in 1971 when he took his young sons, David, Morris and Douglas, fishing at Rough River. He hoped to show them a few fishing tricks but hardly could have hoped for what happened. Using a hellbender lure, he boated a limit catch that totaled 70 pounds, including an 8 ½-pounder, two seven-pounders, and two six-pounders.

Another Louisvillian, Jim Mivelaz, also discovered that Rough River is a good spot for largemouths. Fishing with Mel Borich, Mivelaz cast a plastic worm with a spinner attached and almost immediately pulled in a bass weighing eight pounds.

Walter C. "Pat" Wohlgemuth of Louisville has fished many places and experienced many thrills, including filling his boat with coho salmon in a stream emptying into Lake Michigan. But the piscatorial delight of his life came early in the '70s when he boated a largemouth bass at tiny Guist Creek near Shelbyville which weighed—you won't believe it—nine pounds, five ounces. Fishing with Roger Smith, also of Louisville, Wohlgemuth caught the fish while trolling a deep running artificial lure. Naturally his fish is the largest known bass ever taken from Guist Creek.

The largest pair of largemouth bass ever reported in the state were caught by Bill Cooke of Middletown. The fish weighed just over eight pounds each. Cooke boated the beauties at Mud River off Green River near Rochester. He was fishing at night with a black hula popper. Just two weeks earlier the same angler took two seven-pounders out of the same stream between 2 and 4 a.m.

When William H. Walker of Brooks was only 12 years old, he made the catch of his young life. Fishing at Nolin Reservoir with his father, Sherman, and two friends, Jimmy and Billy Owen, he boated an 8 ½-pound largemouth. The boys started fishing at dawn and young Walker made his catch about 9 o'clock when he pitched a Rapala-type lure along a rocky bank in fairly shallow water. Needless to say, the prize was mounted.

Jim Coakley, Earl Ruby, former Gov. Ned Breathitt and Gim Dossett had a lot of fun and a few fish.

Nolin Reservoir was also the scene of a believe-it-or-not catch made in 1966. You've heard of a lot of bass being caught on odd rigs and big and little hooks, but have you ever heard of one being caught on an anchor? Well, Mr. and Mrs. Elmer Thompson of Louisville once fished the reservoir with Bill Turner of Louisville and Cliff Turner of Elizabethtown. When they returned to Rex Bailey's dock they had 11 big bass. The largest, a four-pounder, was brought in with their anchor.

Originally caught on an artificial lure, the lunker made one last bid for freedom just as it was about to be boated. It got tangled in some brush, and in desperation somebody tossed the anchor overboard to see if it would shake the line loose. It did the job. The line came up, floating free. But no fish and no lure. Dejected, Thompson hauled in the anchor, only to discover the bass, one hook of the lure in its mouth and another caught in the anchor rope.

And here's another unusual bass story: Bob Blandford and Jackie Wade of Louisville went fishing at Lake Barkley one April morning and boated 11 bass on 13 strikes. They used surface lures and cast to stickups along the shoreline. Their biggest prize, a 7 ½-pounder, was a double-barreled surprise. Blandford boated it while casting stickups in the middle of the lake. He got hung on one cast, finally jigged it loose, and got hung on another stick about a foot out of the water. Before Blandford could yank it loose again, the bass lunged out of the water and took the lure, and Blandford got the fish.

But the strangest catch of all was made by Tom Myer of Louisville, who was fishing Reelfoot Lake one April day with Larry Cassidy, Bernard Popham and J. Ed Brown, all of Louisville. Myer cast a surface lure and was retrieving it with slow, gentle jerks, expecting any second to see a big splash as a bass struck the artificial minnow. Imagine his surprise when the splash came not from a fish but from a large owl. The owl missed on its first strike then quickly dived again and got the lure securely in its claws. It flew up into a tree, still holding tight to the lure, until Myer finally had to reel the bird in. His guide pried the talons loose and the owl flew away, angry but unharmed.

Many nice strings of bass come across the docks at Kentucky's major lakes, but many of the real lunkers are taken from farm ponds and small lakes.

W. L. Carter of Lawrenceburg came within five ounces of catching a new state record largemouth bass in 1972 at a pond in Anderson County. Fishing with plastic worms, he captured his prize at 3 o'clock in the afternoon and didn't have it weighed until six hours later. After that drying out, the fish still weighed 13 pounds, three ounces.

Raymond Ferguson of Louisville brought in a 10 ½-pounder from a lake at Ft. Knox. It was the biggest largemouth caught in Kentucky in 1969 and the largest ever taken at Knox. Second largest that year was a 10-pounder taken from Shanty Hollow by Randall Farris of Bowling Green.

John Davis of Valley Station may have set a record for farm pond fishing in 1972 when he hauled in three largemouth bass that together weighed 18 pounds. The largest tipped the scale at seven pounds. Davis, fishing at a pond near Jeffersontown, used a small casting outfit and a purple worm with no weights or spinners. He caught all three about 10 feet from the bank by casting ahead of himself as he walked around the pond just after daybreak one July morning.

Sherrill Baker of Okolona has been fishing a small lake in Lincoln Homestead State Park near Springfield for many years and called it "the best bluegill pond I ever saw, but that's about all." His mother, Mrs. Catherine Baker of Mackville, scoffed at the idea. Mrs. Baker, one of the best bass anglers in the state, said, "I've hooked into a bass in that lake so big he broke my line."

Mrs. Baker and her husband, Richard, went to the 2 ½-acre lake twice in one week. Walking the bank and casting purple worms toward the center, they caught 21 largemouth bass, all of which weighed more than a pound and a half.

Mrs. Baker lost no time in relaying the news to her son, and the next chance they had, Sherrill and Judy Baker headed for Springfield. They arrived at the pond at 6:30 a.m. and began walking the bank and spincasting purple worms toward the center. Baker got two strikes and pulled in one bass weighing about one pound and another that went more than a pound and a half.

Then, about 9 o'clock, Baker threw his lure far out and let it sink to the bottom. He waited a bit and gave a slow, gentle pull. He waited and pulled again. Then again. When the lure was about 25 feet from the bank, Baker felt a mighty tug. He quickly set the hook and gave a whoop. "I think I've got him!" he cried. Afraid that his 10-pound test line would break, Baker cautiously maneuvered the fish into shallow water and asked R. C. Caslow of Mackville, who also was fishing the pond, to give him a hand. Caslow waded out about seven feet, grabbed the fish by the gills, and dragged it to dry land.

Hep Taylor, the park superintendent, was present when Baker set the monster on the scale. The fish weighed 10 ½ pounds, the largest bass caught in Kentucky in 1968.

But the darndest story I ever heard about fishing in Kentucky concerned a lady angler, Mrs. Drane (Ruth) Scott of Louisville. Mrs. Scott set an all-time state record for women in 1971 when she hooked a largemouth bass that weighed nine pounds, seven ounces and boated it all by herself.

Then there is her husband, a man who owned 30 tackle boxes chock-full with more than 2,500 artificial lures. This gentleman caught one nine-pounder and three eight-pounders in one season to establish something of a record for Kentucky anglers.

But there's more. All the monsters were caught in the same lake. Not Kentucky Lake or Lake Barkley or Lake Cumberland, the state's three giant impoundments. No. They were taken from a small lake—most call it a pond—built near Louisville by Louisville sportsman Dave Wilson for his own enjoyment.

Speaking of ponds, I can think of several good ways to fish a farm pond. Here they are, along with the companions I've watched use them successfully:

Glen Beyl of Sellersburg, Ind., washes his hands with kitchen soap to eliminate all human odor. He hooks a big night crawler in the head or tail, strokes it with a finger dipped in oil of anise, and casts the worm as far as he can out into the pond, using no sinker. Beyl takes all the drag off the line, rams the butt of the rod into the bank, then sits back and waits. When a bass takes the lure the line begins to strip off the reel. He lets it run out until it stops. When it starts up again he figures the bass has swallowed the worm, and that's when he sets the hook. Beyl has landed many a slab with this method.

Hope Carleton of Frankfort has found a way to take big bass from beneath heavy moss lining banks. He casts an eight-inch weedless white pork rind on the moss as he walks, then retrieves it in short jerks. A bass strikes at the pork rind and leaves a hole in the moss. Carleton lets the lure drop into the hole, and he gets his fish.

Zeke Morgan of LaGrange, a man of many improvisations, uses his hip waders to work his way

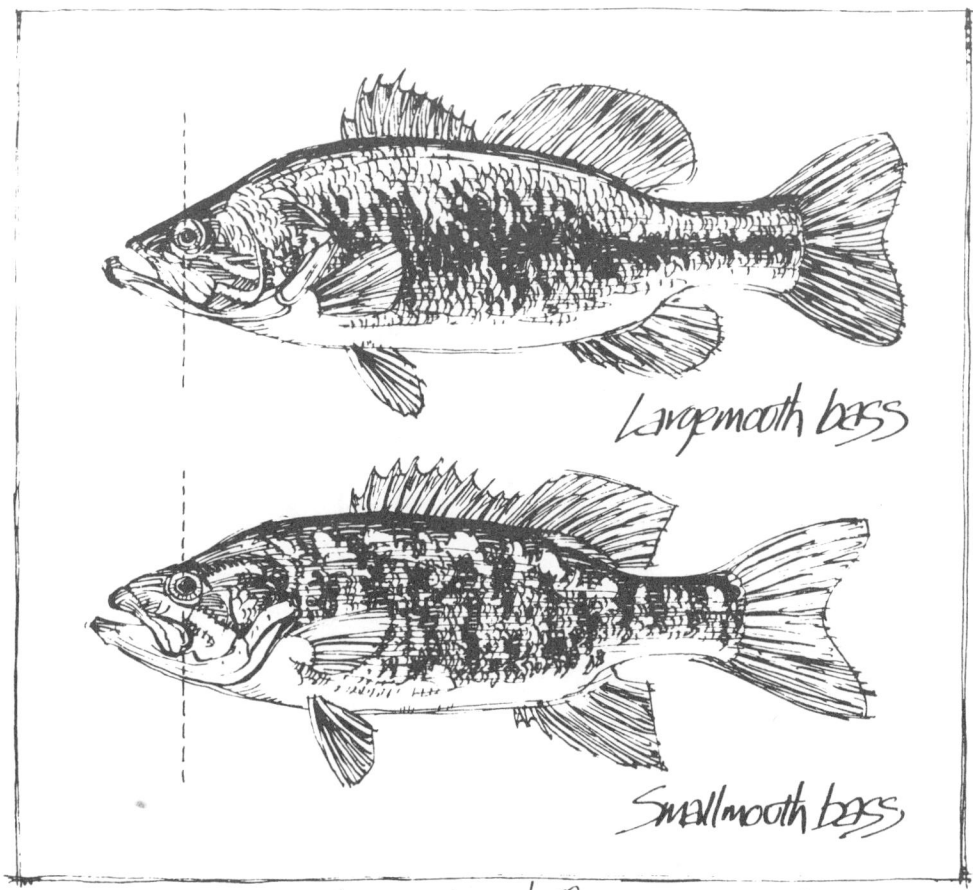

Largemouth bass

Smallmouth bass

How to tell a Largemouth from a Smallmouth bass

out into the pond to the edge of the scum. He casts small spinners and beetle-type lures to the edge of the moss. He always brings back more fish than his partners who stay on dry land. Morgan employs a most unusual procedure when faced with two much bottom vegetation. Using a hypodermic needle, he shoots a bit of air into a live night crawler at three points. When he casts the worm out into the water, it floats just above the vegetation, very much alive and wiggling. It's a sure catcher when retrieved in short, gentle flips.

A farm boy with whom I have fished uses a 12-foot bamboo pole, a six-foot line, and a treble hook full of night crawlers. He jigs the worms just beyond the scum and gets a lot of action, especially around sundown on the shady side of the pond.

I prefer live crawfish for bass fishing in ponds. Every bass I took from one pond one year had big craws in its stomach. In fishing with a craw, you have to be careful it doesn't back into a hole and hide. Try to keep it just off the bottom and retrieve in short pulls.

Smallmouth Bass

The smallmouth bass originally thrived in mountain streams but now is found primarily in Kentucky's large impoundments, where this prowler of lake bottoms has reached its largest size. Because the cagey smallmouth is such a hard fighter and is less common than the largemouth, it generally is considered to be the more treasured catch, even though it is smaller. A five- or six-pound smallmouth is a braggin' catch.

The smallmouth is a species of northern climates and prefers cold, clear water. Usually you'll find it hiding deep among submerged rocks. This is not to imply that the smallmouth cannot be taken with surface lures, but even at night this is unlikely.

If you plan a search of smallmouth bass, go to a large, deep body of water where there is plenty of space.

Dale Hollow has to be the smallmouth bass capital of the world. It not only has produced the world record of 11 pounds, 15 ounces, caught by David L. Hayes of Leitchfield in July 1955, but also a 10-pound, 14-ounce monster taken by John Gorman of Planfield, Ind. Gorman's catch is believed to be the second largest smallmouth ever taken on a hook and line in America.

And those two catches were not flukes. Dr. Herman Mahaffey of Louisville and his wife,

The world champion smallmouth bass is held by David Hayes of Leitchfield, who caught it at Dale Hollow.

Evelyn, caught eight nice smallmouth bass there one afternoon. The fish ran from two to 7 ½ pounds.

Another fisherman who proved that Dale Hollow is worthy of acclaim was seen by Jim Reneau at Holley Creek dock just as he had caught a limit of smallmouth on a day when nobody else had more than one or two.

"I wasn't having any luck until I tried a little wrinkle of my own," explained the angler, whose name is unknown. "I took a dollfly and placed a live spring lizard on the hook. I cast this to the bank and let it hit bottom. Then I retrieved by short jerks, letting it hit bottom each time. When it hit bottom about 10-feet out and 10-feet down, I got a strike. From then on I had a lot of fun."

But now for the real story—the taking of that world record. Hayes and his wife went out together one July morning in 1955. About an hour before the big catch, Hayes hooked a good-sized walleye and, after 10 or 15 minutes, worked it alongside the boat for Mrs. Hayes to net. But unfortunately, just as Mrs. Hayes dipped the net into the water, the fish threw the hook.

That bit of bad luck was soon forgotten when a huge smallmouth hit about 75 feet off Shale Point. After 20 minutes of battling, the fish began to weaken, and Hayes started wondering about netting it. After all, he had just lost one beauty in trying to boat it. After another 10 minutes of fighting Hayes had the fish next to the boat. Mrs. Hayes took the

68

net and, showing the form of an expert, dipped the net into the water and hauled the fish aboard.

Hayes said that he had only one regret. His two fishing partners from Leitchfield, Walter B. Lowry and Maurice K. Willis, were not present to witness his catch. With Lowry and Willis, Hayes had brought in many remarkable bass before latching onto his record-setter. Their joint catches included a nine-pound largemouth, an eight-pounder, and 30 largemouths that weighed between six and seven pounds each.

Hayes got his champion smallmouth by trolling, just as he had taken all those largemouths. He had a 40-horsepower outboard on a 25-foot cruiser. The boat sported a sun canopy and trolling chair like a deep-sea fishing boat. He used five-foot trolling rods and large star-drag reels seldom seen this far from the coast. He tied bombers on 15-pound test lines, let them out 300 to 700 feet (depending on the speed of the boat and the depth of the water), placed the rods in holders, and began trolling just fast enough to keep the lures knocking the bottom.

"The biggest thing about catching big bass is to know where they are," said Hayes, "and you can only find that out by trial and error, troll, troll, trolling days at a time. When you catch a big one mark the spot and go back and forth over the same area. Usually where one is feeding others will be feeding. The big ones seem to hang together."

Hayes found that gravel and shale bottoms seem to be the preferred feeding grounds of smallmouth bass. If the lure snags and comes up dirty with weeds and other debris, the fisherman knows he is in the wrong area.

The process of trial and error often is costly. Even expert fishermen frequently lose half a dozen or more lures on snags during one day's outing. They run their lures about 15-feet deep in the spring, when they use only about 300 feet of line, and 40- to 50-feet deep in the summer, when they let out 700 to 800 feet.

Here are their tips: Know the spots. Have the deep-sea trolling equipment with monofilament line. Learn to get the feel of the lure, the vibration; it has to have motion. When you hook into a big one reel it in under power; don't cut the motor or it will get away. If it's a big one and fights hard, take care with the monofilament; it may stretch and cause the spool to spread and bind. It's best to pump the fish in; haul up on the rod and then reel in, alternately.

Kentucky Bass

The Kentucky bass was so named in 1927 because it was believed to exist only in the commonwealth. Since then, however, it has been found throughout the South and now is known generally as the spotted bass.

The Kentucky bass falls between the largemouth and the smallmouth in size—it averages from one to two pounds in this climate—and in habitat. It enjoys modest temperatures and prefers rocks to weeds and moving water to still.

Usually caught by anglers casting for largemouths, Kentucky bass are found in virtually all Kentucky lakes. Most any lure used on largemouths may be employed in pursuit of Kentucky bass. They feed for the most part on minnows and insects but will strike at crawfish, worms, grubs and small frogs. Look for them along rocky banks and in stickups along those banks.

Because of this fish's wide distribution throughout Kentucky, it was named the official state fish by the 1958 General Assembly.

The state record is seven pounds, 10 ounces, taken by A. E. Sellers of Louisville from a Nelson County lake.

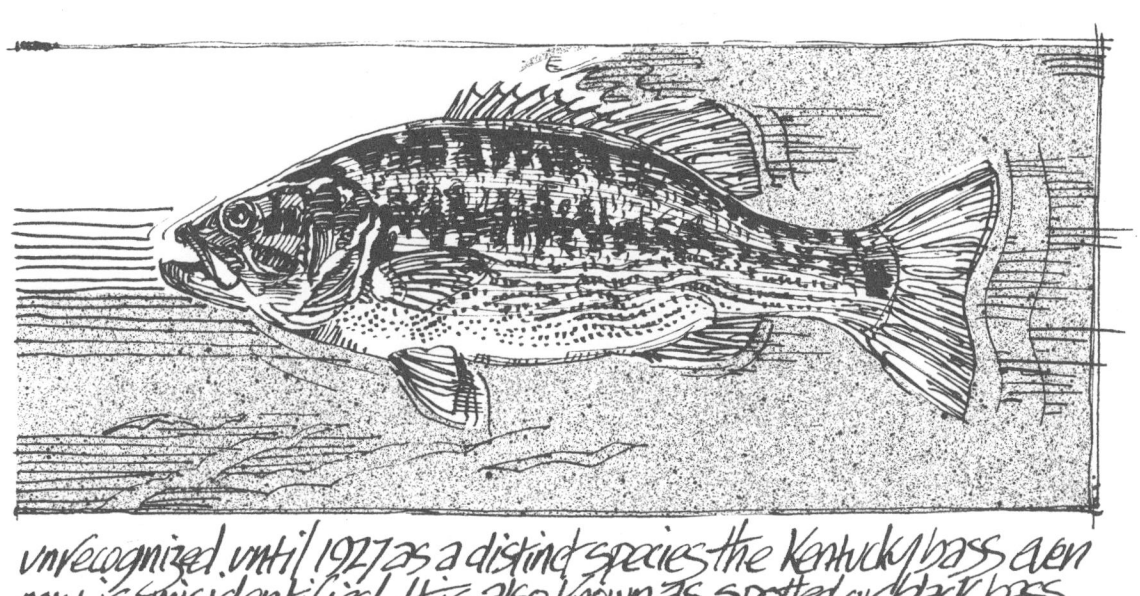

unrecognized until 1927 as a distinct species the Kentucky bass even now is misidentified. It is also known as spotted or black bass.

White Bass

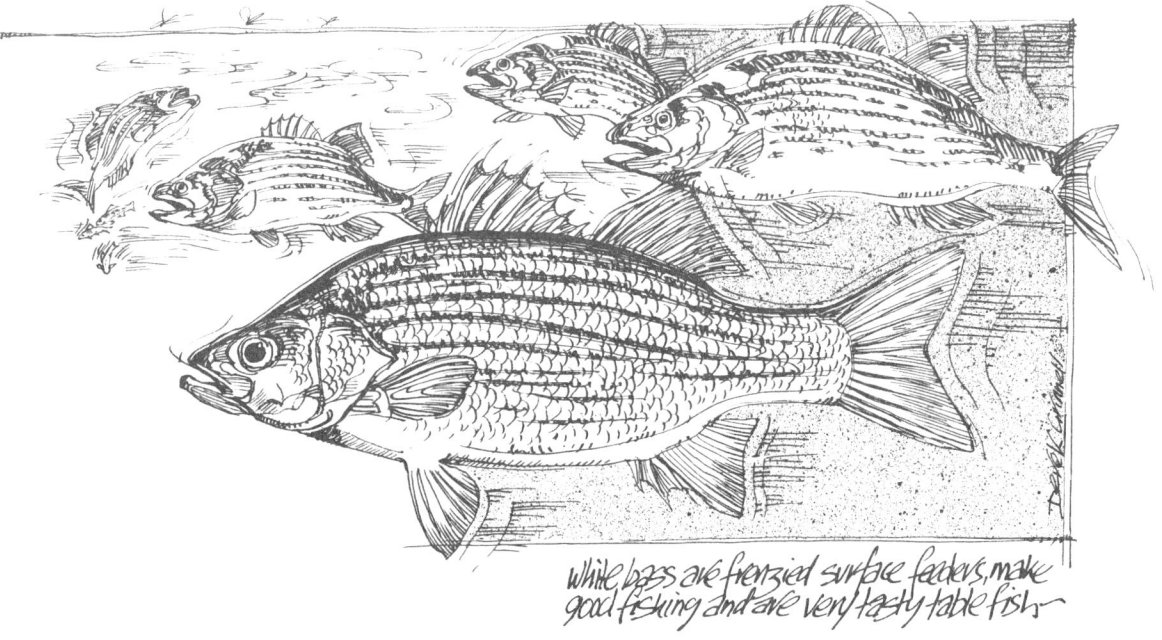

White bass are frenzied surface feeders, make good fishing and are very tasty table fish.

Feast or famine is the story of white-bass fishing in Kentucky. You either catch a tubful of the sleek, silvery fish, or you go home with none.

Not until the construction of large impoundments in Kentucky began did the white bass, formerly considered an unimportant species of fish, become recognized as an amazingly prolific fish that made a delicious meal. And because white bass travel in schools and gorge on shad in large, open lakes, the fishing action is fast and fun.

The white bass, also known as the striped bass, silver bass and barfish, is found in every lake of any size in the state. The fish is primarily silver toned with a greenish back and has narrow rows of dark spots from gill cover to tail on the upper sides. A sure way to distinguish the white bass from the rockfish, which it resembles, is the presence of 11 to 13 spines on the anal fin, a slightly outthrust lower jaw, and a single patch of teeth on the base of the tongue instead of two patches. The white bass feeds principally on small fish, crustaceans, insects, minnows and gizzard shad.

The white bass, which averages from one-half pound to two pounds, has a small mouth, so it is important that you use a small lure.

The best outfit is a light spinning rod and reel with a four- to six-pound test line. If you'd rather use a bait-casting outfit, get a light one. A rod about six-feet long is best with lines testing eight pounds. A heavy rig will make if difficult to cast the small lures.

Anglers concentrate on white bass during three periods of the year — when the fish are on their spring spawning runs up feeder streams, when they are in the main lake feeding on schools of shad, and later in the year when they are deep and can be taken at night.

White bass make their runs up virtually all feeder streams above Kentucky's major lakes. The two most spectacular spots for the spring action are on the Dix River above Lake Herrington and on the South Fork of the Cumberland at Yamacraw. To reach the Dix River area take U.S. 52 between Danville and Lancaster to the bridge over the Dix. Or run up Rankin Road just west of the bridge to Rankin's Bottom, where hundreds of anglers line the bank almost daily during the run. For the Yamacraw area take U.S. 92 out of Stearns.

Other popular spots are on the Cumberland River near Corbin, the South Fork at the Alum Ford Recreation Area, the Rockcastle at Bee Rock, the Barren headwaters near Fountain Run, the Nolin near Millerstown, and the north and south forks of Rough River. Also, you might try the tailwaters below most dams where whites join other frustrated game fish trying to find a way upstream.

After the spawning, the white bass returns to the main lake very hungry and goes searching for schools of new shad. If you keep a sharp eye out you can see a school of small shad boil up on the surface, chased by bass. You can catch a barrel of the whites by gunning your boat to the edge of the "jumps," as they are called, and casting a small spoon or spinner into the heart of it. Usually a bass will strike immediately. You reel in quickly, drop the fish in a bucket or on the floor, and cast again as many times as you can before the shad go deep and the action ends. They'll surface again, sometimes as close as 50 yards away.

A successful white-bass fisherman from whom others can take a lesson is Glen Beyl of Sellersburg, Ind., who always washes his hands with laundry soap before he handles his lures to eliminate the human odor. When you are casting repeatedly in jump fishing, the washing isn't all that important, he says. But other things are.

Beyl and Jim Weber, another Hoosier, went jump fishing at Nolin Lake and caught the limit each of two days. Other fishermen, taking only eight or 10, wondered what Beyl's secret was. The two fellows had put in the lake near Wax Boat Dock about 4 o'clock in the afternoon. The lake was calm — ideal for white bass fishing — and they could see the swarming action—the jumps—in every direction. At one spot near a small island they flipped 28 whites into the boat before they could stop to put them on ice. The next morning they decided to go for black bass, but when they ran through a large school of shad they forgot the blacks and began casting the jumps again.

"There is a science to jump fishing," Beyl said. "These fellows would see me catching a mess and gun their motors until they were on top of the jump, then cast way past it. No wonder they didn't catch any fish. You have to ease up short of the jumps and cast neatly into the thick of them and work your lure like it was a shad."

Beyl uses a small spinner with a fuzzy tail. The size lure depends somewhat on the size of the shad, he believes. "Some schools I saw were made up of shad less than an inch long," he said. "There's no lure small enough to help much there, and bass aren't likely to be chasing the tiny ones anyway. The little ones will grow and provide good jumps later, in October."

Night fishing with artifical light and live minnows can fill a stringer in no time when a feeding school, which usually will be around a deep rock wall or near a steep rocky point, is located. The depth at which a school might be feeding can be determined by allowing a hooked minnow to sink to the bottom, then winding it in slowly until action is felt.

These schools have a way of moving on, and the angler eventually is left with a motionless bobber. He can either use a fish finder and move with the school or wait until it or another school comes along.

There is no substitute for experience in white bass fishing, as in any kind of angling, and that includes timing and choice of lures as well as efficiency in casting and setting the hook. One April day several years ago I went for whites in the Dix River above Lake Herrington. After turning at the bridge on to Rankin Road, I traveled as far as I could by car, then walked to Rankin's Bottom. Anglers of all ages lined the bank.

"Anybody have any luck?" I asked.

"Nobody but the preacher," came the answer.

"Who is the preacher?" I asked a fellow fishing from a stump 10 yards upstream from me.

"I don't know who he is, but he sure catches the white bass," he replied. "He gets 'em when nobody else can buy a strike."

An angler a few yards downstream said, "He teases the fellers by saying ya gotta live right to catch fish. But I think he knows something we don't know. About fish. Not people."

Not long after that a big fellow came lumbering across the slippery rocks in waders up to his armpits. He was carrying a string of fish as long as his waders. Two young fishermen were scrambling along beside him, asking how he did it. He was the preacher, the Rev. C. E. McCracken of Lexington. He had been fishing Central Kentucky waters for several years and had earned a reputation for never leaving a stream empty-handed.

I watched him catch his last bass of the day. He was standing midstream in water about four-feet deep, casting toward a boiling riffle and retrieving with a graceful, easy motion. Flip and reel, flip and reel. When I caught up with him later, McCracken had counted his catch for two admiring youngsters — 40 white bass, one largemouth bass and one big buffalo.

"There's no big secret to catching white bass or any other kind of fish," he said. "You just have to understand fish. You have to try to think like them and act accordingly. It isn't easy sometimes. For instance, fish like to feed early. I was out here at daybreak. There wasn't another soul fishing. I was able to wade out to the best possible spot to cast into that ebb side of the riffle so that the lure would be carried from shallow water back toward deep water and me.

"I picked a small yellow do-jig today. Yesterday it might have been a white one." He held up his lure. It was a jig consisting of a small drop of lead painted yellow to which was attached a hook and a small skirt of yellow bristles.

"You probably saw that I was fishing the second riffle (shallow water over a rocky bottom causing broken water above Lake Herrington backwater). "I always pick the first or second riffle for the more shallow water — never anything farther downstream. If the lake had been lower, I would have been fishing farther downstream. If the lake had been up, I would have been fishing farther upstream.

"I had most of my fish before any other fisherman arrived. By the time fishermen were beginning to crowd each other on the banks, I had all I could carry. I was ready to quit — and so were the fish. That was about nine o'clock. I always quit about nine. Occasionally I'll return around sundown, but not often."

Lorne Eli of Dawson Springs holds his state record white bass, and his wife Bertha shows one she caught that was almost as big.

The state white bass record is five pounds and is shared by Lorne Eli of Dawson Springs and B. B. Hardin of Mount Eden. Eli bagged his prize at Kentucky Lake in July 1953, and Hardin caught his June 1957 at Lake Herrington. With Eli was his wife Bertha, who caught one weighing 3 pounds and eight ounces.

A catch of a four-pounder at Guist Creek a few years ago earned Ralph Elkin of Louisville a certificate from *Field and Stream* as first prize among white bass fishermen using 12-pound test lines. His catch remains the all-time record for white bass taken from Guist Creek, that picturesque little lake near Shelbyville.

The daily limit on white bass of any size in Kentucky is 60, subject to possible change.

Croppie

Croppie (crappie)

nicknamed "croppie eyes" croppie do not like sunlit pools so you'd best find a deep "croppie hole" to fish—

"This is Minor Clark," said the voice on the phone. Clark was commissioner of fish and wildlife for Kentucky from 1958 to 1971. "We have a popular and prolific resident of our state which deserves better treatment," he said. "He has so many names, I think we do him a disservice by letting him be known by his worst.

"I would like you to announce through your column that henceforth in Kentucky this popular fish being taken in such large numbers at most of our lakes will bear the official name of 'croppie.' Where it picked up that inferior-sounding name of 'crappie' is beyond me. But I do know he is far from inferior. In fact, he is one of the top table fish taken in Kentucky. From now on it will be 'croppie' in all our records and periodicals." This was welcome news to sportsmen and outdoor writers who had found it difficult to identify the fish properly.

When I first heard of the fish it was called a "newlight." Some folks said it got this name from a congregation of churchmen in Grant County called the New Lights, or Campbellites, after a stout old Scotsman, John McLeod Campbell. They were said to have found the fish in abundance in nearby Eagle Creek.

More recently, a fisherman from Tennessee joined a discussion about the fish at Lake Cumberland. "If you mean these black ones," he said, indicating several on his stringer, "you're talking about 'calico bass.' And these big white ones here"—he pointed to one of considerable size—"we call them 'strawberry bass.'"

A dock worker listening to the argument said, "It doesn't matter what you fellows call them, the only name that fits them is what we call them here—'papermouths.' They got a mouth that tears like a paper bag, and if you try to horse them you'll lose them every time." It is because of this fragile mouth that most fisherman like to give the croppie plenty of time to swallow the bait before slowly retrieving the fish.

So much for that. The official spelling for the Kentucky delicacy was "croppie" until Clark retired. The present wildlife commission has returned to "crappie," although most anglers still refer to the fish as "croppie," as I will here.

No matter what you call the silvery fish, both kinds—the black croppie and the white croppie—are beautifully marked and easily identifiable. The former has the deeper body, a black back, and is darkly mottled. The latter is somewhat light in color. The white usually has six dorsal spines; the black has seven or eight. Both average about 12 ounces in weight.

There are many ways to hook a croppie, but the most reliable method is to use a long cane or glass pole and live minnows. Croppie also will take crickets, worms, grasshoppers and artificials. Use a sinker heavy enough to take the line to the bottom readily. Attach two one-foot leaders and two croppie hooks one foot and two feet above the sinker. Bait with minnows and let the sinker bump along the bottom while you troll slowly with an electric motor or by using oars. The croppie rigs of sinker and two leaders and hooks are available at all docks. The hooks are made of a wire that straightens out easily when caught on a snag.

You generally will find most action at drop-offs, but during the spring spawning run to the banks you will find them in bushes and brush along the banks. Most women and many men use bobbers when fishing the banks to better judge how deep the minnow is running.

Another popular method, a favorite of Minor Clark, is casting a small artificial lure attached to a barbless floater. This little lure is a small-sized jig that consists of a painted piece of lead on a croppie-sized hook camouflaged by a skirt of yellow, red, or white bristles. The jig is retrieved slowly about three feet behind the floater.

Croppie are sought more avidly in the spring than in the fall, probably on the mistaken assumption that the fish tend to school up during the spawning season. But when the harvest moon rises over the brown cornfields of October, the croppie are just where you found them when that same moon was shedding a romantic glow over the green willows sprouting along spawning beds.

Gim Dossett of Calvert City and I set out one October afternoon to see in what kinds of spots croppie might be found during the fall. In his leisure hours, Dossett managed to drop pieces of brush into various parts of Kentucky Lake and mark them with signs only he could read. I tell you this only to explain why he and I probably had better luck than the average fisherman would have had and to suggest that there is no law that says any fisherman can't plant similar cover to create marvelous croppie spots only he would know.

We got our boats into the water about three o'clock. The sun was shining, the sky was blue, and a bit of wind was blowing. We traveled less than 200 yards from the Kentucky Dam Village boat dock to first try out the shallows. Dossett was using a fly rod to which he had attached a croppie hook. He fixed a small split-shot about a foot above the hook and a light float about three feet above the sinker. All of my gear was rigged with double hooks and a heavy sinker for deep-water fishing. I borrowed a fly rig, and it proved to be an interesting and new experience. By manipulating the line with my left hand as fly fishermen do, I could cast the minnow quite a distance with my right. This enabled me to drop my minnow into brush without disturbing the water.

Because the lake was about five feet lower than it usually is during the spring, we had to shorten our lines to a depth of three feet in places where we found a depth of eight feet in the spring. Despite the wind, we picked up 25 good-sized (one-pound)

croppie in about two hours.

The next day was rainy and we couldn't fish the shallows because of the biting wind, so we headed for the eastern shoreline near the channel where we found some slight protection and deeper water. We slipped our bobbers back to allow us to fish deeper and found larger-than-average croppie about seven feet down near the opening of the canal connecting Kentucky Lake with Lake Barkley.

The next croppie hole we tried was about a quarter of a mile up the lake. With rain trickling down my neck and water sloshing around my feet, I began casting minnows into a 12-foot hole out from an old stump that marked the hole. Dossett was hauling in a good croppie when another hit my minnow. By noon we had 50 very good fish.

That outing took place in 1966, the best year for croppie in the history of Kentucky Lake. I was also there during the spring of that year, and each day I fished, the lake was covered with boats. The banks were lined with men, women and children using every kind of fishing rig imaginable, and limit catches of 60 fish were reported regularly.

Joe Young, Joe Coulter and two other friends from Harrodsburg left the lake with at least 200 dressed. Terry McBrayer and three others from Greenup, took 200 fish with them when they left. Charles Rich of Highland, Ind., boated a slab that weighed three pounds, three ounces—near the record in Kentucky.

One Saturday I decided it would be best to get out early to beat the weekend crowd. I told Fred Tracy, a part-time guide, that I'd need him at seven o'clock the next morning. "If you think that will get you out ahead of the crowd, you're crazy," he said. "But seven o'clock is early enough for croppie anyway."

Despite high winds, low clouds and rough water, the lake was alive with fishermen when we shoved off. Yachts were anchored in the open water, and smaller boats were in and around protected coves. I saw one man in waders about 30 yards off a rocky point. He had a dip net hanging from one hip and a stringer from the other. He was casting live minnows as if they were bombers, but even he was catching fish.

We tried several inlets that were protected from the wind. Tracy hauled in three good croppie before I could get my rig into the water. We enjoyed only fair success until it started to rain at 11 o'clock. "A lot of people would say it's just insane to fish in

weather like this," Tracy said as other boats were racing for the dock. But we kept right on fishing—not just to wait out the storm, but because the harder it rained the faster the croppie hit. We just couldn't pass up the opportunity.

When the rain let up a bit and the wind died, we moved out into the open water, where we used to be able to spot a productive ridge by sighting from a large tree on one bank to a red buoy located a couple of hundred yards out from the dock. We called the marker Gladys Ward's buoy, for a reason I will mention later.

For some reason known only to themselves, the lake engineers moved Gladys Ward's buoy several hundred yards to the right. This threw all our calculations out of kilter. Tracy made some adjustments, however, and it didn't take us long to find the ridge. From then on, we boated one slab after another.

Kentucky Lake has provided good croppie fishing in other years. One spring day in 1968 my boat was coming out of a creek when I passed Dick Christman, who came to Western Kentucky from Evansville, Ind. to build a motel. He had so much trouble getting ready for the season that he decided the heck with it—he'd go fishing and forget work for a while. Christman usually fished by himself and always brought back croppie.

One autumn day when nobody but Christman was catching croppie, Tom Clark, who worked at the dock, followed Christman with his binoculars. Clark saw the angler run his boat right up to a stickup and shake the bush vigorously with one hand while he dropped a minnow on a four-foot pole and line into the water just at the edge of the brush. The more he shook the bushes, the more croppie he caught. Clark couldn't believe his eyes.

"You can't go by that," Christman told him later. "I just do that when everything else fails. Most of the time, I have to be quiet like you guys."

And then there was the morning I was fishing some bushes on a ridge almost in the middle of Kentucky Lake just above the dam when Don Phelps, the old University of Kentucky football player, and Bennie Hager of Gilbertsville chugged past on the way to the Dam Village dock. They had such a large string their boat tilted.

"We got out early," Phelps said. "We ran up to Taylor Creek (about a half-mile upstream) about 4 o'clock. We located three bushes underwater. We went from one to another and picked up three or four croppie out of each, every time around.

And then there were eight anglers from Jefferson County who found no action at Kentucky Lake one spring day, so they switched to Barkley and had excellent luck. The fellows were Walter Goins, Bud and Charles Waits, Harry Gilliland, Al and Tommy Miles, Jimmie Cottrell and Bobby Walls.

On their first of five days on the water they decided to do a little experimenting. Those in one boat would fish the banks, those in the second boat would drift over deep water, and those in the third would set their minnows for five or six feet and drift over drop-offs. What happened? Well, sir, when they returned to camp they found that there wasn't a quarter's worth of difference in any of the catches. Surprisingly, all the females were still carrying eggs and, presumably, were not quite ready to make their beds.

One thing the men did not do was anchor anywhere. When you anchor over any hot spot you may catch six or seven fish and then none at all. If you drift back and forth across the same spot you usually will continue to get strikes.

They learned something else. After two days of delightfully calm, warm days, strong winds began to blow. Boats all around them sped back to camp or to protected coves as waves up to three feet lashed at them. Those who tried the coves caught only small croppie. Rather than settle for the little ones, my angling friends headed out to the middle of the lake and let the wind blow them across the white caps. "It will beat sitting around camp all afternoon," Bud Waits reasoned. And so it did. Their good luck continued, and they caught near-limits by bumping heavy sinkers along the bottom. They ran out of medium-sized minnows and began tossing tiny ones and large ones. It made no difference; the croppie kept right on biting. Their catches averaged more than a pound each, and at least 100 of the fish went to two pounds or more.

The hottest spots they found were in Donaldson Creek. In an area of unusual activity, Waits got a snag and pulled up a section of old rusted wire fence; indicating they were over an old roadbed or fence row. This is one of the big differences in fishing conditions between Barkley and Kentucky. The submerged brush and stumps at Kentucky Lake have mostly rotted out and disappeared, while at Barkley there are still great hiding places for all kinds of fish.

When it comes to croppie fishing, women seem to have an edge over the men. It must be their gentle touch, or perhaps their ability to feel the slightest nudge on their lines. Gladys Ward, after whom that Kentucky Lake buoy is named, probably knows more about croppie fishing than anybody else I know, including Dutch Owen, a veteran guide.

Bob Patterson and I and our wives were fishing Kentucky Lake for white bass one June day when we ran into Henry Ward, former state parks commissioner and state highway commissioner now retired in Florida, and his wife, Gladys. The Wards were about to shove off on a pontoon boat—one of those contraptions that look like a big sea-going playpen. You can guess what happened. Our wives forsook us for the luxury of the Wards' floating patio, and Patterson and I said we'd go ahead and meet them later when they caught up.

We hadn't been gone 15 minutes when here came that pontoon, its canvas top fluttering in the breeze. It was about to pass us up, with all hands laughing, when we decided to tie on and go aboard. Mrs. Ward was gracious enough to try our fishing spot for a while, but she soon pulled anchor and let the patio drift until the women located croppie in about nine feet of water some 40 yards offshore. Mrs. Ward pulled three nice ones out of the hole, and from then until we ran out of minnows we all had a picnic, catching an occasional croppie and watching Mrs. Ward pull in one almost every time she dropped her line into the water.

I couldn't compete with her. I tried oil of anise. I washed my hands in strong soap. I tried a tight line and later a bobber. But she still kept flipping those croppie on board, usually at my feet where I could take them off her line, put on new minnows, and place the fish on the stringer.

When we returned to the dock, we all conceded that Mrs. Ward was the undisputed champion of croppie anglers. But we also voted another laurel to the Ward family. Her husband, we agreed, was the most relaxed fisherman known to man. Ward fished from a reclining deck chair, his feet propped up on the rail. Once a croppie took his bait and was swimming about while Ward watched with amused interest.

"Henry, you've got a fish!" cried his wife. "Bring him in!"

"What for?" asked Ward with a disarming grin. "Just to let another one get on?"

Of course, Mrs. Ward is not the only expert woman croppie angler. One of the largest croppie caught in 1969 was a 2 ½-pounder taken by Mrs. Edward LeVin of Gilbertsville. She was fishing the shallows of Kentucky Lake above the dam with her husband. Together they boated 22 croppie by drifting back and forth over the bushes, far out from shore.

But you can't talk about the feminine touch for catching croppie without mentioning Mrs. Gilbert A. Bryant. Just ask her husband, a frustrated sportsman from Eastwood. Bryant once took his wife and son fishing on Lake Cumberland near their cottage at Conley's Bottom. Gilbert caught two croppie, his son three—and his wife took 51!

"I'm not sure about that feminine touch," Mrs. Bryant said. "It seems like anybody should be able to feel a fish on his line and set the hook. I think the most important thing is finding the fish. We use an electronic depth finder. We knew a spot far out in the lake where we caught a lot of croppie last year. We went looking for it."

They worked their way toward it. Finally they found the spot—an old treetop and a sharp drop-off. It was in 30 feet of water. Almost immediately Mrs. Bryant began pulling in fish. She used a regular light spinning rod and reel—very similar to those handled by her husband and son. The only difference was that Mrs. Bryant let her line out until it hit the bottom, raised it up a few inches, and locked her reel. Then she hooked a finger of her left hand under her line while she held the pole in the other hand.

"The instant I felt a little nudge on my minnow I set my hook," she explained. What she did—and she said this was important—was pull the line in hand over hand, never disturbing the reel. To do this she held the line loops in her mouth. "This way I was able to keep my line exactly the right length all the time," she said.

The Bryants found the spot around 12:30 p.m. An hour later Mrs. Bryant had 29 croppie, the biggest about 17- inches long. She went out alone again after lunch to try to boat the limit.

Her sensational luck continued, but, without the boys to applaud, Mrs. Bryant gave up when she had a total of 51.

More and more Kentucky anglers seeking croppie are turning to electronic depth finders and, like Mrs. Bryant, are having great success. "I'd just as soon go fishing without a pole as to go without my depth finder," said Vard Curtis, a Paducah restaurateur and one of Kentucky's most

Dr. Ronnie Babb of Murray picks a 2½-pound croppie from Kentucky Lake.

Mrs. Henry (Gladys) Ward was such a great croppie catcher they named a buoy after her.

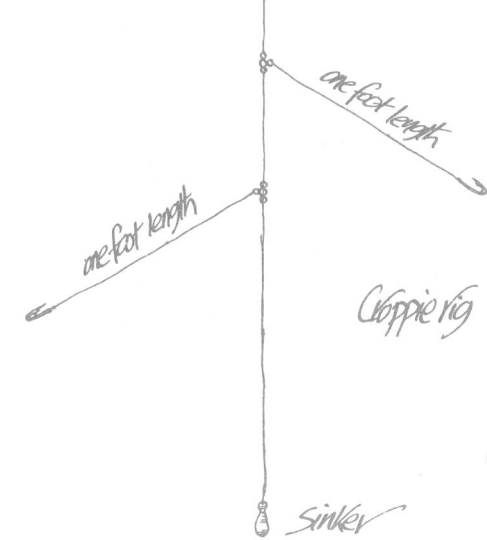

one foot length

one foot length

Croppie rig

Sinker

consistently successful croppie fishermen. The electronic age apparently has invaded the ancient sport of fishing, and soon the little battery-operated gadgets that have made Curtis a champion may be as common as corks and sinkers.

Curtis at one time fished Kentucky Lake two to five times a week, 12 months of the year, and he considered it a poor day when he and his mates didn't hook a one-man limit of 60. He rarely brought in that many, however, because he believed in releasing the small ones. But during one 12-month period in 1966, if memory serves correctly, he counted more than 2,000 cleaned and dressed croppie.

Curtis and his frequent companions, Joe Wallace and Leon Carney, also of Paducah, were so sold on the electronic guide that they took along a spare in case one would break down. On one trip Carney boated a slab that weighed three pounds, 2 ½ ounces and had 40 other croppie on his stringer, all caught in the main lake near the mouth of Sledd Creek. Curtis came in that day with 48 slabs that weighed 50 pounds. He had taken three friends out at 10 a.m. and returned six hours later.

The unofficial all-time record croppie taken in Kentucky was caught by Charles E. Jenkins of Gilbertsville in 1957. The fish weighed 4 ¾ pounds and was 20- inches long. It was taken below Kentucky Lake dam on a live shad minnow not much more than an inch long. Unfortunately, Jenkins failed to have his catch weighed before witnesses.

The recognized state record weighed four pounds, three ounces and was caught by David C. Crowe at Lake Pewee near his Madisonville home in April 1969. His catch topped by three ounces the old state record set by Darrell Whitmer of Louisville in 1951. Tom Prather of Campbellsburg also is numbered among the elite of croppie anglers. Not too many years ago he boated a three-pound, seven-ounce beauty at a Henry County Lake.

Muskellunge

It's big and it's savage and it's unpredictable and it's a fighter. Add these characteristics to that of scarcity and you'll understand why the muskellunge is considered the most awesome challenge to the Kentucky angler.

Like all pike, the muskie has big, alligator-like jaws, sharp teeth and a long body. The muskie's back is green or olive colored, and its belly is white. Although the marks are often indistinct on larger fish, the muskie sometimes has darker spots and stripes on its sides. These markings set it apart from the pike, which has light markings on a darker body. The muskie also can be distinguished from other members of the pike family because it has no scales

The muskellunge is a fierce fighter and very high on the list amongst prized game fish.

on the lower half of the gill cover or the cheek.

Regarded as a prodigious feeder that will eat almost anything that moves, the cannibalistic muskie "not only eats its own young but also could devour every fish and frog in its domain and wouldn't hesitate to top off its meal with a chipmunk or a duck swimming on the water's surface," says one biologist.

An old-timer from deep in the woods once told me, "Lots of men fish for muskies down here, but don't none of 'em know how." I asked him what he'd suggest as a surefire method.

"Just ketch you a half-grown squirrel," he said. "Tie a gang hook onto his back, and throw him out and let him swim. Iffen they's a big muskie anywhere near, you'll get 'im!"
This method would not be approved by the Department of Fish and Wildlife or the Humane Society, but I wonder how many trophy muskies adorning walls of fishing lodges were taken by such an outrageous rig.

The muskie is a solitary fellow, and prefers to hide under overhanging vegetation in deep pools and wait for its dinner rather than to search for it. Some anglers have reported seeing a muskie move out of its hideaway to inspect a lure several times before making up its mind to either ignore it or crunch it.

No other fish is meaner or more contrary than the muskie. When the muskie lunges at a passing carp or bass, the whole lake quivers.

Fishing for muskie requires a good amount of hunting, says Ed Thompson of Louisville, 1978 president of the Kentucky Silver Muskie Club. First he searches out the most likely area of a lake or stream. Then he sets about provoking it to strike. He advises a beginner to try first around the mouth of a creek or river, where the old boy may be lurking, waiting for a small fish or whatnot to come by. Do this, he says, on an overcast day in early autumn when the air pressure is falling, or is low, and the day is warm. It might even be raining, with a bit of a breeze to keep the boat moving.

When nothing else brings any action, try working your lure in a figure eight all the way up to the boat. Even dip your rod a couple of feet into the water and speed up the figure eight or move it in a circling action. Ray Ostrom, a muskie expert and winner in international muskie competition, says he has used the figure eight technique many times with surprisingly good results.

The best muskie bait you can use is a live sucker, preferably eight- to 12-inches long, but artificials, such as a Bill Norman's Deep Runner, a spoon, or a bucktail spinner, are good at times. Try gold color in murky water, silver in clear water. And be sure to use lures large enough to entice the muskie to strike.

When casting, you generally should retrieve the lures fairly fast, although in some instances slow retrieves might better catch the muskie's attention. There's no way to know which retrieve will work best, so try both.

Ed and I try trolling deep and fast when casting isn't productive. In shallow water you won't need a weight on your line, but you may want to use a lead trolling weight to get the lure down 15 or 20 feet in deep water.

Don't plan to use your regular bass or trout tackle if you go fishing for muskie. It's just too light for this large, vicious fighter. Ed uses a stiff bait-casting rod from five- to six-feet long and bait-casting reel that holds at least 100 yards of line testing 15 to 20 pounds. For casting, use a six- to seven-foot spinning rod with monofilament line testing to 15 pounds. The lighter lines and rods can be used to fish for small muskies in open water.

When the muskie finally strikes, give it line so it can swim away and swallow the bait without feeling a pull. After you think the bait has been swallowed—and this sometimes can take quite long—give the rod one or more hard jerks to set the hook in the fish's tough jaw.

The hottest spot in Kentucky for muskellunge, perhaps for years to come, is Cave Run Lake in the heart of Daniel Boone National Forest a few miles southwest of Morehead. Formed in 1973 when the picturesque Licking River was dammed, Cave Run is the newest and fourth largest lake in the state, almost three times the size of Herrington. The water is unusually placid, protected as it is from winds by high, lush green hills.

The northern half of the Cave Run Lake aptly could be called the Reelfoot of the mountains. Except for a narrow, winding channel, dead treetops and brush protrude everywhere and provide marvelous cover for fish, undisturbed by skiers, who are forbidden by law and nature. The southern half is a direct opposite—a wide, clear lake set in the midst of a park-like setting where skiers and pleasure boaters may frolic unchallenged.

Cave Run is fed by the Licking River, North Fork of the Licking, Cave Run Creek, Beaver Creek

and Cane Creek, all well known for the muskie and bass. To the resident native fish, the Department of Fish and Wildlife Resources has added thousands of six- to 12-inch muskies The stocking will continue as the young become available and until a satisfactory balance of the fish population has been reached

"This is the greatest place for muskie and bass I've ever seen," says Arnold Greenhill of Olive Hill, former president of the 250-member Kentucky Silver Muskie Club. I ran into Greenhill at Cave Run Lake just after he caught and released three muskies.

"I come here every chance I get, " he said. "It boggles the mind to think of how great it may be in a couple of years."

The muskie's favorite haunt in a lake is cold, clear water in weedy, shallow areas and coves, around sunken trees, brush piles and logs, and under any other type cover. Ordinarily it feeds not more than two- to 15-feet below the water's surface, except during the summer weather.

I kept this in mind on my first trip to Cave Run in 1975. Ed Thompson and I trolled the channel and cast the stickups, then trolled the channel deeper, and cast the stumps. The yield included several good strikes and three muskies in the boat.

Doing everything we could to attract muskie strikes, Thompson sprayed each lure with detergent, and I rubbed mine with oil of anise. During one trolling run Thompson held his lure deep with the aid of a heavy sinker set about seven feet in front of his lure. He got one bump that stirred him into action, but he lost the fish halfway to the boat.

In the same part of the lake in a narrow lane between big groves of dead birches, I got a strike and saw the muskie break water. Then it too flipped out, leaving me a badly frayed leader.

Licking River and Green River are the state's best muskie streams. Licking produced a state record—a 42-pounder, taken by Glenn Terrell of Morehead on one cold February morning in 1973.

And it was the picturesque little Green River that yielded a state-record 36-pounder in 1955 to Mrs. Ruby Skaggs. It was also at Green River that Willard Parnell of Edmonton boated a muskie in 1969 that weighed 39 pounds, 14 ounces. It reigned as king until Terrell came along four years later.

Since that time many extraordinary catches have been reported across the state. Owen Chelf took a

Glenn Terrell

Glenn Terrell of Morehead held the
state record for muskie several years with
this beauty.

Portor Hash of Edmonton holds his
state record Muskie.

30 ½-pounder from the Licking in 1975. Chelf
caught his less than 30 minutes after shoving off in
a john boat about nine o'clock in the morning. He
changed baits three times in that period, and the
muskie struck just after he switched from a white
bomber-type lure to a black bucktail.

It remained for Dale Hollow, however, to
produce a new state record catch in 1978—a 43-
pounder taken by Portor Hash of Edmonton, in
early March. Portor had to break through ice to get
his boat in, and was hampered by wind and ice when
he cast a Bill Norman Deep Runner, a 7-inch silver
plug with a black back, and a flange in front to take
it down. The strike was his only one of the day.

On an earlier day at Dale Hollow, three anglers
scored almost simultaneously. Edwin Kaiser of
Fern Creek caught a 16 ½-pounder, his son, Shug
took one weighing 17 pounds, and Dr. Herman
Mahaffey of Louisville followed them with a 13 ½-
pounder taken from the same area.

Another unusual catch was made by Lum Gravil
of Brownsville. He was fishing Green River when he
took a 24-pound muskie on a trotline. Other notable
catches were made by Jerry Fannin and Gene
Mullins of Raceland, who simultaneously boated a
22-pounder and a 15-pounder, respectively.

An unprecedented catch of three giant
muskellunge on three successive days by John
Gaines of Bowling Green proved that Barren River
also is a productive muskie stream. The Bowling
Green publisher, who kept a boat and small motor
tied to a small dock within 10 minutes of his office,
fished by himself almost daily when the weather
seemed right. He went out at noon a few days
before Christmas several years ago and caught a 16-
pound scrapper. The following afternoon he boated
a muskie weighing 16 ½ pounds, and the next day he
got an 18-pounder.

"I've found that the best time for muskies is
between noon and 3 p.m. during extremes of the
weather—either very hot or very cold," he said.
"The colder the weather the more I bend the lip of
my pike minnow to make it run deeper. I troll the
river with a three-horsepower outboard, but when I
get into my best fishing areas I cut the motor
and scull the boat with one hand and fish with the
other."

Ed Thompson, who was named Conservationist
of the Year and chairman of National Wildlife
Week by the League of Kentucky Sportsmen in
1969, suggested a trip to Green River for muskie
one March day that year.

"During Wildlife Week, what could be more
fitting than a trip into Kentucky's most magnificent
wildlife sanctuary?" he demanded. Well, I didn't
know Mammoth Cave National Park was our most
notable wildlife haven. I thought that Ft. Knox held
that distinction.

(There is one big difference between the two
sanctuaries. At Ft. Knox, all wildlife is protected
except from post personnel, friends of post
personnel, and a number of outsiders drawn at lot.
At Mammoth Cave, all wildlife except fish is
protected. Thus fishing on Green River has an
added attraction—the abundance of wildlife. There
are deer, wild turkeys, ducks, birds too numerous to
identify—everywhere.

I had taken float trips down Green River from
Mammoth Cave to Houchins Ferry, about 14 miles
downstream. I had caught a few fish and had
bagged a few frogs, but I never had fished for
muskie there.

We fished with surface and shallow running
muskie lures, which are about twice the size of bass
lures. Thompson used a homemade copy of a bayou
boogie that was as big as the palm of his hand. We
fished hard. I mean real hard; my arm became
numb. But a muskie fisherman is nothing if not
patient. My patience finally gave out, and I devoted
my full attention to observing the wildlife.

The average muskie fisherman is content to get
one keeper (30 inches or longer) two or three times
a season. A small muskie (about 40 inches) is good
eating, but a 10- to 12-year-old (40 inches or up)
would look a lot better on the wall than on a
dinner table.

Most fishermen release any muskie not wanted
for the trophy room or the table. And this is good,
because, being the cannibals they are, muskies
don't allow enough of their children to grow to
keeper size. One suggestion here: If you are going to
release your catch, be sure to do it without taking
the fish out of the water. A net can so damage its
gills that it will die.

Some muskies grow very large, but most that are
caught weigh between 15 and 25 pounds. The world
record muskellunge is 69 pounds, 15 ounces,
recorded in the St. Lawrence River in 1957. But
operators of the ferryboat across the Green River
insist that they have seen monsters that would
exceed the world record fish float past their ferry
during quiet hours.

Rockfish

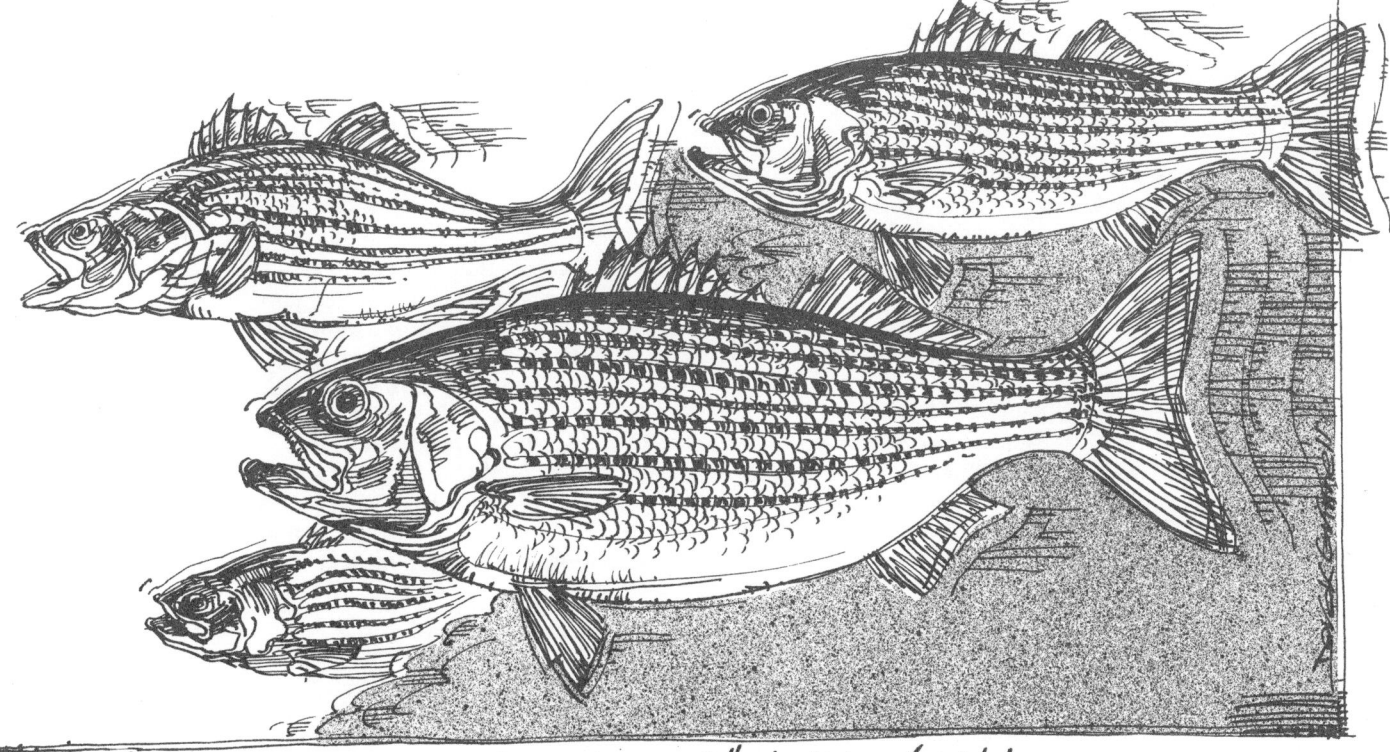

Rockfish (striped sea bass) are very selective about their diet and catching them may need a frequent change of lures to find the right combination.

Kentucky's long effort to establish the rockfish in its major lakes is paying off handsomely. The rockfish (striped sea bass) became landlocked in the Santee-Cooper Reservoir in South Carolina more than 30 years ago. Kentucky wildlife officers, hopeful of planting rockfish in this state, were granted permission to take as many fish as they liked from the reservoir—by hook and line. Only 12 fish were caught that first year, 1958. The number jumped to 50 the following year and to 433 in 1963.

With each new spring, Charlie Bowers, fisheries chief for the state, hopes that some male and female rockfish will manage to get together. Although more than five million rockfish have been introduced to Kentucky's lakes, few males and females meet at the child-bearing stage because they are so scattered. Rockfish are believed to have begun to reproduce in Barkley, Herrington and Cumberland lakes, but we're not sure. Meanwhile, increased production through artificial means is continuing at the hatcheries. In 1978, more than four million rocks were raised at the Frankfort hatchery, and released into Kentucky lakes. The rockfish were far above average in size, which should result in a greater survival rate and bring them up to legal keeping size—15 inches—as much as a year earlier than usual. The daily creel limit on rockfish in Kentucky is five.

The rockfish should not be confused with the rock bass, also known as the redeye or rock sunfish. It resembles the white bass in coloration but has a slimmer body and a relatively shorter second anal spine. The body is marked with seven or eight dark horizontal stripes on a silvery background.

The rockfish is an excellent game fish and superior table fare. Its rapid growth and its predatory tendencies mark it as probably the best thing that ever happened to Kentucky anglers.

Not until 1975 did any Kentuckians go fishing exclusively for the rockfish. Some marvelous catches have been reported, especially on skipjack herring caught below the dams at the major lakes and on saltwater-sized artificials.

The state record rock is 44 pounds, four ounces, caught by James Fugate of Burlington and Ronald Warner of Burgin at Lake Herrington in July 1970.

Fugate and Warner aren't likely to forget the day they landed that monster. They stuck their cane poles in the muddy bank, and, when eating lunch, noticed that one pole was bobbing up and down in the water several yards from the bank. They gave chase in their boat, but only after several unsuccessful efforts to grab the bobbing pole did they manage to hang on to it. The anglers slowly led the fish back to the bank, where they waded in, grabbed it by hand, and lugged it onto dry land.

In 1976 I almost caught a rockfish that would have challenged the record they set, but it was one of those many fish that got away. Joe Fay Britt of Madisonville, Cy Layson of Frankfort, Brad Fable and Ronald Skinner of Madisonville and I went fishing for rocks in the Cumberland River below Barkley Dam. Skinner caught our bait—skipjack herring about six-inches long—on a six-foot line dotted with tiny flies, which he jigged along the riprap, or rock pilings, near the dam.

Skinner, who was in a boat with me, took one look at my 20-pound test outfit, laid it aside, and handed me a stubby trolling rod equipped with 50-pound test line, an eight-ounce weight, and two No. 3/O hooks on which he threaded the herring. "Now you will know," he said, "if you get a big one on you won't lose it." How little he knew.

First we fished close to the dam, held securely by a large anchor and 50 feet of rope. We let our sinkers walk along the bottom in the rushing water out to a distance of about 100 feet. We caught

several channel catfish but had no explosive strikes, so we moved nearer a bridge that crosses the stream several hundred yards downstream. We hadn't been there long when I got a powerful strike that almost yanked my rod out of my hands. But that was all. The fish took the herring and departed.

Twenty minutes later, as I felt my sinker bumping the bottom, the big fish struck. It ripped off 50 yards of line before I flipped my drag to tighten it a bit. That was my first mistake. I found out later I had pushed the drag too far and locked it. My second mistake was that I failed to take into consideration the force of the current.

The fight continued as I gradually reeled it toward the boat. The big fellow broke the surface about 30 yards away and laid there, apparently too tired to battle further. Britt, in the other boat, raced around and snapped pictures of the fish. I gave another heave and started to reel again when— pow!—the line broke. The fish disappeared.

"Gad," Britt cried, "he must have been four-feet long. Maybe a new state record." Then he grinned. "What was the matter, Ruby, did you choke?" If he had been in my boat, I know who would have choked.

Joe and Barbara Parsons of Lyndon brought in what might have been a new record rockfish, but lost out to Father Time. They were casting for black bass in the summer of 1976 at Lake Cumberland near Beaver and Otter creeks. At eight o'clock in the morning they hit the lake, and at three in the afternoon their stringer hung dry in the boat. Parsons suggested that they either return to the dock or switch lures and go for rockfish. Mrs. Parsons fortunately voted for the rocks.

They selected a couple of saltwater Rebels that they had bought at Beaver Creek Resort dock. Parsons gunned the boat to deep water out from the mouth of the two creeks and began trolling. Almost immediately he had a strike as the line peeled off his level-wind reel. "I've got a good one," he cried. "Give me room." Mrs. Parsons reeled in her line, grabbed the net, and hauled in the rockfish, which later was found to weigh 13 pounds.

Less than 15 minutes later Mrs. Parsons' reel screeched and her line zinged out. "Let him run," Parsons cried. He gunned his outboard and followed the fish while his wife maintained a tight line—as tight as she dared with her 17-pound test line. After nearly 25 minutes of racing back and forth, the fish quit fighting, and Parsons, with the net

Norman Pepper of Louisville missed the state record by ounces with this monster rockfish.

around the monster's head and the tail in his other hand, heaved it into the boat.

They raced back to the dock, but the only scale there could weigh only up to 28 pounds. The fish was placed in an ice machine where it remained until Ed Meece, the dock manager, arrived several hours later. Using a bathroom scale, Meece weighed himself then picked up the fish and weighed again. A bit of subtraction indicated the fish weighed 42 ½ pounds. "If you had weighed it before it dried out you might have had a new state record," Meece said. That was bitter consolation.

Fishing for rockfish is a "whole new ball game," according to Larry Snyder of Louisville, who had just returned from Lake Cumberland in the summer of 1976 where he and his wife, Wanda, had fought two good fights with rockfish—and won. "July and August have been nothing months for us in Kentucky," he said. "Now I can hardly wait until next weekend to go out again."

Snyder had been bass-fishing Cumberland for more than 15 years with consistently good luck, except during July and August. "We were just about to give up for the summer when we decided to give it one more try on my birthday," he said later. "We threw every kind of lure we had and hadn't gotten a strike. Then Wanda reminded me that it was a day like this that we had taken a rockfish at Cherokee Lake in Tennessee. We decided to give it a try. We began a slow scan of the bottom, trolling as we went along the riprap and dam. We found nothing. Then we headed into open water."

The depth finder registered 100 feet. Suddenly there was an abrupt rise and with it came blips telling them that a big school of shad and several big fish below the shad were moving with them. At that moment Mrs. Snyder got a powerful strike and her line peeled off. Snyder quickly reeled in his trolling lure and put on a king-sized dollfly. He made one cast and also got a strike.

There they were, two in a boat, each with a rock running crazy through the water. Fortunately Snyder's fish had swallowed the lure and didn't put up much of a tussle. It was so big that only half of the fish went in the net. When Mrs. Snyder saw it she got excited and started horsing her catch. "Don't do that!" he cautioned. "Take it easy." She was using a 14-pound test line that could have snapped at any second. Mrs. Snyder slowed down her retrieve and the fish reeled off the line faster than she was taking it in. A grueling 25 minutes

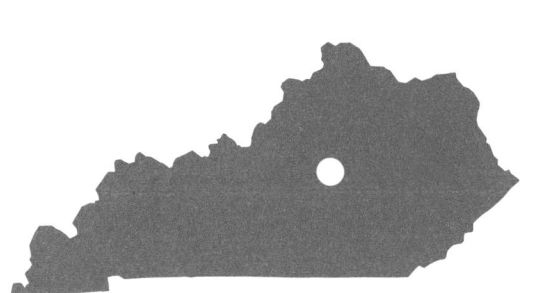

Herrington Lake where 90% of the Rockfish are caught.

later the fish surrendered.

After an unsuccessful attempt to relocate the rocks, the Snyders returned to the dock. Mrs. Snyder's fish weighed 22 pounds and was 37 ½ inches long; her husband's fish hit exactly 20 pounds.

Skiers and pleasure boaters ruin fishing for some anglers, but not for Russell Gooch, Kalip Cole, Clyde Neil and Preston Jones of Richmond. The more roaring craft the better on days when the water tends to become static and clear, Gooch says, and he has many successes to prove it.

What the boaters do is churn up the water, causing it to wash on the banks. After several hours of this the water along the banks becomes murky as far out as 10 or 12 feet. The sloshing creates air bubbles, adding oxygen to the water, and washes minute food particles off the bank into the water. Small fish move in to the bank to dine and are pursued by large bass and rockfish.

Gooch and his friends wait until the heat is out of the sun (about 7 p.m.), then they troll back and forth in the murky water close to the bank. They troll bass lures on the shore side and rockfish lures on the lake side.

One Sunday afternoon at Herrington, Gooch and his pals, in two boats, gunned their way to a long stretch of good bank between Paradise and Kennedy docks that showed plenty of abuse from party boaters. They baited with diving-type lures, which figured to run about 12-feet deep, and in no more than three hours they boated several keeper bass and three keeper rockfish in the eight-pound class. And what was more interesting, they hooked two mighty rockfish that pulled the boat around as they lunged out into deeper water and snapped the 15-pound test line as if it were thread.

"We are going to heavier line," said Gooch, "to hold these monsters. Even the smaller rockfish of seven or eight pounds give fishing tackle a beating, and a big one is simply overpowering."

Fishing the same general area of Lake Herrington six times during a period of two weeks, the four men had 25 rockfish strikes and boated six. "We used to wash the banks ourselves," Gooch explained, "beating it hard by running our boat as close to the bank as we could get safely. We'd wait a while and then go fishing." A good rain and wind storm creates a similar water condition. Right after such a storm Gooch hooked three rockfish and netted two.

Herrington is a very special place for Woodrow and Lucille Meier, also. Curious and envious anglers gather around the Paradise Fishing Camp there whenever these fishermen from Burgin pause after a morning on the lake. "How many this time? Where were you fishing? What kind of lure were you using?" To these questions I added, "What do you know that these others don't know?"

They catch rockfish with seemingly no effort, and together they brought in more than 20 in one week, all well above the minimum size.

"We work at it," Meier said, "if you could call any fishing work. You can't catch many of them on a one-day or two-day fishing trip. Sometimes it takes us a week to find them. They travel in schools. We find them by trolling and then we catch them by trolling. One thing I know for sure, we have never taken one by casting.

"We use deep running lures such as the hellbender and waterdog, and we troll just fast enough and use just enough line to take the lure down 15 or 20 feet. Once we locate a school we start trolling across the nearest point, usually at the mouth of an inlet. If the school is a big one, we get a strike almost every time we cross the point. The rockfish usually hit silvery or pearl baits best, so if we can't find some that color, I paint some myself."

Meier, who makes many lures from scratch, said the fish seem to like to follow a lure quite a way before striking. For this reason the Meiers rarely do any casting.

Herrington, which has enjoyed saturation stocking, has produced 90 percent of all rockfish recorded so far in Kentucky. Others have come from Kentucky, Barkley and Cumberland tailwaters.

Robert M. Barrow would not agree with the Meiers on casting and lures. He boated two large rockfish below the dam at Kentucky Lake while fishing for catfish. His lines were heavy with smelly catfish bait. One explanation for his success might be that rockfish are such voracious feeders throughout the summer and winter that when they are very hungry they will hit anything.

Rainbow Trout

rainbow trout have an excitment for white waters and offer the angler some spectacular leaps and runs

Rainbow trout are cold-water fish and are not native to Kentucky, but thanks to the Department of Fish and Wildlife's generous stocking program in lakes, streams and tailwaters, there is fair to good stream action in some parts of the state most of the year.

The beautiful rainbow trout gets its name from its vivid coloring—a green or blue back fading into silvery green on the sides with small dark spots covering the whole upper side of the fish. A wide crimson or pink band running along the side from head to tail often can be seen on older fish and especially on males during breeding time.

Because rainbows are not native to the region, most trout fishing is on a put-and-take basis. The one exception is a section of Upper Martin's Fork in Cumberland Gap National Historical Park, where there has been evidence of reproduction.

Eight- and nine-inch rainbows are stocked several times a year in about 40 small, cool Kentucky streams. These are fished out rapidly by anglers of all ages using kernels of corn, small balls of cheese, bits of worm and salmon eggs. Larger fish placed in lakes and tailwaters live longer and grow to remarkable sizes in a few seasons.

Many fishermen have wondered why it is necessary to stock adult trout. Why not fingerlings, like bass, and let them grow? The answer is that while some of Kentucky's streams are cold enough to make year-around life comfortable and attractive to trout, the best trout streams can accommodate only 40 to 50 rainbows per mile. "Under the stocking program we can put in as many as 500 per mile," explained Charles Bowers, director of fisheries for the state. "This affords much better fishing, as you can imagine.

"Naturally," he added, "no stream could provide food enough for so many fish for very long. We want the fishermen to catch them all within two or three weeks after each stocking."

Rainbows like fast-moving waters—rapids, around waterfalls, at the mouths of creeks or rivers in lakes—and the hottest spot for catching this colorful fish is Cumberland River below Wolf Creek Dam. The three biggest rainbow trout caught so far in the state were taken from that stream.

Ervin Moffett, one-time manager of the dock at Lake Barkley State Resort Park near Cadiz, established the early rainbow record in 1963 with an 11-pound, three-ounce jumbo. Danny Antle of Louisville went to Cumberland River in March 1971 and tied into a rainbow that weighed 13 pounds, 12 ounces. His record had stood a little more than a year when Jim Mattingly of Somerset brought out the present record-holder. His catch weighed 14 pounds, six ounces.

Fly fishermen are hard put to find streams suitable for their art. Once found, they guard the secret with their lives.

Fishing techniques for big rainbows vary, but worms and night crawlers have lured more rainbows to the net than any artificials. Many anglers, however, still prefer small spoons, spinners and flies. In lakes near a dam, trout usually are taken at night with night crawlers and from water anywhere from two- to 40-feet deep.

When a rainbow trout is hooked, it generally will put up an exciting and thrilling fight, accented with stirring leaps.

Fishing at night—specifically on a stormy and dark night—is one man's secret to catching limits of rainbow trout in Lake Cumberland above the dam. Let the thunder roll and the lightning flash. Let the wind blow and the rain fall. Anchor off a point near the dam, well removed from other

Rainbow trout of this size are stocked in many Kentucky streams on a monthly basis.

Mike Smith flips a fly in a cool stream.

fishermen, and drop live night crawlers to depths ranging from 20 to 40 feet. If you can't find any night crawlers, take creek chub minnows—but no shiners.

This is the advice of Gene Stice of Louisville, who played an important role in taking two large strings of rainbows from Lake Cumberland on successive nights several years ago. First, Stice went out with Gary Oaks of Louisville and Jim Huckleby of Glasgow. Their one-night haul was 25 rainbows ranging in size from one to three pounds.

Stice was so elated over his catch that his parents, Mr. and Mrs. Ragmon Stice, also of Louisville, went out with his uncle, John Branstetter of Glasgow, the following night to the spot where Stice had had his wonderful luck. Mrs. Stice wasn't sure she liked sitting out there with all that lightning and rain, but she went. And they came back with 24 big rainbows.

(While the daily limit is eight, a new day starts at midnight.)

"There's nothing new about our method of fishing," the younger Stice said after posing for several pictures. "I don't mind telling you everything about it—except the exact spot where we tied up." He said he didn't think the exact spot meant much anyway. "It's just that we don't want to be crowded," he said. "The worst thing you can do while night-fishing for rainbows is to get in a crowd. We got out early, fought rough weather and water, and stayed longer and worked harder than anyone else."

When you think of an angler fishing below the dam at Lake Cumberland, you picture the fellow struggling against the churning water just below the turbines. But some of the best fishing for rainbow trout in those cool tailwaters is found downstream as far as 16 or 18 miles.

Probably the best known spot is the rock house, a sheer rock wall with a hole in it close to the small community of Creelsboro on KY. 379. D. A. Parker of Louisville with his wife, Geneva, and his uncle, Jim Parker of Owensboro, fished this area regularly, and rarely failed to return with several rainbows. One trip they made about five years ago was more spectacular than most. All three limited out in just four hours of hectic angling.

Trout stamps are required for all trout fishermen, except those persons not required to have fishing licenses.

Streams and Counties

1. Casey Cr., Trigg
2. Claylick Cr., Crittenden
3. L. Whippoorwill Cr., Logan
4. Sulphur Spring Cr., Simpson
5. Lick Fork Cr., Simpton
6. Trammel Cr., Allen
7. Long Cr., Allen
8. Beaver Cr., Barren
9. Big Brush Cr., Green
10. Lynn Camp Cr., Hart
11. Roundstone Cr., Hart
12. Rough Cr., Hardin
13. Sinking Cr., Breckinridge
14. Raven Cr., Harrison
15. Boone Cr., Fayette/Clark
16. Goose Cr., Casey
17. Beaver Cr., Wayne
18. Laurel Cr., Elliott
19. Caney Cr., Elliott

20. Kinniconick Cr., Lewis
21. Schultz Cr., Greenup
22. Laurel Fork Cr., Harlan
23. Fugitt Cr., Harlan
24. Greasy Cr., Leslie
25. Station Camp Cr., Estill
26. Sturgeon Cr., Lee
27. Hood Cr., Johnson
28. N. Fk. Triplett Cr., Rowan
29. Swift Camp Cr., Wolfe
30. Middle Fork Cr., Wolfe
31. E. Fk. Indian Cr., Menifee
32. Big Double Cr., Clay
33. War Fork Cr., Jackson
34. Indian Cr., Jackson
35. Cane Cr., Laurel
36. Bark Camp Cr., Whitley
37. Dog Slaughter Cr., Whitley
38. Rock Cr., McCreary

The five streams listed below are stocked only once each year, usually in November, with sub-adult, or fingerling, trout. These waters are located in remote portions of the Daniel Boone National Forest.
a. Craney Cr., Rowan Co.; b. Brushy Cr., Menifee Co.; c. Big Buck Lick, Jackson Co.; d. Hawk Cr., Laurel Co.; e. Laurel Fork, McCreary Co.

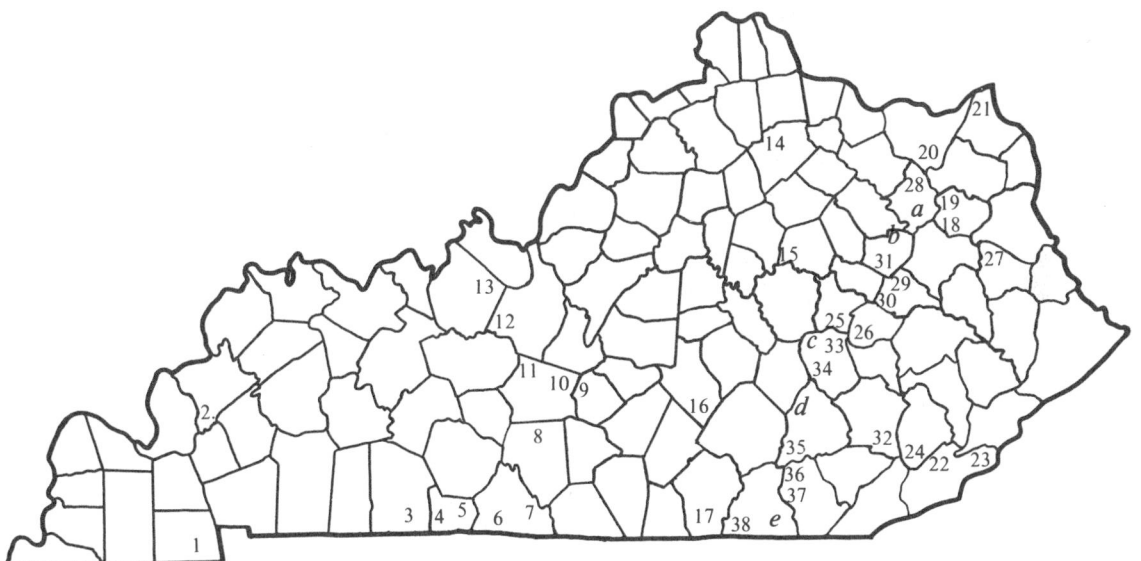

Here's where the trout are in Kentucky

Walleye & Sauger

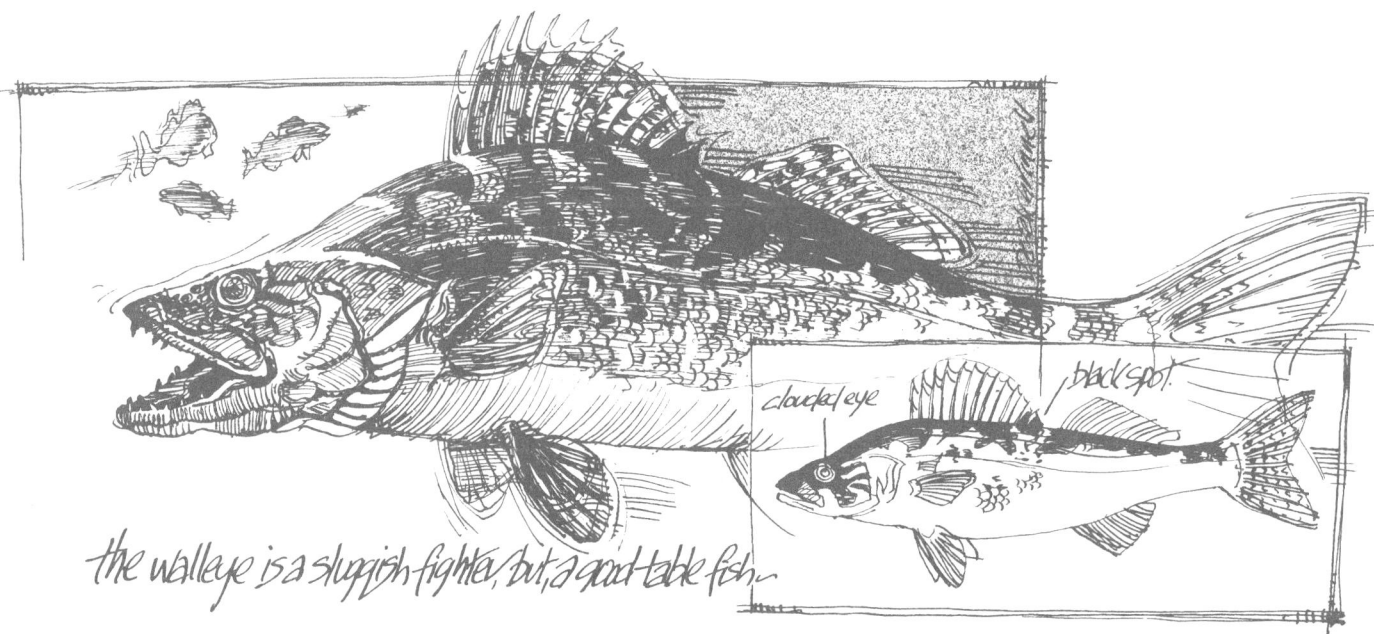

cloudedeye

black spot.

the walleye is a sluggish fighter, but a good table fish.

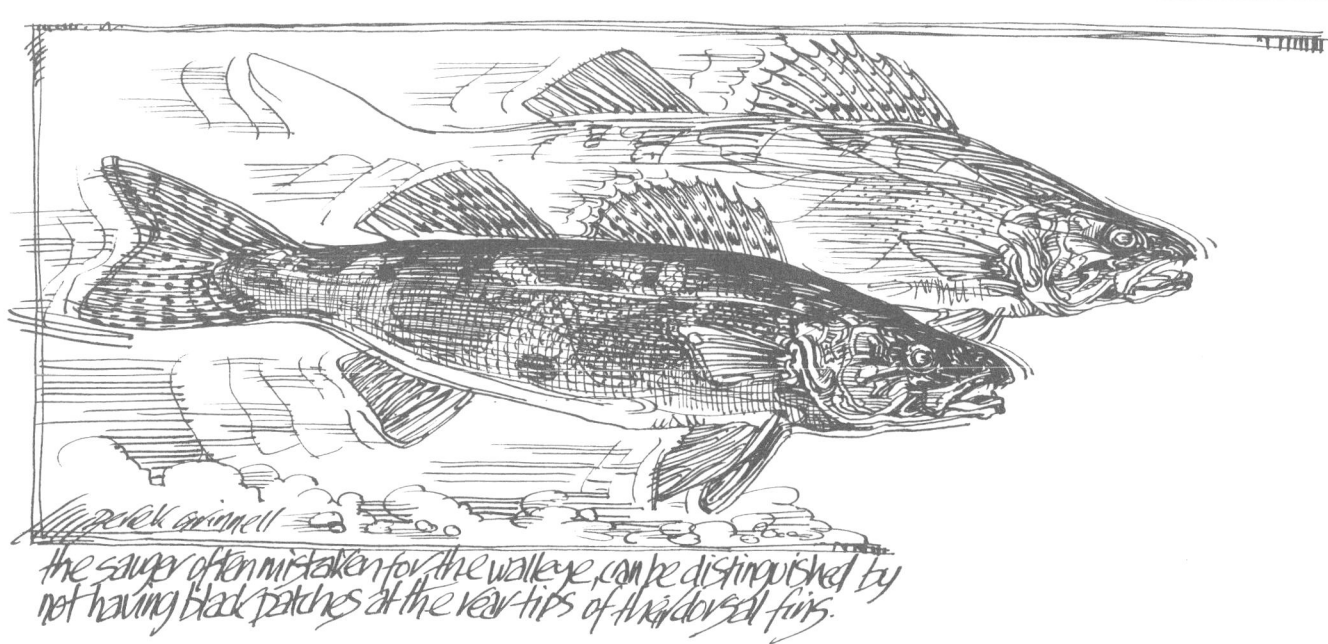

the sauger often mistaken for the walleye, can be distinguished by not having black patches at the rear tips of their dorsal fins.

No two fish caught in Kentucky waters confuse more anglers than the sauger and walleye, both erroneously called walleyed pike, jack salmon and jackfish.

The fish are much alike in shape. Their bodies are long and almost cylindrical and taper toward the tail like most fast swimming fish. Both are highly migratory and subject to decline when impeded by dams.

There are simple ways to tell the walleye and sauger apart. The walleye has a single black spot at the base of the posterior membranes of the dorsal fin, usually a white spot on the lower part of the caudal fin, and lacks the oblique rows of smaller spots in the middle part of the dorsal fin that are distinctive marks of the sauger.

In addition, the walleye generally grows to be much larger than its look-alike. An average walleye will weigh from two to eight pounds; the typical sauger will tip the scale at no more than one pound.

Walleye

The walleye gets its name from its large eyes, which look as if they have a cloudy film over them. It is bronze, gold, or yellow with darker markings on its sides. Because of its strong fin spines, spiked gill cover and sharp teeth, this fish should be handled carefully.

Although young walleyes feed upon insect larvae, adults dine almost exclusively on other fish, especially bluegills and gizzard shad.

The walleye does not put up a fight at all. What makes it a popular catch is its quality on the supper table. The walleye is neither fatty nor oily and therefore can be stored in the freezer longer than most fish.

The state has stocked more than two million walleye in Lake Cumberland since 1973, and the increase in big catches has been nothing short of sensational, especially in the spring spawning runs up the Cumberland River, the South Fork of the Cumberland, and the Rockcastle River. Because the walleye is a cold-water fish, it moves up to spawn very early in the spring. The day might be bitterly cold, but when the runs start, usually in February, you'll find the banks lined with anglers.

If you prefer summer fishing, stick to early morning, late evening and night hours, or on cloudy, rainy days. Like most cold-water fish, the walleye will be in shallow water during the cooler hours and much deeper when the sun is hottest.

No special tackle is needed to catch walleyes — almost any bait-casting, spinning, or spincasting outfit should do — and light tackle will provide the most exciting sport. Artificial lures such as spoons and bombers work best in taking this fish. Natural baits such as lively minnows, soft-shelled crawfish, and especially night crawlers, are good for still fishing.

Walleyes are often difficult to locate, but the best methods are slow trolling or drifting with the wind across a lake. Because they prefer deep, cool water, trolling can be spectacularly successful once you have found the proper depth. Also, because walleyes enjoy the company of other walleyes, where you hook one you may hook several. Casting also can be effective especially during the fish's spring spawning activities.

The best locations for finding walleyes in lakes are around rocky points and weedy bays or at the mouths of streams and rivers entering the lakes. You'll seldom find one over a mud bottom.

Once you have found the walleye and it has found your bait, give the fish plenty of time to swallow before you set your hook. The walleye won't jump or make fast runs, but if you use light tackle, bringing the fish in can be fun. Have a big net handy for boating a larger walleye, and watch out for the sharp teeth when removing the hook from its mouth.

Abe Black of Shaker Heights, Ohio, caught the state record walleye at Lake Cumberland in October 1958. The fish weighed in at 21 pounds, eight ounces.

Sauger

Almost everything said about catching the walleye can be said about the sauger, except that it will tolerate murky water that the walleye will not. The feeding habits are similar, although the sauger frequently will be found in even deeper water. Anglers can take it by trolling, casting, or still fishing with live bait.

The best sauger catches usually are made below dams, where their upstream schooling runs are blocked by man-made walls of concrete.

The sauger, like the walleye, has made a spectacular comeback in Kentucky, and now is found in abundance in Lake Cumberland, Kentucky and Barkley lakes. I have found them especially active around the canal joining Kentucky and Barkley. Anglers are continually surprised to find them in the Ohio and Kentucky rivers.

One of the best places to catch sauger is in the Ohio River from the Indiana shore just below McAlpine Dam at Louisville. Hardly a day goes by, winter or summer, that someone isn't wetting a line from the bank or from a well-anchored boat. No Indiana fishing license is required; a stretch of land at that location is part of Louisville, and, of course, the Ohio River is owned by Kentucky.

There is no size limit for the sauger, but a walleye must be at least 15- inches long.

The state record is held by W. H. Price of Murfreesboro, Tenn., with a 6 pound 1 ounce prize.

Dr. Herman Mahaffey of Louisville was justly proud of this 29-inch walleye caught at Dale Hollow.

Panfish

Rock bass

Bluegill

Shellcracker

Redear

Pumpkinseed

Warmouth

Perch

In the category of small game fish appropriately known as panfish, probably because they can be cooked in small pans, fall the bluegill, rock bass, redear or shellcracker, pumpkinseed, white and yellow perch, and a whole batch of sunfish species going by scores of unofficial names.

Bluegill

The most popular panfish is the bluegill, which can be found in almost every river, lake, pond and stream in Kentucky.

A member of the sunfish family, the bluegill, also known as the brim, bream, or blue sunfish, has a blue-green or olive-green back, lighter sides and an orange-toned breast. It can be distinguished from other sunfish by these characteristics: The pectoral fins are long and pointed, the entire gill cover flap, is dark, without a border of another color, and is squared at the back; the mouth is small; the dorsal fin has a dark blotch near its rear end.

While sought mostly by children using cane and glass poles, the bluegill provides hours of sport for anyone using very light casting and spinning outfits or a fly rod. Casting and spinning rigs should carry two- to four-pound test line with rod and reel to match. A heavier outfit like that used to catch bass robs bluegill fishing of its excitement.

For those fishermen using bait, a single little split shot, a tiny hook and a light bobber will suffice. Bluegills go for red worms and will take crickets, grasshoppers and insect larvae. Because bluegills are notorious for stealing bait, it is best to thread the worm on the hook, leaving very little dangling.

Only occasionally found in streams, bluegills prefer lakes and ponds surrounded by vegetation.

Although bluegills bite throughout the fishing season, the best time to look for them is in late spring or early summer. At that time of the year the fish are spawning and easy to locate. You usually can find them close to shore guarding their nests.

When you get a nibble, don't set the hook too fast. Like all sunfish, bluegills have small mouths and need plenty of time to swallow the bait. A very small, light bobber provides real excitement. First it will bob up and down, and, when the fish pulls it under, you can set your hook. Despite its size, the tiny bluegill will put up a powerful struggle.

Although a half-pound bluegill is considered to be a fish worth bragging about, some bluegills grow to unusual sizes. The state record bluegill, caught by William S. Wolley of Campbellsville in May

1955, weighed three pounds, six ounces. He took this monster from a pond in Taylor County.

Rock Bass

Another popular member of the sunfish family is the rock bass, also known as the redeye, goggle-eye, or rock sunfish. It has an olive-green or black back, yellowish, mottled sides, and a lighter belly. The body of the rock bass is oblong and compressed. The mouth is large and the lower jaw projects forward. As its alternate names imply, its eye is large and usually red. Teeth are found on the tongue.

Like the bluegill, most rock bass are taken by young fishermen using 10- to 12-foot-long cane or glass poles, bobbers and natural baits. A light spinning or spin-casting outfit also will work well, but a fly rod may offer the best sport for taking these weak fighters.

Because the mouth of the rock bass is much larger than that of other sunfish, an angler may use a larger hook than would be selected for catching bluegills. Natural baits—worms, crawfish, minnows—are best, but artificial lures also will work occasionally.

Early or late fishing probably will provide more rock bass on the stringer, although deep fishing can be worthwhile in midday. Once on the hook, only the bigger fish will put up much of a struggle.

Remember the rock bass's name when you fish for it, because this panfish usually is found around rocks, under trees, or wherever it can find shade. Young rock bass often swim in schools and are easy to locate and catch, but the older and wiser fish keep to themselves in deeper waters.

The rock bass may reach a weight of a pound or a pound and a half and a length of a foot, although the average specimen will tip the scale at less than one-half pound.

The Kentucky record rock bass, caught by H. S. White of Cadiz in Trigg County's Casey Creek in May 1975, weighed one pound, 10 ounces. He topped the record of one pound, seven ounces set by Ronald Pitcock of Louisville in 1972.

Warmouth

The warmouth, or warmouth bass, warmouth sunfish, or lady perch, has a shape very much like that of the rock bass. It is usually bronze or greenish bronze but does not have the dark spots of the rock bass, but has vertical markings. Easily distinguishable from the other sunfish because of its large mouth, the warmouth is a husky, red-eyed fish with a patch of small teeth on its tongue. To find the warmouth, try weedy, muddy, quiet spots and fish with worms and small minnows attached to lines on cane poles.

On the whole, the warmouth is not a very popular fish because of its muddy taste.

Redear Sunfish (Shellcracker)

A panfish that closely resembles the bluegill is the redear sunfish or shellcracker. It also has long, pointed pectorals but can be distinguished from the bluegill by the red and white border on its gill cover flap.

The redear sunfish is olive green above, generally with brassy tones, and yellowish to brassy or silvery below. The shellcracker is larger than the bluegill; it commonly is six- or seven-inches long but rarely reaches a length of 10 inches.

Primarily a bottom feeder, it is a rare catch that is taken from the surface of the large rivers and lakes it inhabits. The shellcracker is so named because it eats shells and other small shelled creatures which it crushes with teeth in the back of its throat. It can, however, be coaxed to strike worms.

Rupert Zwigard of Louisville caught a state record shellcracker in 1969 but has not received proper recognition because he cut it up and even buried the head and tail before learning that he had taken a champion. The mark of two pounds, five ounces, established by R. C. Masters of Louisville on Memorial Day in 1964, still is recognized in Kentucky. Masters caught his beauty at a lake in Taylor County.

Pumpkinseed

The brilliantly colored pumpkinseed, only occasionally found in Kentucky waters, closely resembles the redear sunfish. The main differences are a blotch on the posterior part of the dorsal fin and bluish bands on the sides of the light orange head.

Many pumpkinseeds are taken on hook and line along with the bluegill and in the same areas, at the same time, and with the same type of bait.

H.S. White of Cadiz displays his state record rock bass, along with a near-record he caught the same day.

Richard Masters of Louisville took this state record shellcracker.

Catfish, Carp & Gar

Carp eat most anything and will often destroy lakebed plants while churning them up for food.

No doubt the least appreciated fish in Kentucky waters are the catfish and carp. Both put up good fights and provide excellent table fare. However, they are regarded lightly in angling circles mostly because of an abundance of better game fish and because of the work that is required to make them ready for the table.

You will find these fish in virtually every farm pond, stream and lake within the state's borders. When nothing else is biting, you can bait up for cats and carp and not go home empty-handed.

Carp

The carp is the most important freshwater food fish in the world. Not a native of the United States, it was first brought to this country around 1830. In 1877 a large supply was imported from Germany, where carp was staple table fare. Izaak Walton, writing in the 17th century, called the carp "the queen of the rivers, a stately, good, and very subtle fish."

Because of its wide distribution, the carp has developed many variations in color, including shades of silver, yellow, gold, green and brown. Its sucker-type mouth is toothless, but it does have teeth in its throat. The carp also can be recognized by the two barbels of "whiskers" on either side of its mouth. The average carp weighs anywhere from one to 10 pounds, but fish over that weight are not uncommon.

The carp isn't classified as a game fish, but an increasing number of Kentuckians are finding sport in catching it on light tackle, and bow and arrow anglers find the carp an exciting target.

The carp is a hardy fish and thrives and multiplies in many Kentucky ponds, rivers and lakes that would be unsuitable for other fish.

All kinds of tackle are employed by carp fishermen, with the weight of the rig determined by the size of the fish that usually are found in the particular lake or stream.

Artificial lures can be used, but natural baits are best. And no carp fisherman should forget about the highly popular doughball, made from flour or cornmeal, a sweetener and water. (See recipe on page 127.) Other good carp baits are fresh bread, corn, peas, beans, meat, crawfish and worms.

Good carp fishing will be found throughout the day during the spring and fall and during the cooler morning and evening hours of the summer. Carp are most likely to be found in warm, quiet, slow moving streams with mud bottoms and a lot of vegetation.

The state record for carp is 54 pounds, 14 ounces, caught in March 1971 by Ricky Vance of Paris. Vance, who was fishing the Licking River, had trouble landing his spectacular catch and swore he'd never again go fishing without a net.

Vance bought some night crawlers and drove about 15 miles to a point on the Licking River where Mill Creek enters it, just below Cynthiana. He had been fishing an hour or so when something took his night crawler and hung on. Vance thought he had a snag at first, but then whatever had his bait moved slowly to one side. Vance kept a tight hold with his 10-pound test line. More moves and he let out a little of his line, fearful that a quick move would break the monofilament. Then came a long battle. The fish moved back and forth but fortunately did not make a run too far out to deep water.

A half hour passed. Finally the fish began to give way, and Vance was able to reel in most of his line. A large fin appeared on the surface; Vance had never seen a fish big enough to own a fin that long. A gentle pressure on his line brought the fish in to where its belly rested on the muddy gravel bottom. It then turned slowly on its side and flopped weakly about.

Having no net, there was only one thing for Vance to do, and he did it—shoes, socks and all. He waded into the water and grabbed the big fellow under the gills with one hand while he held his line taut with the other. Then with both hands he lugged his prize up the bank to dry land. What a fish! It was a carp, he was sure, but how big?

With the fish in the back of his car, Vance drove to Richard L. Emmons's place in Paris, where he had purchased the night crawlers. The fish swung the indicator on the scale to 54 pounds and 15

ounces. They telephoned Harry Towles, then record keeper for the Department of Fish and Wildlife in Frankfort. "You sure have a record carp for Kentucky," Towles said, "and if it weighed seven more ounces, it would be a world record!" (The world record carp, which weighed 55 pounds, five ounces, was caught in Minnesota in 1952.)

The state record for a carp taken with a bow and arrow is held by Jim Farthing of Harrodsburg. Farthing and his wife drove to Herrington Lake one summer day in 1976 and went by boat to the muddy and grassy flats at the head of Cane Run Creek to look for gar, which like to float on the top of the water during hot days. As they pushed their boat into water less than two-feet deep, they came upon a sight thrilling to a bow fisherman—no gar, but huge carp rolling in the throes of spawning.

The carp took no notice as Farthing inched his boat closer to pick out a prize. On his first shot he sent his arrow through a 21-pounder, yet the amorous rolling continued without a pause.

Farthing let the arrow go again, and this time he hauled in a 26-pounder, a new state record for a carp taken by bow and arrow. (The old state record, so far as is known, was a 24-pound carp taken 10 years earlier in Salt River by Larry Chauvin of Shively.)

But Farthing was not content with his second fish. He spotted the rolling belly of a carp that made the others look like bream. The arrow found its mark. The giant carp struggled to get into deeper water, but Mrs. Farthing held the line and pulled the fish close enough for her husband to grab it by the mouth.

After a struggle to get the monster into the boat, the Farthings returned to the dock, where a scale showed the fish to weigh 47 pounds, 12 ounces, a new state record almost twice the size of the earlier champion.

The Farthings discovered that springtime, especially during the month of May, is the best time to go for carp with bow and arrow. That is when the egg-laden females, escorted by males, move into grassy sloughs. The female holds her eggs until grabbed by the gills by a male (in some cases by two males), which thrashes its body against the female's. This causes the female to deposit the eggs, which are then sprayed by male sperm.

Anglers thinking of trying bow fishing should acquire a short bow, a bow reel, a metal or glass arrow with one or more barbs at the point, and about 50 feet of heavy gauge fishing line. The reel is attached near the handle section of the bow, with the line attached at one end to the reel and at the other to the arrow. Due to water refractions in distance and distortions over water, the hunter must shoot from six inches to a foot lower than the carp appears to be. And he must shoot quickly.

Catfish

Like the carp, the catfish is a hardy number that thrives in low-oxygen, warm, torpid water where more delicate game fish cannot.

There are numerous varieties of the catfish, but the one that offers the best game in the cleanest, fastest moving water is the channel catfish. This smooth, streamlined, bewhiskered fish is usually gray or grayish blue on top with many dark spots along its silvery sides. A sure indicator of a channel cat, which has no scales, is its deeply forked tail and its long barbels, used to help it find food.

All kinds of tackle and all kinds of bait have been

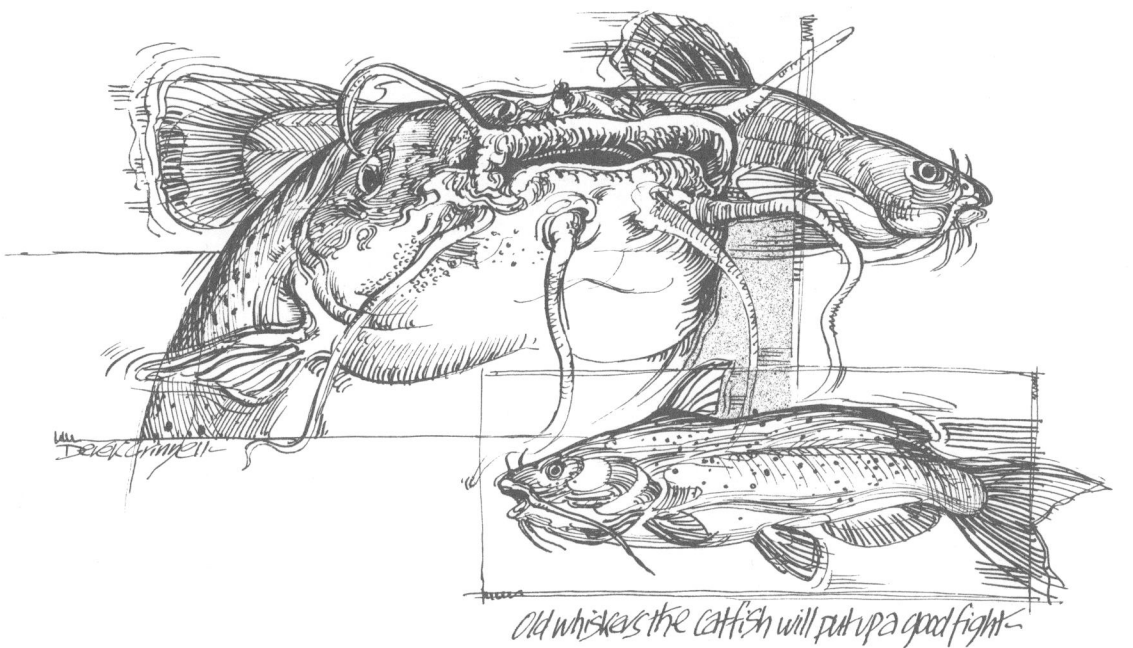

Old whiskers the catfish will put up a good fight.

Fred Cornett with state record channel cat

Jim Farthing with his state and national record gar (by bow and arrow)

used to take catfish. For the best sport, just be sure to use the lightest tackle that is practical for the size catfish generally found in the water you're fishing.

If you are fishing in quiet water, all you need do is let your baited hook sink to the bottom. When distance is needed, a small sinker may be added a few inches above the hook.

Catfish are largely nocturnal bottom feeders, but they often are caught during the day in deeper holes. They will take almost any kind of lure, but the best are natural baits, such as night crawlers, chunks of meat, crawfish, gizzard shad and guts of certain other fish. These live and cut baits are usually more productive than artificial ones, although jigs, spoons and spinners can be used. Like the carp, let the catfish nibble at the bait at its leisure before you set the hook.

One modern version of an old invention employed to catch cats is called jugging. Attach a hook and line just long enough to keep the bait near the bottom to an empty beer can or a plastic container like that used for bleach or milk. When the "jug" starts bobbing, you know you have a catfish.

Anglers using jugs at night have been known to force a small rock or two into the container. When the fish strikes, the rocks will rattle and let the fisherman know he has some action and where it is.

The best time to go catfishing is after a rain when the water is discolored and catfish are eating the foods washed into the river. When the water is clear, stick to the early morning and evening hours and particularly the night, when cats leave their hideouts, usually under overhanging banks.

The state record holder among channel cat fishermen is Fred Cornett of Lexington. His championship catch weighed 15 pounds, six ounces and was caught in Beaver Lake in Anderson County in April 1973.

A Kentuckian holds a world record for another catfish.

Jewell Copeland of Benton caught a 100-pound blue cat below the dam at Kentucky Lake in 1970.

The blue catfish is larger than the channel cat. Although both have the same blue tone, the blue is not spotted. It does, however, have a deeply forked tail. The easiest way to distinguish between the two is to examine the anal fin. The blue has 30 to 36 rays and the free edge is almost straight; the channel's anal fin has 24 to 30 rays and its free edge is rounded.

Copeland had eaten his blue cat and discarded everything, including the head and jaw, when he was told he had a world record. It bested the old record of 97 pounds taken from the Missouri River in 1965.

Kentuckians also go for bullhead cats, which frequent farm ponds as well as most streams and lakes. Like the blue and the channel, the bullhead is a good table fish.

There are three species of bullheads—black, brown and yellow. They are attracted to baits with strong odors. Barbels under the jaw are whitish on the yellow and dark on the brown. Tails lack the deep fork of the channel and the blue. Bullheads rarely are found to measure more than 18 inches.

There are no size or creel limits on catfish, which form the bulk of all fish caught commercially in the state.

Gar

You can't talk about carp and catfish without mentioning the gar, which is a favorite quarry for bow anglers. The gar has a slender, cylindrical body covered with diamond-shaped scales in diagonal rows. It can be identified easily by its long beak and numerous sharp teeth.

There are four species of gar in Kentucky—the longnose, the shortnose, the spotted and the alligator. The longnose is yellowish to olive above and whitish-yellow on the underside. The beak is long and narrow. The shortnose can be distinguished from the longnose because its snout is wider. Although it is similar to the spotted gar, which rarely is found in this state, its spots are confined to the median fins while the spotted has large spots over most of its body. The alligator has two rows of large teeth on each side of the upper jaw, in contrast with the single row found in the other species.

The record gar was taken in August 1956 by Kelsie Travis Jr. of Paducah. It weighed 40 pounds and was taken from the Ohio River. Jim Farthing, mentioned above, holds the national as well as the state record for gar taken by bow and arrow.

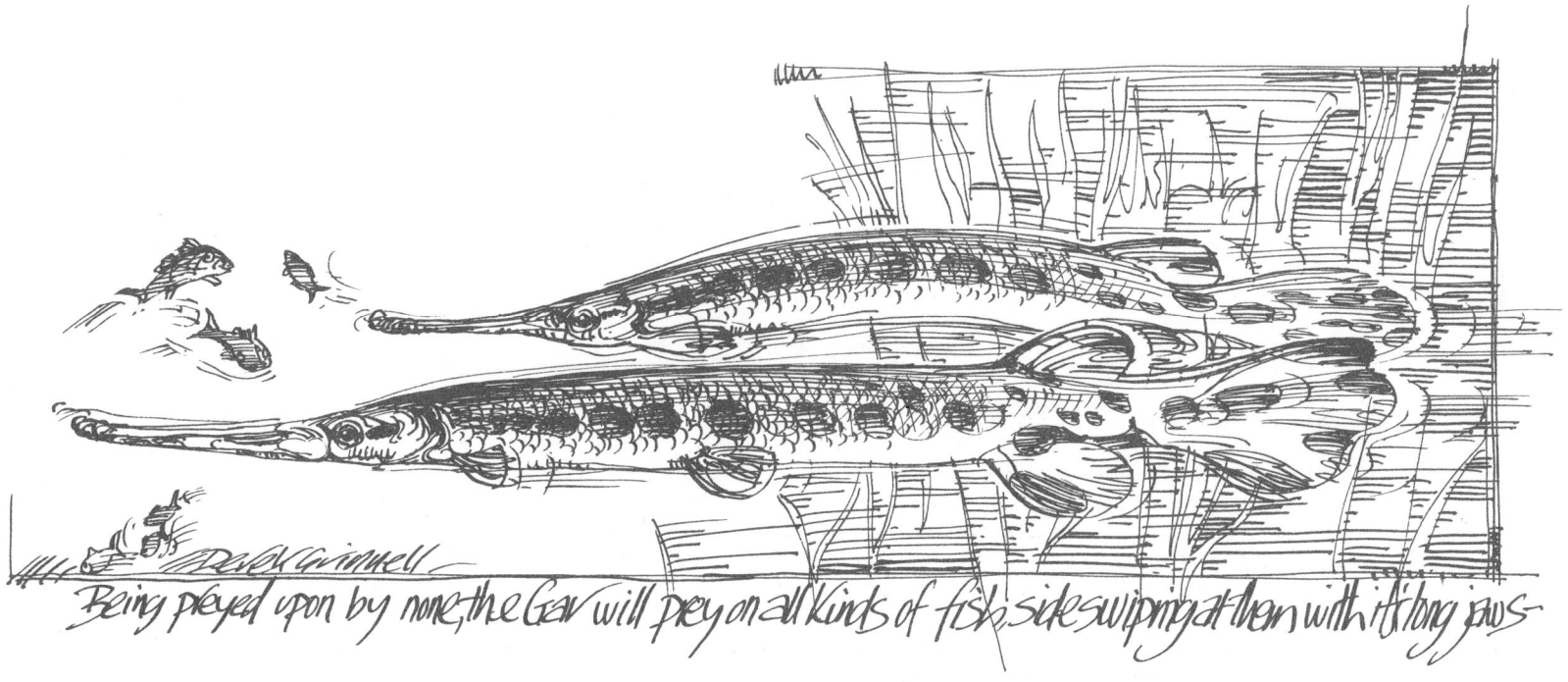

Being preyed upon by none, the Gar will prey on all kinds of fish sideswiping at them with its long jaws

Frogs

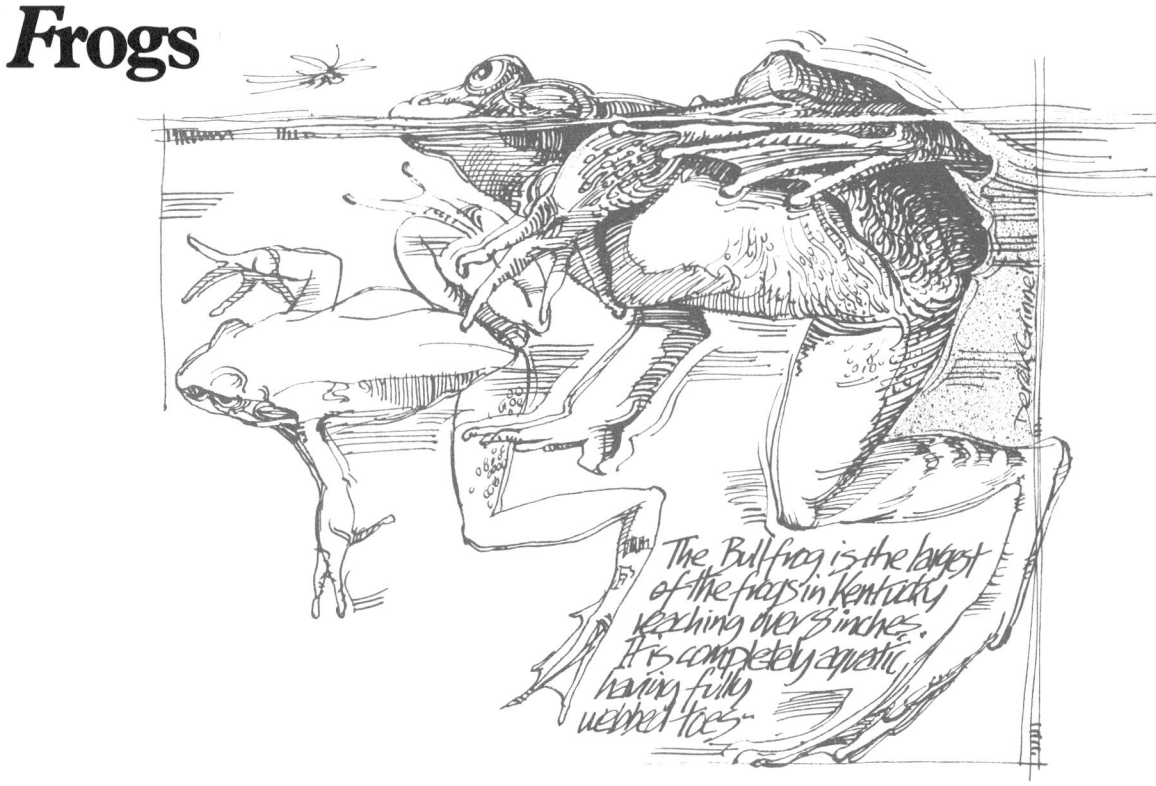

The Bullfrog is the largest of the frogs in Kentucky reaching over 8 inches. It is completely aquatic having fully webbed toes.

You come across some unusual characters when frog hunting in Kentucky. For instance, I used to go frogging with Harry Lazarus of Bowling Green, who floated every stream in his part of the state and never carried a gig. He bagged hundreds of frogs each spring, picking all of them up by hand, in the soft light of a small carbide lamp. Near daybreak at the end of those journeys he and I slept on cots while our driver, who met us at a bridge crossing, cleaned our frogs and cooked our breakfast on a sandbar.

Then there was Acree Higby of Henry County, who hunted frogs by day and night with a long fishing pole, a three-foot line, and a fishing hook baited with a bit of red flannel.

And a commercial hunter who for years waded many small streams in Southcentral Kentucky with no equipment except a carbide lamp affixed to his cap and a long sturdy pole he used to poke his way along. He picked up his frogs by hand and stuffed them into his ample shirt. He could carry up to 100 that way. "If I come across a lawman all I have to do is pull out my shirttail and, wham!, all the evidence is gone," explained the man, who obviously would prefer to remain anonymous.

Dr. Herman Mahaffey of Louisville and Davis "Zeke" Morgan of LaGrange are such avid frog hunters they sit up the night of May 14 so they can be the first to hit a special lake when the season opens at midnight. They pick their lakes by fishing

them by day and counting the number of frogs they spook off the banks.

And then there's Buddy Williams of Maud, a small town near Bloomfield. Williams hunts frogs by day and gets his limit of 15 in no time at all by riding shotgun on a farm tractor. Using a .22 rifle and hollow-point bullets, he circles the ponds on his tractor, stops above each frog, and shooting left-handed, never misses. "They hold still as long as I keep the tractor motor running," he said, "but if I turn it off or climb off the tractor, they all jump in the water."

Williams was with us on one night expedition when he came back to the car soon after dark with a sack, heavy with frogs, hanging from his hips. Two others in the group returned from another pond with only five. "We saw several more under bushes and out on the moss but couldn't get to them," one said.

"I can tell from your dry pants why you didn't get 'em," said Williams, who was wet almost up to his belt.

"How far out did you wade?" he was asked.

"Just as far as I needed to," he said, patting his hip pocket, "but not up to my money. I don't like wet money."

Williams joined Mahaffey, Morgan, John Hughes of Maud and me on a two-day, two-night hunt for frogs and fish at ponds and lakes around Maud. Hughes had obtained permission from the owners of the ponds before we arrived, an act of courtesy no frog hunter should ignore.

The first night was dark and stormy; a radio voice told us the temperature was 56 degrees. "Just about too cold for frogs to be out," I said and quickly was proved wrong. We took turns from pond to pond and gigged our limits before a full moon came out about 1 a.m. I prefer a three-inch-long, three-prong gig attached to a light pole that measures about 10-feet long when I go gigging. Most of the frogs we sacked were so large we saved the front legs as well as the back ones by cutting the skin around the neck and pulling it off with a pair of pliers. In cleaning whole frogs, I cut the white tendons in the back so the legs won't draw up when cooked.

You're never too old to learn something new about hunting frogs, and I found this out when I accepted an invitation from Eddie Jungbert and King Stratton of Louisville to go frogging with them one June night in 1970. I said, "We've got a bright moon. I don't think we can do much good." They told me to just pack a lunch and bring a good flashlight. I prefer the old-fashioned miner's lamp that burns carbide, but I couldn't find one at the neighborhood hardware store. Instead, I took a flashlight with a heavy-duty battery and a handle.

We drove several miles east of Louisville and turned off on a long, winding country lane. Finally we came to a neat white farmhouse. Stratton, who had made the arrangements, knocked on the door. An affable lady told him, "If you don't get frogs tonight, it's your fault. They've been croaking so loud we can hear them all the way up here."

The moon reflected in the quiet water, and there wasn't a sound of a bullfrog. "I just don't see how we can get many frogs in moonlight that bright," I said.

"That moon is nothing," said Jungbert. "Wait till they turn on the lights." Just then the lights came on, four of those big, tall vapor lights that illuminate so many farmyards around the state. They showed the outline of the lakes, the fences, trees and bushes all around.

"My gosh," I said. "Who ever heard of frogs under lights like these? We can't get close enough to gig any frogs in those lakes."

Stratton and Jungbert were pulling on boots and adjusting their lights. "All I know," ventured Stratton, "is that we have got them here before."

An aluminum boat was shining under a nearby tree. We shoved it into the water. Jungbert took the front, I sat in the middle with a wet gunnysack for the frogs, and Stratton manned the oars. By then the deep voices of several bullfrogs were echoing across the water. Jungbert looked back at me and grinned. We were moving along a bank on our left. The moon was shining in back of us now, and one of the bright farm lights was directly ahead on the far bank.

Jungbert's light picked up two frogs, but both were too small — only about eight-inches long. We slowly and quietly made the turn and had the big light almost overhead when we spotted a jumbo squatted almost flat on the mud bank. "There he is," Jungbert said in a hoarse whisper. He guided the boat directly toward the frog. Holding his gig steady until it was less than six inches from the frog, he gave it a quick push forward. "What did you say about that light scaring frogs away?" he cried as he raised the frog high in the air. I said I guess the frog was too busy catching flies attracted by the light to

see us coming.

We cleaned the frogs before leaving and found that some of them, not content with flies for food, had dined on some of their young. Most of the frogs we caught were real jumbos — about 14-inches long. "Well, that proves that we don't hurt the frog population by harvesting a lot of granddaddies," I said.

"Yep," said Jungbert, "and I guess we proved something else."

"Yeah," I admitted, "that you can take frogs in the light of the moon and under a bright farm light."

And that's not the only lesson I've learned about frog hunting. I was taught another at John Hughes's farm at Maud in 1971. "Well, I'll tell you what you can do," Hughes told me. "You can go down to one of these ponds and try fishing it. Then after dark, you can frog it."

Morgan and Mahaffey were with me, and we headed for the pond, really a small lake, as I offered the sage observation, "You just don't get bass and frogs — that is big bass and frogs — out of the same pond. One or the other dominates the water." That afternoon Morgan caught a tremendous bass on a tiny Gay Blade. It tipped the scales at eight pounds. He carefully put his prize on a stringer and placed it back in the water so it would stay alive. A light rain began to fall as darkness closed in while we waited to start our frog hunt.

"Well, I guess there won't be any frogs in this pond," Mahaffey said, "if Ruby is right."

Just then the deepest, most vibrant "belly-deep" imaginable shook the willows. "There's at least one," I conceded. So we shoved our boat into the water, and Morgan rigged up his electric trolling motor — a real must for easy frogging some big ponds. We rounded a bend and my light fell on one of the biggest bullfrogs I'd ever seen.

"You take him," Morgan said.

"Heck no," I said. "You got the biggest fish, now you can take the biggest frog — both from the same pond — and prove I'm crazy." He took it easily, and we were off and running on an all-night hunt that produced several very large specimens.

I checked later with Charles Bowers, director of the Division of Fisheries in Frankfort and a real authority on fish. He explained that while it usually is true that bass and frogs can't remain together long in most ponds, there are exceptions. "If there is enough shallow water to give the frogs protection,

Paul Ruby of Louisville was just a kid when he went well-armed for frogs one dark night.

Davis (Zeke) Morgan of LaGrange says "How's this for size?"

they will survive and grow big," he said. This lake was that kind — plenty of shallow water for frogs as well as deep water for bass.

Soon after that excursion I received another invitation I couldn't refuse. "Come on a round of ponds with us," said Frank Smith and Bobby McCullough of Lexington. "We'll show you more frogs and bigger ones in Bourbon County alone than you ever saw on a creek. And it'll be easier hunting."

Well, we saw a heap of frogs. And we gigged a mess apiece. The limit is 15 per customer a night, and much as old creekers will dispute it, I think we got some frogs in those limits that were bigger than any ever seen on a creek. "It's natural," explained Smith. "Pond frogs just sit and eat. Creek frogs got to get around some."

There is very definitely an art to frogging. It's like learning to catch a slick bar of soap in the bathtub. In fact, a bit of practice with that bar of soap isn't a bad idea, especially before frogging by hand at night.

One of the most consistently successful froggers I've known was J. T. Lewis Jr. of Lexington. This gentleman preferred to "gun in the sun rather than float in a boat." And not because he was 72. "I was shooting frogs when I was so young back in my hometown of Hardinsburg that my mother wouldn't let me carry anything bigger than a BB gun," he said with a smile. He later switched to a .22 rifle with a scope sight on it.

"I scout around before the season opens and find the good frog ponds," he said. "Then I ask permission to frog. When the season opens I usually have several nice ponds waiting for me.

"If it's rainy or wet I stay home. After all, I frog for fun, and it's no fun sitting in mud in a chilly rainstorm. If the sun is shining I try to get set by my pond around seven o'clock in the morning. I usually can limit out with 15 good-sized frogs by 3 or 4 p.m. If I'm very quiet in approaching the pond I might get a shot before I sit down. If I don't, I just sit and wait.

"The only equipment I take along, besides my rifle, is a garden rake to which I have tied a few feet of rope. When the first big frog appears above water I let him move as close to the bank as he acts like he intends to go. Then I draw a bead on him and try to hit him in the head. I've heard of fellows shooting in the water just under the frog and knocking him out on the bank, out of breath and sorta temporarily

paralyzed. But I'm not that good with a gun. All I want to do is get a bullet into the frog.

"Then I lay down my gun, pick up my rake, and run over and rake him out of the water. If he's too far out for the rake, I toss the rake out and pull it back by the rope. I seldom fail to bring him in, but I must say a hit frog sinks fast, and you can't fool around much."

I mentioned that some froggers contend that a dead frog will float. Lewis scoffed. "If he's real dead he might float," he said. "But how many times do you kill one real dead? A frog always has one last kick, and it usually is away from the bank, aimed at getting him underwater."

The shot and commotion scare all other frogs back into the water. Lewis sits down again and waits quietly until the bigger fellows begin to re-surface, usually about 15 minutes. "Funny thing about a frog," he confided. "You'll notice that each has a favorite spot to sit. Just like a rabbit or a bass or most other wild things. When the frogs surface and go for the pond banks, they will head for the very spots they left when scared off before."

Well, so much for daytime frogging. My favorite method of taking big bullfrogs is by hand at night, floating in a flatboat light enough to be hauled over fallen trees and extra-shallow riffles. I carry a gunnysack in the boat to carry the frogs in and use small carbide lamps to spot the frogs. Picking up the frogs by hand is easier and simpler (except in weeds and reeds) than using a gig, and, best of all, you don't injure the frogs. If a frog turns out to be a bit less than the size you want, you can turn it loose unharmed to be bagged another night.

There's no trick to it. You just grab the frog quickly around the middle while it's temporarily blinded by the light. It's best not to let your hand cross in front of the light; the shadow falling across the frog's face may be all the rascal needs to sense danger coming its way.

There's nothing quite so peaceful and interesting as a night float trip. I started to say quiet, but a successful frog hunting trip is never a quiet one. Unlike most frogs, which sing only to communicate with a prospective mate, a bullfrog will sing for the pure fun of it. Many a night old Harry Lazarus and I floated down the Barren River on all-night trips that might have been boring and unproductive if it hadn't been for the bullfrog's love of music.

After eating supper on a gravel bar waiting for night to fall, we would listen for the first deep

"harrumppp" of a giant bullfrog. If none was forthcoming after we shoved off and got everything ready, Lazarus, who had a deep voice, would croon "Asleep in the Deep," putting emphasis on the deep notes of "sailor beware — be . . . eee . . . eee . . . ware."

Pretty soon the chorus of croaking all around kept us too busy grabbing and stuffing the gunnysack to do any singing. But if we went as long as a city block without a frog, Lazarus would break out again with "Old Man River" or deep notes of other tunes enjoyed by our big-eyed quarry. Almost invariably an answering "harrumppp" would come from a nearby patch of waterside weeds.

Ed Hovious of Bardstown and Bill Mudd, a neighbor, are exponents of the Lazarus system of frogging. They like the cool, calm of night float trips. They prefer the gig to the bare hand, however, calling it "more certain. We decide before we aim a gig at a frog whether he's a keeper or not," Hovious said. "If he is, we gig him. We lose virtually no big frogs this way."

Two other dedicated froggers are Ralph Davis Sr. and James Cook of Vanceburg, who were among the few frog hunters to venture out on the opening day of one frog season when cold weather kept most indoors. They came back with their limits of 15 each in less than three hours every time.

"You may be interested to know," reported Davis, "that while we frequently use the bare-hand method, which you claim to be the most sporting way to take frogs, we have refined our hunting beyond this. The system we now employ exclusively on frogs we intend to keep is to throw a one-tine gig like a spear or javelin. This not only is more sporting but requires skill. We missed our mark only four times on opening night."

An enlightening comment on this system of catching frogs came to me from Mrs. H. M. Bertram Jr., a neighbor of Davis and Cook. "I was interested in your challenge to Ralph and James to use only their bare hands in hunting frogs with you," she said. "I am sure that Mrs. Davis would be delighted if those two renowned frog hunters would start going after frogs with their bare hands.

"The reason? Poor Mrs. Davis probably holds the world's record for cleaning bullfrogs and stashing them in the freezer. Those two stalwart hunters may return home by 3:30 a.m., but long after their snores are rattling the house, Mrs. Davis is standing in the kitchen surrounded by those gigged and bloody frogs, cleaning and freezing them. Maybe if the men used their bare hands, the frogs would live and the men could clean them, themselves, the next day."

The unusual size of frogs caught some years surprises many sportsmen. On a typical hunt one very good year five Louisvillians picked up 75 frogs, all 15 inches or more long at ponds in Jefferson County. The men were Gary Hatfield, Lonso Robinson, Joe Hatfield, Herb Hatfield and Vernon McManis.

State regulations give night fishermen a big edge over frog hunters. The day begins at midnight for fishermen. This means that if you have your limit or near-limit by midnight, you can take your string back to the dock and then return to start a new day's limit at 12:01 a.m.

The froggers were allowed two limits per night also until about 15 years ago. The law was changed then, setting the start of a froggers day at noon. This was a real blow to old-timers who liked the all-night float trip. They found that, with a limit of 15 frogs

in the gunnysack at 11 p.m. or so, they had to continue floating five or six hours with nothing to do. It's not an easy thing to find put-in and take-out points on most of the good frogging streams; in fact, you're lucky if you find such points less than eight hours apart. The new law is a good one, however, since it foils greedy guys who hunted every night and took two limits each night.

While there never has been a size record kept for frogs, I have caught several in the 17-inch class, as have many others. Frogging is confined to farm ponds, lazy streams and some small lakes. Frogs can't survive predator fish in most major lakes.

The presence of frogs in any pond near a road can be detected by cruising in your car after dark and cutting your motor every now and then and listening. Once heard, a knock at the door may mean the farmer's permission to hunt them. Most farmers do not mind froggers who are careful to close gates, gig quietly, and leave no litter.

Either a fishing or hunting license is a passport for taking frogs by hand or gig. A hunting license is

a must for hunting with a firearm.

This simplified method of cleaning frogs was suggested by Buddy Williams of Maud, who has cleaned a million, more or less, in his lifetime. I recommend it highly.

His method eliminates the use of a cutting board and the wear and tear on a good knife cutting through the backbone and foot bones and enables you to discard the innards without contact with the hands.

1. Using a very sharp knife, cut the skin all the way around the belly and back. Using good pliers, pull the skin down and off the legs.

2. Using tinners shears or kitchen shears, cut off legs at the middle.

3. Snip off the toes, and the job is done.

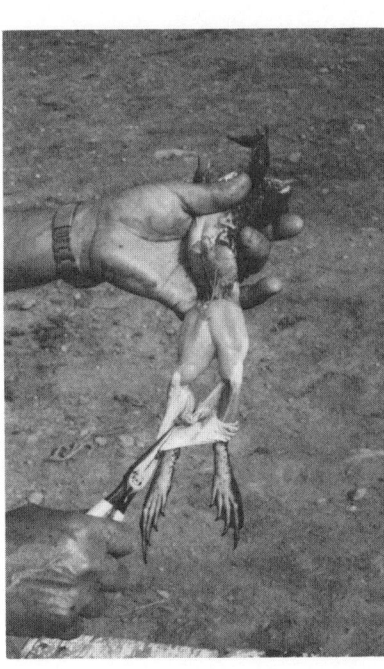  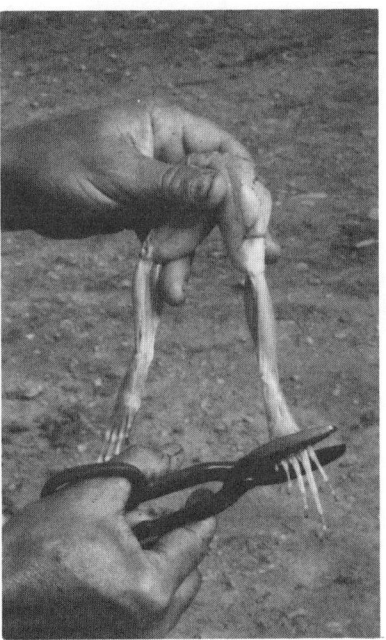

Turtles

Although the turtle family has been around for something like ninety million years, they are still considered by some as a delicious table dish.

Some sportsmen wait for the chatter of the squirrel, the call of the bobwhite, or the haunting note of the mourning dove, but to Dr. Herman Mahaffey of Louisville, there's nothing as sweet as the voice of the turtle.

You didn't know the turtle had a voice? Well, it hasn't, for most people. But Mahaffey hears something—maybe the cry of his ample tummy for fried turtle—and off he goes to Dale Hollow each spring. His friends and neighbors are glad that he heeds this voice they can't hear because he usually brings back enough meat to last until he can find time to go again.

"You've really got to make one of these Dale Hollow trips with me," he said. So we left Louisville at 5:30 one morning and arrived at Star Point Dock about four hours later after traveling through Greensburg, Columbia and Albany.

Dale Hollow is on the Tennessee-Kentucky border, and because we would be hunting turtles and fishing in the Tennessee part of the lake, I bought a three-day Tennessee non-resident fishing license.

Mahaffey had bought 100 No. 8/0 hooks (big enough to hang a country ham on), a couple of balls of heavy-duty cord, and several pounds of the toughest chunks of neck meat of beef he could find. While I manned the outboard motor, Mahaffey cut the cord into six-foot lengths, tied a hook to each, and worked each hook through a piece of the meat. Stowing our lines neatly in the bottom of the boat, we gunned the outboard to a favorite cove and began casting the banks with small spinners, all the while looking for good spots where a turtle line could be tied to an overhanging limb. By dark we had all the lines out and three bass to clean for breakfast.

The next day, after an unsuccessful morning of fishing, we ran our turtle lines and hauled in four good-sized turtles. Mahaffey dangled each turtle above the gunnysack that I held and carefully lowered it into the sack. Dealing with an angry turtle with a razor-sharp mouth, iron jaws and flailing legs can give you a few anxious moments.

Mahaffey came by his turtle-hunting hobby quite by accident. He was determined to teach his sons, Daniel and John, all he could about fishing. On one camping trip he set out a trotline for fish but caught two soft-shelled turtles. By trial and error he cleaned and cooked them. The next day he found a snapper on his line. Again he proceeded by trial and

*Arsel Robinson
and Elmer Maddox go
crawling for turtles.*

error (mostly error) but by then he was as hooked as the turtle. He has been setting lines ever since.

Mahaffey likes Dale Hollow for its marvelous wooded beauty, and the area around Star Point for its seclusion. But mostly he likes the challenge of the turtle.

This brings me to the tale of two youngsters, who would have laughed at the way I gingerly held that sack. Kelly Singleton was 14 and Randy Patterson was 16 in 1975 when this story took place. The two Indiana youths did their fishing and frogging and turtling at several small Hoosier ponds near their homes.

One day they set lines baited with the innards of an old rooster, then they fished until dark. The next morning they found they had made one mistake that would have stumped the average angler but did

not bother them. They hadn't used line that was heavy enough. They found action on five lines and began pulling in turtles. They got the first three with no trouble, but on the next line one boy said, "We'll never get that baby out of the water on this line." The other agreed, and, without hesitating, he waded out into the water and gave the turtle a hefty shove from the rear as his pal pulled on the line. That did the trick. They repeated the process on the next line, switching jobs, and neither got a scratch. The turtles weighed more than 20 pounds each.

What to do with a turtle after it's been landed can be a problem.

Mahaffey has a system for preparing a turtle for the table that I learned during a trip to Dale Hollow.

He first cuts off the head, leaving as much neck

meat as possible. After the body has drained, he lays the turtle on its back, slices off the flat undershell, then carefully cuts the body out of the rounded top shell. He keeps the neck, shoulder, legs, and tail meat. He throws away the rest, except for the tenderloin which remains in the bottom of the rounded shell. He removes this white meat with a hatchet and knife. Then he cleans and freezes the meat.

Some turtle fanciers remove the leg bones, but Mahaffey doesn't. "That would be like deboning chicken," he argues.

Tips for the *F*isherman

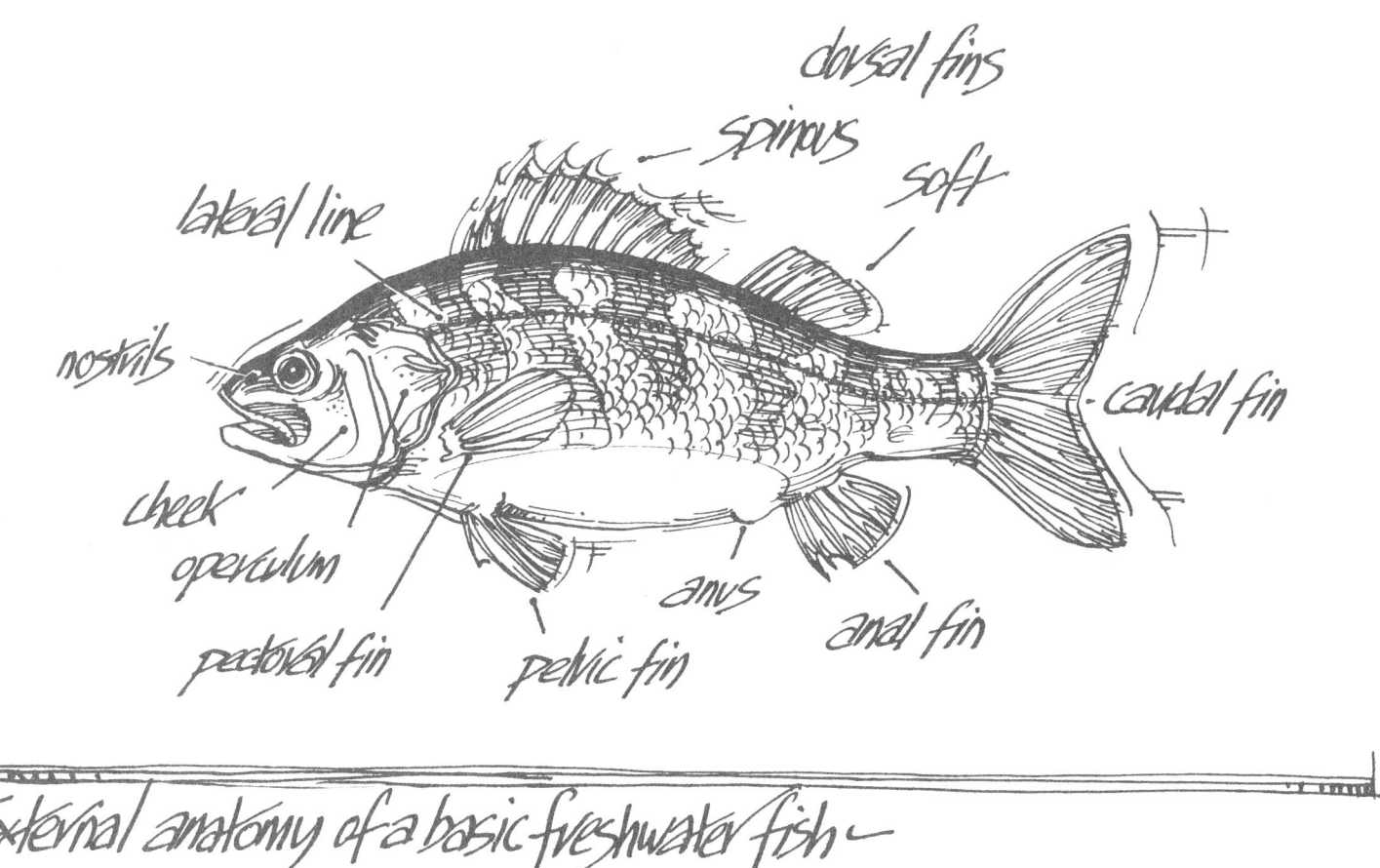

dorsal fins

spinous

soft

lateral line

nostrils

cheek

operculum

pectoral fin

pelvic fin

anus

anal fin

caudal fin

External anatomy of a basic freshwater fish —

Identifying Fish

To identify many kinds of fish, it is necessary to know their external features. This simplified drawing of a fish shows these general features, although naturally they will differ from one species of fish to another.

Tying a Good Knot

I was fishing several years ago with Ken Wisdom, owner of a boat dock on Dale Hollow Lake, when I caught a huge bass that was putting up quite a battle. Wisdom went for the net but I said, "Never mind, I think I can bring this baby in by hand." The words barely had slipped from my mouth when the bass gave one last whirl and was gone.

Also gone was my lure. My knot had not held. I became something of a knot nut after that. I have tried them all and mastered a few. No matter how much money you spend on rods and reels, lines and lures, if your knot isn't tied properly, you and your fish soon will part company.

On a 1975-76 winter fishing trip in Florida with former Louisvillian Jack Gerber, now of Jacksonville, I discovered a knot that is absolutely foolproof and may be used for almost any purpose. Developed by Vic Dunaway, editor of *Florida Sportsman,* this knot isn't totally new but, as he says, is a combination and refinement of known elements.

The basics of the knot were shown to Dunaway in 1972 by Norman Duncan, a veteran light tackle angler from Florida who used it only for tying a fly to a heavy monofilament leader. It dawned on Dunaway that here was a knot that might be adapted easily to replace the improved clinch in tying a leader to a hook or swivel, the end loop knot in looping a line or leader to an artificial lure, the blood knot in tying two lines together, and the surgeon's knot in joining a leader to the line. Dunaway worked at this new knot for a long time and had it tested by Du Pont laboratories in Wilmington, Del., before passing along his discovery.

Of course, if you have mastered any of the other knots, you probably won't want to discard them for the uni-knot, but you might want to add Dunaway's tie to your stock of tricks, perhaps using elements of it along with your other hard-learned hitches. Try it first on the commonest tie of all—joining a leader to a hook or swivel. Once you master that,

you can carry it as far as you like to other connections.

The following descriptions and illustrations of the uni-knot are reproduced here with Dunaway's permission:

First, run the line through the eye for several inches. Turn the end back toward the eye to form a circle as shown in Figure 1. With thumb and finger of the left hand, grasp both strands of line and the crossing strand in a single grip at the point marked X, just forward of the hook. Now, make six turns with the end around both strands of line and through the circle, as in Figure 2.

Maintaining the same grip with the left hand, pull on the end of the line in the direction shown by the arrow until all the wraps are snugged tight and close together. Snugging down tightly at this stage is essential to maximum knot strength. See Figure 3.

Finally, slide the finished knot tight against the eye of the hook by dropping the end and then pulling on the standing part of the line. The excess end can be trimmed flush with the knot after final positioning, as in Figure 4.

It takes just one slight variation to transform the hook tie into a loop arrangement which provides more freedom of action for artificial lures. Instead of sliding the finished knot all the way to the eye, just slide it to the size loop desired. Then, gripping the loop just forward of the hook eye, take hold of the tag end with pliers, as shown in Figure 5, and pull very hard. This locks the uni-knot around the standing line or leader at that point. If it slides down at all it will only be under heavy pressure when fighting a fish.

Tying line to line is actually done the same way as tying line to hook. Compare Figure 1 with Figure 6, and you can see that you handle things the same way, even though the two parallel strands involved are from different pieces of line rather than from the same piece doubled back.

This procedure is simply to form the uni-knot circle with line A around line B, going through six times and pulling down as in Figure 7. Once the knot is formed and tightened, see Figure 8, you then have to reverse the lines and tie another uni-knot with line B around line A. After the two knots are finished, pull on the two main strands of line, as indicated by arrows in Figure 9, to slide the two knots together. Trim both excess ends.

Tying light line to heavy leader is not much

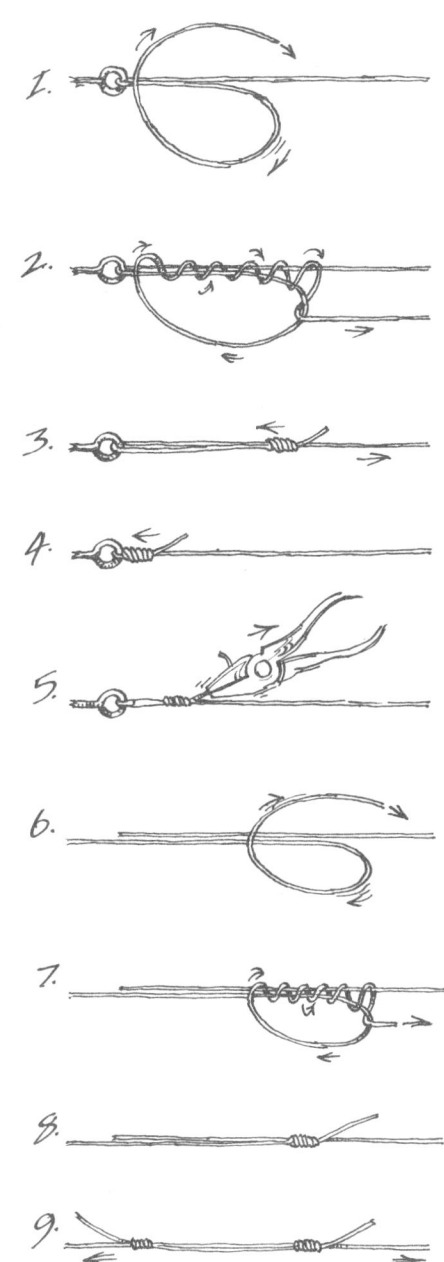

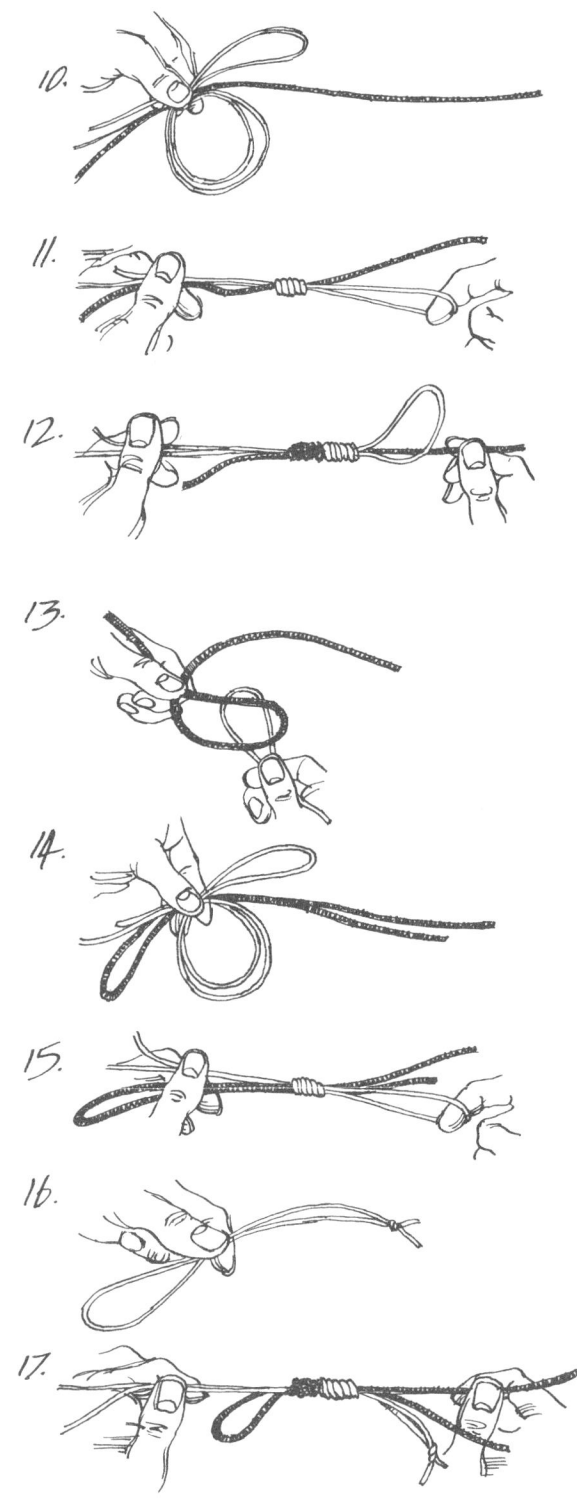

10.

11.

12.

13.

14.

15.

16.

17.

different from the preceding application. It may seem awkward at first because the end of the light line must be doubled to gain maximum strength. But the doubled portion is treated as a single strand and is actually easier to draw down.

Double back several inches of line. Overlap the doubled section with the end of the heavy leader and form the familiar uni-knot circle, as in Figure 10. Go around the strands and through the circle with the doubled end. It is only necessary to go through three times. Now, slip your finger into the loop. Holding all strands on the other side of the knot with the left hand, pull the loop with your finger until the knot is very snug, as in Figure 11.

Reverse the lines and tie another uni-knot with the end of the heavy leader around both strands of line. (There are two strands because the light line is doubled.) Again, only three turns are required. Pull the second knot as snugly as you can manage. Last, slide the knots together by pulling with opposing pressure on the main strand of leader and both strands of line, as in Figure 12.

This is a different line-to-leader tie that should be used when diameters of the two monofilaments involved vary by five times or more in test. It makes a much trimmer tie than the previous one when you use extremely thick leader. And note that it should be used only with greatly different diameters, since the bulk of the larger leader is needed to provide a positive hold.

Double both the light line and the heavy leader. Insert the doubled line though the leader loop upward, as in Figure 13. Make the uni-knot circle, grip all strands with thumb and finger, Figure 14, and then make four turns through the circle. Holding all strands with the left hand, insert finger in loop of light line and draw the uni-knot down very tight, Figure 15, around both strands of heavy leader.

The last step is to take a firm grip on both strands of light line but only the main strand of leader and pull until the knot slides to the doubled end of the leader. Continue pulling hard until no more slippage is felt, then trim off all excess ends.

Done properly, this also is a consistent, 100 percent tie and can be used with seemingly incredible variations in size—for instance, one-pound test line to 100-pound test leader.

To form a maximum strength doubleline, you must use a simple but back-door approach. First you cut off enough line to form the desired length of

double line and tie the ends together with an overhand knot, as shown in Figure 16. Then you proceed to tie the doubleline back onto your line. The overhand knot is for convenience only and will be trimmed away later.

Double the end of the standing line. The procedure that follows is just the same as the line-to-line tie illustrated with Figures 6 through 9. The obvious and only difference is that you are working with two double strands instead of two single strands.

There is one idiosyncrasy, however, that must be catered to in order to get a perfect result. After the two knots are pulled together until they just touch, the final tightening must be done by pulling with both strands of doubleline but only the main strand of regular line, as in Figure 17.

As easy as the uni-knot system is, it may seem difficult at first glance simply because you will be trying to sort and follow all the instructions in your head. Neither this nor any other unfamiliar knot is easy until you sit down with some line and tie it a couple of times, following both the instructions and the illustrations. Do that, and you'll soon be tying everything in the uni-knot system with no trouble—and maybe even coming up with new applications of your own.

Selecting a Rod and Reel

Whether you are a beginner selecting your first equipment or an experienced fisherman adding to your gear, always remember two things when you select a rod and reel: Choose a rig that feels comfortable to you, and pick the rod and reel combination that's appropriate for the time and place.

Like most long-time fishermen, I have accumulated an assortment of rods and reels over the years, and rarely do I go fishing that I don't wish I had taken another rig. One of my old standbys is a heavy Zebco Cardinal 6 spinning reel and a 6½-foot rod, which I bought in 1968 for offshore fishing in British Honduras. I knew the outfit was too heavy for most of the fishing we have in Kentucky, but I have managed to catch a large number of bass with it.

One fishing partner, Bob Budd, would refuse to get in a boat with me if I carried my heavy rod and reel. Budd is a member of the American Casting Association Hall of Fame whose Jeffersonville,

Ind., home is stacked high with trophies he has won in national and international casting contests. Budd fished every chance he got until recently, and almost always returned with a goodly string of fish. His philosophy about selecting a rod and reel is simple—the lighter the rig the better, and the lighter the rig the lighter the line.

Undoubtedly the most used fishing outfit is a cane, or sometimes fiber glass pole ranging in length from eight to 14 feet. These poles are perfect for short-distance still fishing, and probably more panfish have been taken with these traditional rigs than with any others.

But most fishermen need a more adaptable rod, and a reel. Experienced anglers are familiar with the four basic reels: 1) spinning, 2) spincast, 3) level-winding, and 4) fly.

The level-winding reel was invented by George Snyder, a Kentuckian who made watches at his home in Hopewell. He created the first reel about 1800, and some 40 years later two brothers, J. F. and B. F. Meek of Frankfort, produced the first level-winding reel commercially. The modern reels naturally are more refined. They have automatic free-spooling and drags to discourage fouling the line and a level-winding device to allow the line to be spaced evenly on the spool. The spool should be kept full to increase the diameter and reduce the number of revolutions. Most professionals prefer this reel over all others for accuracy and feather control.

The open-faced spinning reel is built around a fixed spool and was invented by an Englishman about 1900. The line spirals out from the spool, which remains fixed in a housing below the rod handle, controlled by the finger either on the reel itself or on contact with the line against the rod. This reel allows free flow of line and comes in all sizes for general use.

With the closed-faced spincast reel, the line feeds through a small hole in the housing and is controlled by thumb pressure on a lever at the rear of the housing. Releasing pressure on the lever releases the line for casting, and renewed pressure locks it in place for rewinding. It is easy to operate, making it a favorite for beginners, but it is not as accurate as the spinning reel.

Budd uses the level-winding and star drag with appropriate line for tarpon and other large ocean fish but selects a light spinning outfit for most freshwater angling. He uses a spincast reel only after rigging it with an adapter that gives him the same fingertip control he gets with a spinning reel. He loves the fly rod and prefers it to all other rigs for quiet fishing where the fly may be flipped almost on the fish's nose without spooking it.

The open-faced spinning reel, which operates on the principle of a stationary spool, can be used for almost any fishing in Kentucky. Contrary to common practices, Budd urges the beginner to start with the light spinning reel rather than with a closed spincast. "There are two reasons," he said. "The beginner can get much more accuracy with it, and he will start catching fish sooner. The thumb button on the closed reel stops the lure abruptly, usually several feet short of where the fisherman is aiming. But by controlling the line on an open-faced reel with one finger, he can soon learn to place the lure near where he wants it."

With the lightest possible spinning reel for beginners, Budd recommends a light, flexible rod of 5 ½ to six-feet long and a test line of four to six pounds.

For the fisherman with some experience, Budd advises the use of the lightest spinning reel that will get the job done. "The commonest mistake made by fishermen in buying equipment is the selection of an outfit heavier than necessary," he said. "Don't forget—the heavier the rig and the line, the fewer lures you can toss and the quicker you tire." Again he suggests a six-foot rod light enough to match the

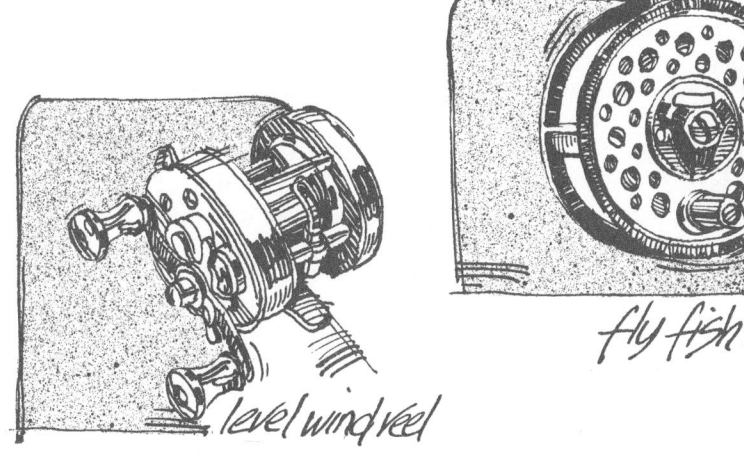

level wind reel

fly fish reel

spinning reel

spin cast reel

reel. "A seven-foot rod will wear you down sooner and not improve your performance," he said. And for the expert angler, Budd recommends a two-pound test line "to get more distance and a thrill a minute."

I might add that Budd has no use for the universal method of braking the flight of the lure from a spinning reel by letting the line run through the crook of the finger. "The way to govern the flow of the line is to curl your index finger around the post and place your first finger on the reel itself," he said. It does make a difference.

The spincast reel also has a fixed spool, but its spool is enclosed. The advantages of the spincast are that, with only a little practice, it can be fairly accurate and fast. With it try a 5 ½- or six-foot rod. The test of the line depends on the size of the fish you are after.

When he fishes with the spincast reel, Budd uses a spinning rod, and rigs the reel to the rod's underside, as he would a spinning reel. This increases the fingertip control of the line. The Jeffersonville fisherman runs the line out from the reel, through a gadget taped to the rod. The gadget is simply a piece of plastic with two holes through which the line passes and an indentation against which his finger can press. With it Budd can control the line with one finger.

The level-winding reels produced today usually have an antibacklash device that makes them fairly easy to cast. Although this reel still probably requires more practice than other reels, it is a favorite among many Kentucky anglers.

When advising other anglers about the level-wind, Budd's original rule still holds—the lightest rod, reel and line for the water and the possible size of fish to be caught. "Those heavy and expensive reels proudly displayed by so many fishermen are too slow and heavy for best fishing," he said.

For fishing excitement, some anglers choose fly rods and reels, which are made in an assortment of weights and lengths. As a rule, shorter and lighter rods should be used for smaller fish and waters, and longer and heavier rods for larger fish and waters.

When he is fishing, Budd prefers an eight- to 8 ½-foot light rod and reel that will hold No. 6 double tapered line. For big bass he prefers a rod with medium action and No. 8 line and a heavy-tapered leader.

(Note: As we were going to press Bob Budd died at age 71.)

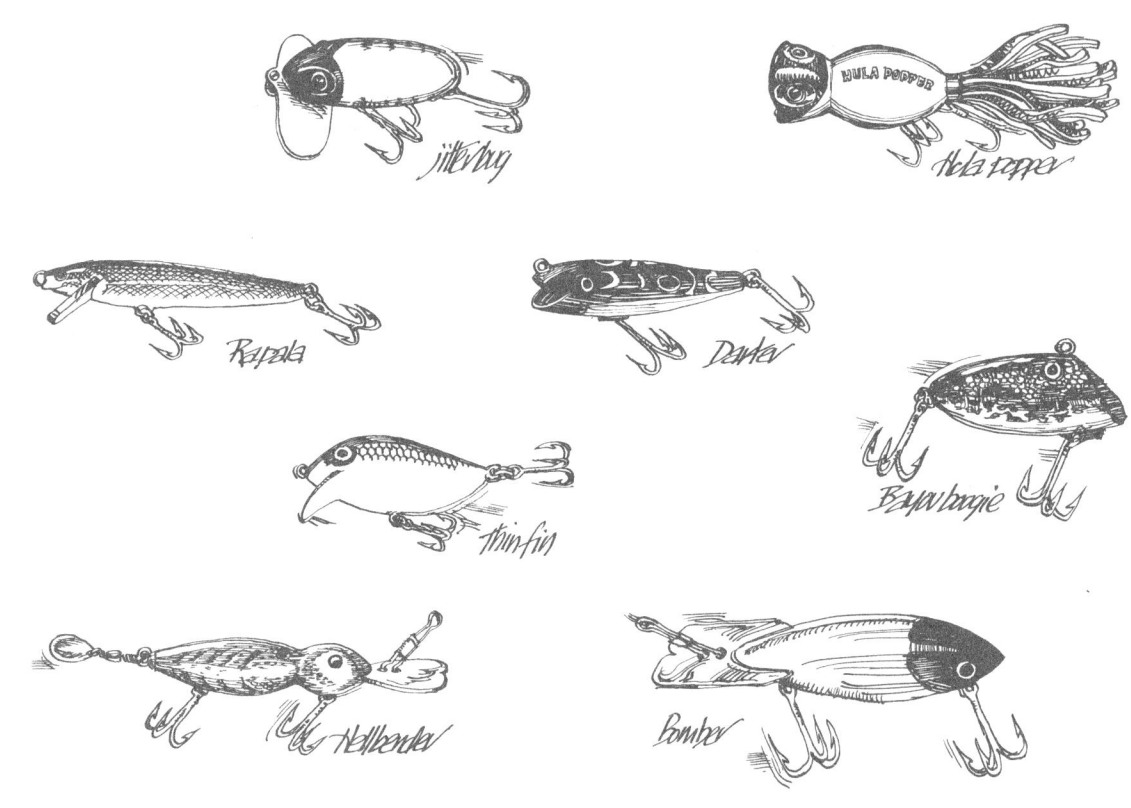

Selecting Artificial Lures

What makes a lure appealing to a bass on one particular day and not on the next remains something of a mystery. But Kentucky anglers, through trial and error, have discovered that there are some lures that they can depend on during certain periods. For those who make a study of lures of all kinds I highly recomend Vic Dunaway's "Complete Book of Baits, Rigs and Tackle." For this book I list simply the lures my friends and I have found most productive in Kentucky.

Surface lures—Most Kentucky bass anglers, like their brothers elsewhere, prefer to fish when surface lures draw strikes. These lures provide exciting, visual action. Some are designed to resemble slim minnows. My favorites among these are the Rapala and Rebel. Try twitching on a slow retrieve.

Popping bugs, such as my old standby the Hula Popper, and chugger make a burping kind of a noise when jerked and are preferred by night anglers.

And then there are the wobblers, such as the Jitterbug, which wobbles and gurgles on a slow retrieve. Night fishermen swear by them, and so do I.

Then the darters, such as the Creek Chub Darter, designed to dart about when twitched. They swim well under the surface when retrieved.

Medium Runners—These lures, such as the Thin Fin and Bayou Boogie (old favorites), run under water on retrieve, and resemble mostly a shad minnow. They get their action from a flattened head or molded lip. Use for trolling or casting.

Deep Runners—These lures are ideal for trolling. The Bomber and Hellbender are almost as old as fishing. Use one of them where you want the lure to bump the bottom, as David Hayes did when he caught that world champion smallmouth at Dale Hollow. For casting I much admire the tiny metal Gay Blade, which Zeke Morgan used to take an eight-pounder out of a lake near Maude, Ky., mentioned elsewhere. It's unbelievable how big a

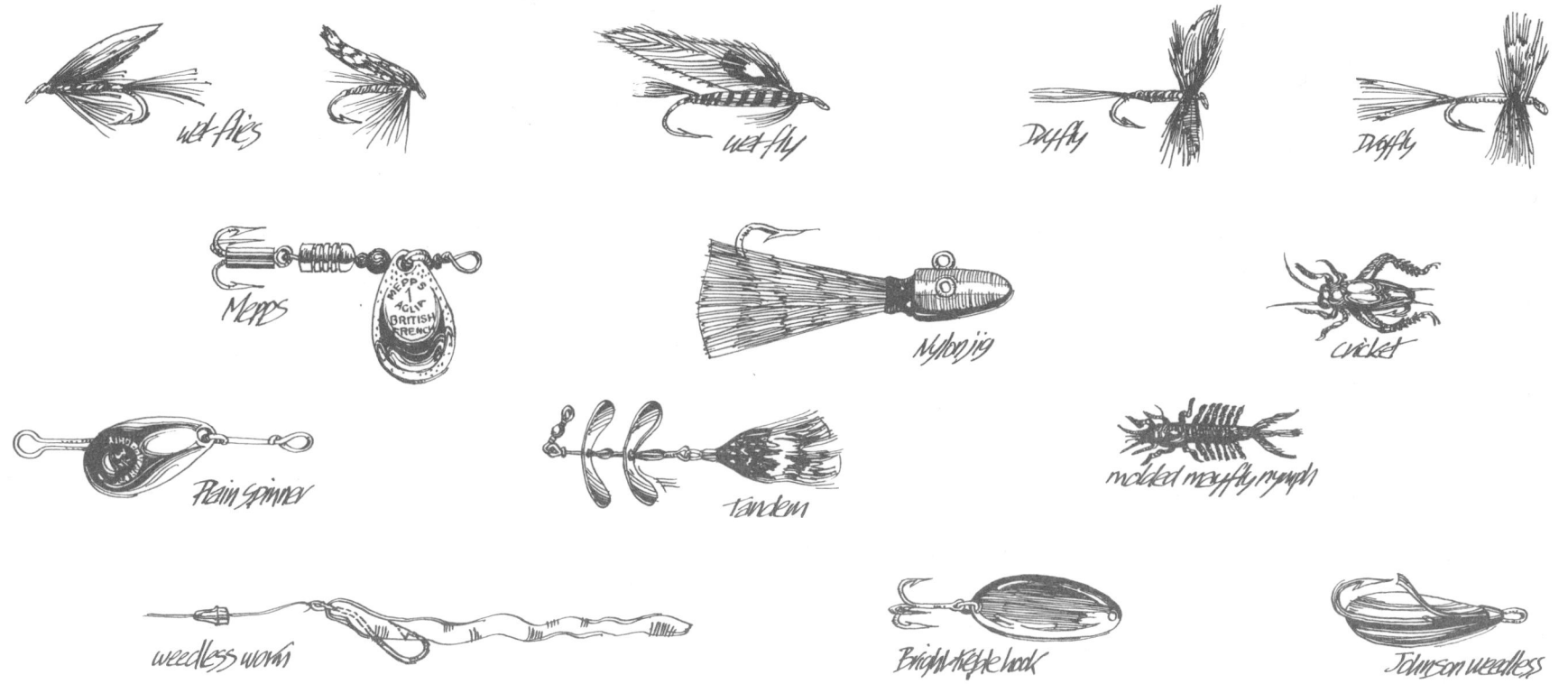

bass can get hung up on such a very small lure. I like it also for trolling for white bass.

Spinners—There is a world of spinners on the market. These metallic lures have shiny metal flanges, which spin when retrieved. Some of the most popular are the Mepps Killer, one of my old reliables, the Beetle Spin, Hawaiian Wiggler and Rooster Tail. Your retrieve should not be too fast with these lures.

Spoons—These lures come in many colors and shapes. A bit of pork rind or plastic worm trailing from one is almost a must. The spoon is great for casting into white-bass jumps, and in fishing deep for black bass.

Jigs—The handiest artificial lure of them all is the jig. It consists of a lead head on the shank of the hook, with a skirt of hairs, feathers, nylon or whatever, covering most of the hook. The jig can be deadly when fitted with pork rind. This is especially true when fishing deep

for bass, or jigging along a bank when the water is too dirty for ordinary fishing. The deadly little Popeye is great for pan fish and white bass on spring spawning runs.

With the smallest gay blade, the Killer, smallest Rooster Tail, tiny Beetle Spin and Popeye I recommend a very light rig and line. Try a four-pound line with them and enjoy the added action.

Plastic worms—Here is the one big advancement in fishing lures made in the last few years. The worm comes in all sizes, lengths and odors, ready-rigged with any number of hooks, plain hooks, weedless hooks and no hooks. I usually buy my worms rigged with one or two weedless hooks, but at times have rigged my own worm and made it weedless by inserting the hook in such a manner that the point is inside the worm.

The worm sometimes works best when weighted with just enough split shot to take it to the bottom, where it may be retrieved in short, gentle flips to

resemble a live worm. When this doesn't work, try retrieving at various speeds until you find out which, if any, attracts strikes. Recent additions to the plastic worm market are some that sport a flat spiraled tail, and some that float, being hollow.

Flies—Because so many fly-rod enthusiasts fashion their own flies, there is no limit to the variations of dry flies, wet flies and streamer flies flipped into Kentucky waters. Fly fishermen have a language all their own, and outsiders hesitate to interpret the lingo. One word most used and least understood is "hackle."

Originally hackle meant any of the long, slender feathers at the neck of a rooster, peacock, or pheasant and used as the legs of an artificial lure. Now it refers to any feathery stuff, either natural or artificial, used in making a lure.

The dry fly is made of hackling designed to make it float. The wet fly is so made to allow it to ride just beneath the surface. Streamers also sink but are made to look like minnows instead of flies.

In Kentucky, where there are so many mayflies hatching during the warm days and where all kinds of panfish abound, fly fishermen looking for a lot of action bait up with small molded mayfly nymphs molded crickets, spiders and popping bugs. The popping bug is the old reliable equivalent of the surface lure in plug casting when going for bass.

I'm not much of a fly fisherman, but have enjoyed reading about it in these books, which I recommend to anyone wanting more knowledge of the sport:

Creative Fly Tying and Fly Fishing, by Rex Gerlach. Winchester Press.

Fly Tying and Fly Fishing For Bass and Panfish, by Tom Nixon. A.S. Barnes & Co.

The Complete Book of Fly Fishing, by Joe Brooks. Outdoor Life.

Making Doughballs

Doughballs are by far the cheapest and best bait for catfish and carp, and the best recipe for doughballs came to me from David Bennett, a former commercial fisherman on the Ohio River. In the days when Bennett's father made twice-daily rounds of their lines, he perfected his own concoction for catching these river fish.

I made a mistake the first time I tried Bennett's catfish bait. I carelessly used self-rising flour, and my doughballs became full of air holes. So be sure to follow these directions carefully.

Catfish—Use plain flour (no mixtures), a little sugar, and enough water to hold it all together. Mix up a ball about as big as a tennis ball. Flatten it like a pancake and drop it into a skillet of boiling water. Let it boil for about half an hour, then allow to dry. Cut to bait-sized bits. Each is guaranteed to bounce like rubber.

Carp—Fill a saucepan half full of water. Add salt. When it starts to boil, add cornmeal with one hand and stir with the other. Cook until it is too thick to stir. Place on a board and knead numerous tufts of cotton into it until every pinch you take off for bait will have a bit of cotton in it.

Another proven recipe calls for one cup of cornmeal. Place the cornmeal in a saucepan and add boiling water, a little at a time, until the meal can be worked into a ball. Add one teaspoon of brown sugar to the water, then place the whole ball into a cloth bag or wrap it in a rag and squeeze tightly.

Leave overnight in the refrigerator. Cut into bait-size bits.

Hope Carleton of Frankfort prefers this variation: Use one part flour and three parts white cornmeal, sugar and anise. Drop bait-size balls into boiling water, remove them after several minutes, then let them stand for several days until they sour.

Selecting Natural Baits

The live minnow is far and away the best live bait used in Kentucky waters. It will attract croppie, black and white bass, and most panfish. Because the minnow is a fragile bait, don't hook it though the back or tail; it is best always to hook it through both lips or the eyes.

Bass anglers around Lake Herrington say there's no bass bait like a soft-shelled crawfish, which the fishermen catch themselves in small feeder streams at night. They use lanterns and catch them by hand or with small dip nets. Hook the crawfish through the tail, or else it may back into a rock crevice.

Night crawlers are a must for most spring angling. These worms, measuring up to a foot long, can be found during most warm nights on the top of the ground with the aid of a flashlight.

Red worms, the perfect bait for panfish, can be found in most shady locations and especially under rocks and rotted wood. Although crickets are hard to catch, they also provide great panfish bait. If you have no luck in grabbing them, crickets can be purchased at nearly all docks and bait houses.

Rigging a Sliding Bobber

If you want to cast a bobber rig some distance from the shore or from your boat, try a rigging that permits the bobber to slide down to your sinker or swivel when you make your cast yet stop at a preset depth when the bobber hits the water. To do this you need a sliding bobber and a tiny plastic or glass bead.

Tie a rubber band to your line where you want the bobber to ride when fishing. Thread the bead onto the line below the rubber band, then thread the bobber onto the line below the bead. And finally, tie on your hook and sinker or leader. When you complete your cast the bead will stop at the knot, and the bobber will stop at the bead. The knotted rubber will pass through the rod guys with no trouble and can be raised or lowered at will.

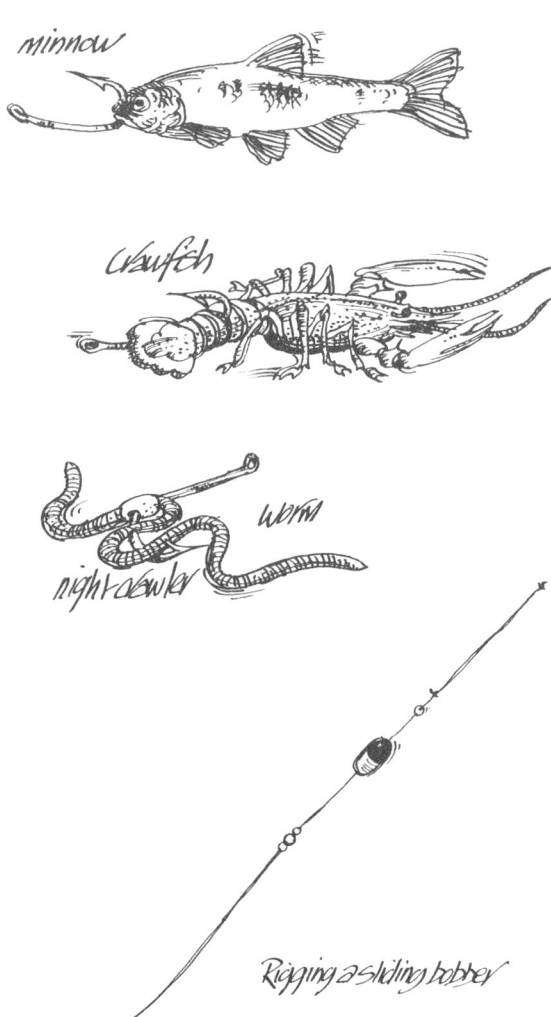

minnow

crawfish

worm

night crawler

Rigging a sliding bobber

Planning Float Trips

Float fishing on any one of Kentucky's roaring little rivers is a great sport for the young at heart and strong of limb. To really make the most of the sport, you should take from two to six days and camp and cook along the way. But as I said, that's for the rugged young adventurers. Old timers will be content with pushing five or six miles upstream with the help of an outboard motor and floating and fishing back to the starting point. The long one-way trips are best through July, August, September and some days in October.

Most young explorers who have tried the long hauls will tell you that the lighter you travel, the easier and more enjoyable the trip will be. Even the best of the small fishing streams have shallow riffles, an occasional fallen tree, or log jams. This means that you may have to carry the boat around or over the obstruction.

It's almost a necessity to use two cars or trucks—one to be driven to the take-out point, and the other to be used to carry you to the starting point.

For the beginners I might caution that it is essential to have at least one experienced boatman, preferably a professional guide, on any float trip. Some of the state's streams are marked with big, sharp rocks and narrow gorges, and they might become raging after a sudden heavy rain.

Two of the calmest, safest and shortest trips for beginners are along the Green River and along the Rough River. The best part of the Green for such an excursion is from Mammoth Cave National Park to a ferry landing about 10 miles downstream, and the Rough River's choicest location is from Hardin Springs to any take-out around the headwaters of the Rough River Reservoir.

But for the real explorers, let me suggest any one of four trips carefully tested several years ago by Hope Carleton of the Department of Fish and Wildlife Resources. Here they are:

Red River, as most people know, is a very scenic stream with tremendous bluffs and rock formations. Under normal conditions the river is clear and cool. A beautiful two-day trip would cover approximately 25 miles of good bass water. Make your start in the Sky Bridge area of KY 715 (see map) and take out near Bowen, which is a few miles above Stanton. The easiest route to the put-in spot is the Mountain Parkway. Exit at Pine Ridge and take KY 15 to KY 715 to the point where that highway crosses the Red River.

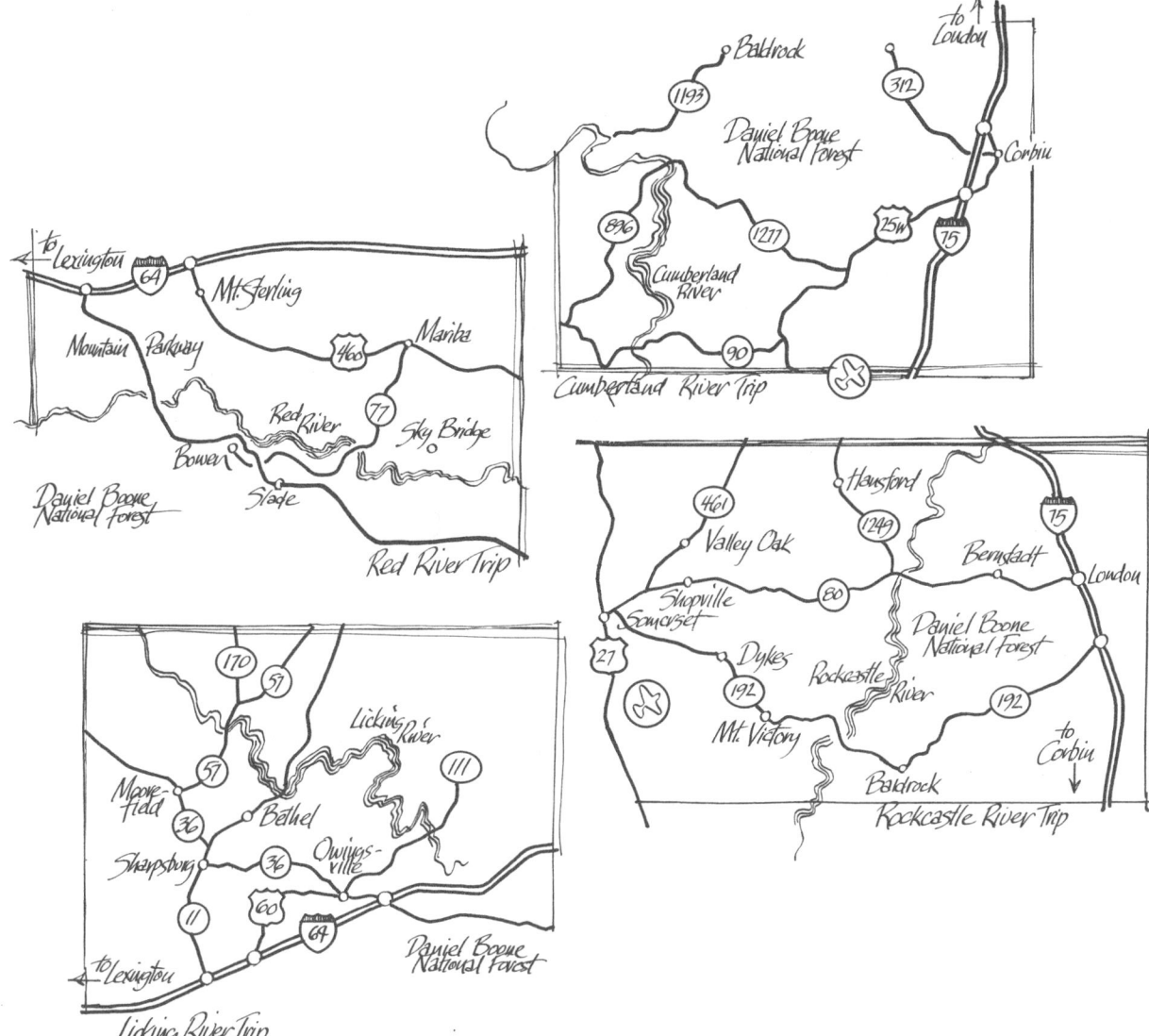

One of the most picturesque trips in the state may be made down Rockcastle River. But the 17 miles inspected by Carleton include some fast, dangerous water not suitable for a beginner. The trip can be made in one day but would be more enjoyable in two. Fishing tapers off during July, but the beauty of the forest, gorges, waterfalls and riffles remains all summer. Put in at the Rockcastle Bridge on KY 80 between Somerset and London and take out at Bee Rock Camp near Mount Victory (see map). There is no boat ramp at the bridge, so the lighter the boat the better.

Remember, this trip can be tricky, so be careful.

The exciting and frequently dangerous white waters below Cumberland Falls provide one of the most challenging trips the state offers. Remote and rough, this 12-mile journey into yesterday has been made in as little as four hours when the water was swift. But it provides better fishing if conditions permit you to go the route in a day and a half. Giant rock outcroppings, magnificent trees and spectacular cliffs mark this stream as it drops from one deep pool to another through narrow gorges. Carleton suggests, and I surely agree, that you let your boat pass from one pool to the next by itself. You walk the bank and hold on to the boat with a long rope. No sense in taking a dunking in those cold and often dangerous waters. Put in below the falls at the state park, carrying the boat to the water's edge. The take-out point is Noe's Dock, which is on KY 1277 (See map).

Long, fast and crooked—that's Licking River in Fleming County. But it isn't as dangerous as the other rivers mentioned. Many boats have capsized on spring floats, but by July and August the waters tame a bit. Channel catfish are plentiful, and trotlines set each night usually produce good catches. Black bass fishing tapers off during the hot weather, but good fishermen will be successful. Put in at a bridge on KY 111, which may be reached via KY 32 from Flemingsburg. You have to carry your boat to the water since there isn't a ramp there. After 35 miles of wilderness, which could take as many as six days to fish well and leisurely, you take out at Upper Blue Licks, located on KY 57, which will take you back to Flemingsburg (see map).

Wherever you go, be sure to wear a life jacket at all times and carry a small first-aid kit for scratches and cuts. And don't forget the long rope for walking your boat over the worst riffles.

Fly Fishing in Kentucky
Are there any streams in Kentucky suitable for fly fishermen to wade? This question was raised by Nicholas W. Carlin of Louisville. The answer is yes, the state has many miles of wadable streams and quite a few streams with banks suitable for fly fishing. Kentucky has more miles of fishable streams than any other state except Alaska, and 38 of the streams are stocked with rainbow trout. Virtually all of the others carry a good number of bream, rock bass and black bass. This brings up three more questions.

1. How can a newcomer find access to such streams?

2. Is it legal to wade a stream through a farmer's property?

3. May you float a boat down a stream that runs through private property?

In answer to the first question, there are two ways to determine the locations of the wadable streams. If you are after rainbows, see chapter on Trout. Or, if you wish information on the other streams and lakes, you can get a free booklet that includes price lists of a great number of maps of streams, lakes and forests by writing the Department of Commerce, Map Sales, 133 Holmes St., Frankfort.

The answer to the second question is no. It is unlawful to wade a stream that runs through private property without first obtaining the owner's permission.

The answer to the third question is yes. You may float a boat down any stream, regardless of whose property it penetrates, because you will be afloat on what the law says are "waters of the commonwealth." But any use of the banks may be challenged as trespassing.

The most wadable streams in the state are Elkhorn Creek in Franklin and Scott counties, Brashear Creek in Spencer County, Upper Salt Creek in Mercer County, Hanging Fork Creek in Boyle County, Floyd's Fork in Jefferson County, Upper Trammel Creek in Logan County, Boone Creek in Clark and Fayette counties, and Middle Fork of the Red River in Wolfe County.

There are occasional public access points on these streams, but some of the best fly fishing areas pass through private property and permission to wade and fish must be obtained in advance. There is no easy way to do this. Knocking on farmhouse doors is about the only place to start.

Of course fly fishing is popular on all our lakes.

Registering a Fish for Record
If you think you have caught a record fish, follow these directions to have it properly certified:

1. Have witnesses who can testify that you caught the fish.

2. Have it weighed on a good scale with two witnesses.

3. Have the fish properly identified by a qualified biologist. This will be done by a Department of Fish and Wildlife official, so don't eat the fish before you have this done.

4. Write the Department of Fish and Wildlife Resources for an official registration blank, fill it out, have the witnesses sign it, and return the registration to Frankfort.

Understanding Hook Sizes
The method of designating hook sizes can be very confusing to the beginner. Hooks are divided into two classes. In the smaller class, the smaller the hook the larger its number. The very largest of this class is the No. 1, and the smallest in general use is the No. 14. Now for the confusion. The larger class of hooks—all hooks bigger than the No. 1—start with No. 1/0 and run up in size through No. 2/0, 3/0, and so on to a whopper 8/0 in freshwater fishing.

This chart shows actual comparative hook sizes:

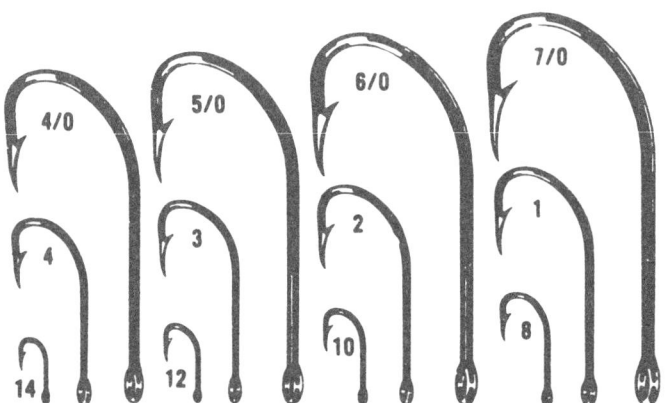

Filleting Fish

Cleaning fish is something best learned before the angler finds himself face-to-face with a boatload of them. I find that filleting wastes a lot of flavorful bits of meat around the bones. Some of the best fish meals I've ever served were headlined by small channel cats that I had skinned with the help of a sharp knife and a pair of pliers. I cut the tough skin around the base of the head, then pull the skin down and off. For catfish specialists there is a new skinning board on the market that makes the chore considerably easier.

Filleting larger fish is a simple art easily mastered. The fillets give bone-free pieces ready for the stove. In addition to being the cleanest and quickest way to prepare fish, it also cuts down on space required for freezing.

Here's how to do it, say experts, including Hope Carleton of the Department of Fish and Wildlife, Frankfort, from whom I obtained these photographs:

1. Insert the point of your knife along the back and cut from the head to the tail.

2. Make a cut behind the head down to the backbone.

3. Start at the cut behind the head and slide the knife along the backbone through to the tail.

4. Using a slightly sawing motion, separate the fillet from the rib cage.

5. Turn the fish over and repeat the procedure. Discard the remainder of the fish.

6. Place the fillet skin down and hold it by the narrow end. Place the knife flat on the skin and with a sawing motion cut through between the skin and the meat, leaving the skin and scales on one side and a beautiful, clean fillet on the other.

1

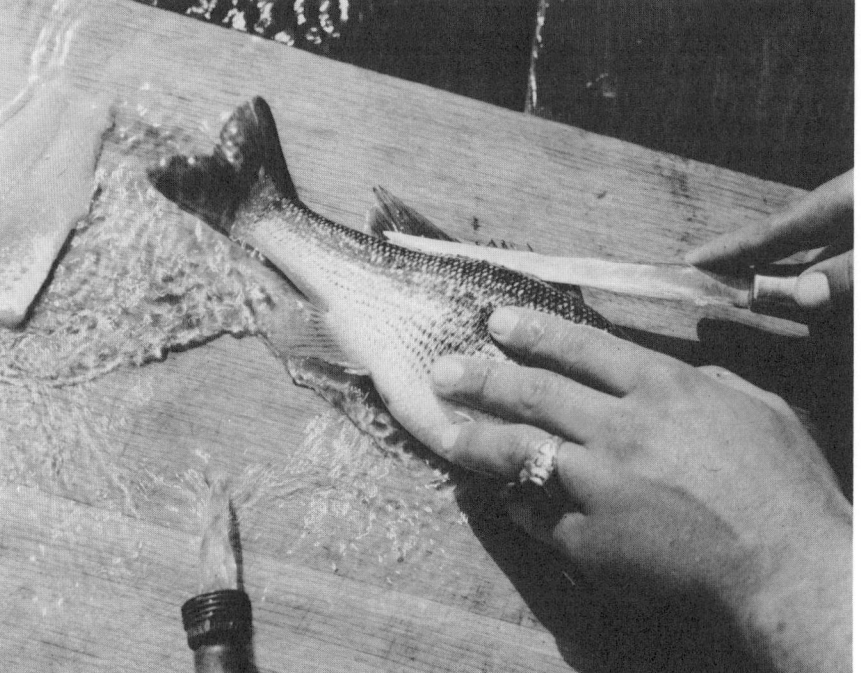

2

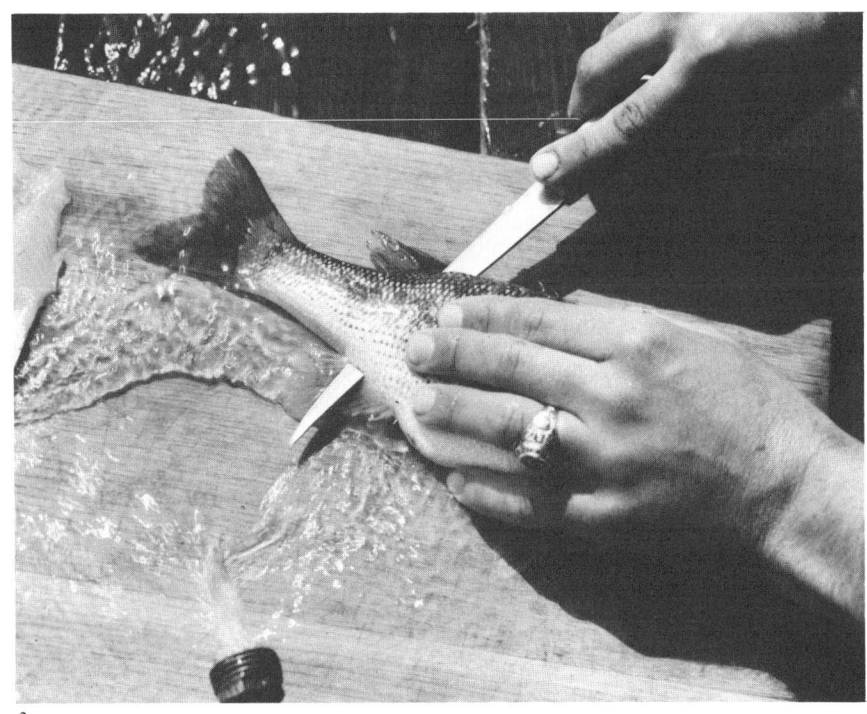

3

5

4

6

Freezing Small Game and Fish

For a long, long time, my freezer was a jumble of oddly shaped packages wrapped in foil, freezer paper, and even newspaper. Finding what I had was a game of hit-and-miss, mostly miss. Wrappings came loose, and most everything got freezer burn if left as long as two months.

Then I learned about one- and two-quart milk cartons. Now my freezer accommodates more food, and everything is tagged and orderly. Freezer burn is impossible.

Whatever I have to freeze—fish fillets, quail, doves, even parts of rabbit—I stuff into a carton and fill to the top with water. The game remains fresh indefinitely in the block of ice that forms around it.

Making a Smokehouse

If you are an avid fisherman or sportsman, you doubtless on occasion have caught more fish or game than you could use at the moment and have frozen the surplus. If your freezer isn't any larger than mine, things can get a bit crowded. Why not add to the fun of the trip and the enjoyment of your catch by smoking some of the bigger specimens? With just the minimum equipment you can produce a real treat for yourself and your neighbors.

An old Florida fishing companion, Ted Farley of Canada, has smoked almost a ton of fish using nothing more than two old garbage cans and a lard bucket. What heavenly flavor! And what a kick he gets out of serving the delicious morsels to his friends.

Farley cut the lard pail about four inches from the bottom and used the bottom part for his firebox. He then turned one garbage can upside down, over the fire box, and punched a lot of holes in the bottom of it.

He then cut off the bottom fourth of the other can and set it down upright on the inverted can. He suspended old circular barbecue grills on heavy wire from the cover of this can, after he had punched several holes in the top to let the smoke sift through. After loading these grills he lowered them into the can and shoved the top down tight. This was his smokehouse. If you prefer you can punch holes in the side of the top can, shove metal rods through and place the grills on them.

Farley builds a charcoal fire in the bottom of the lard can and covers it with any good hardwood

except pine. Applewood is excellent. The fish are laid open, exposing the entire inside. Farley leaves the head on so that he can tell what kind of fish he is serving. He soaks the fish in brine (salt water just strong enough to float a potato) for two or three hours. Then he dries the fish, places them on the racks, starts the fire, places the combined garbage cans over the fire, and lets nature take its course. Be sure there is space for air to enter under the lower can.

"Just watch out that the fire doesn't get too hot," he warns. "If the upper can gets too hot to touch, you've got too much fire. Slow it down."

With the properly regulated fire, the fish should be ready to serve in four to six hours. Of course, you'll want to lift out the fish two or three times to be sure everything is okay and to remove any smaller fish that might be done sooner.

Another simple way to smoke fish or game is to utilize your outdoor fireplace. All you have to do is make a smoke box, set it on the grill, stop up the chimney with almost anything, and bend a sheet of aluminum or tin to make the thing as airtight as possible.

If any of your fish or game comes out too hard, just freeze and thaw a few times and it will soften up nicely. If refrigerated or frozen, smoked fish will keep indefinitely.

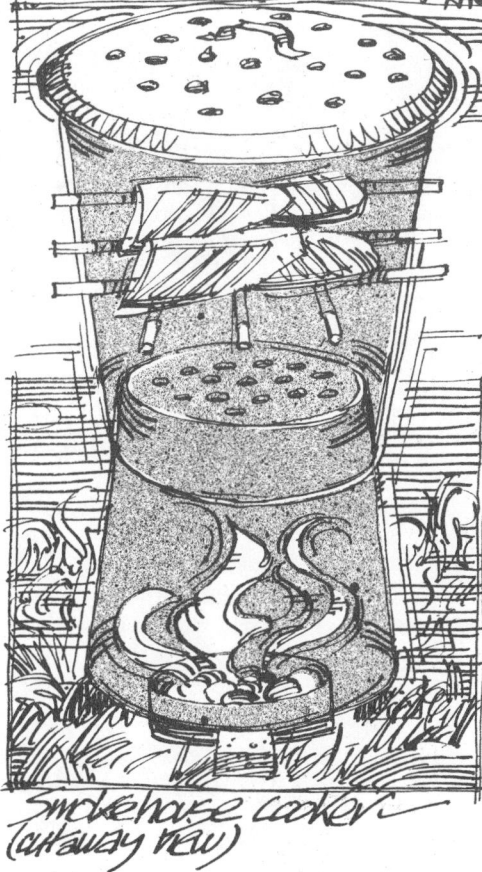

Smokehouse cooker (cutaway view)

Cooking Fish & Wild Game

Recipes for Wild Game

Whether it is a coincidence or a carefully laid plan, Thanksgiving Day falls around the opening of the hunting season, and many bountiful holiday feasts are planned around freshly killed birds and game. This includes in some too-rare instances spring-killed wild turkey kept frozen for the memorable occasion. Here are a few suggestions on how to present a banquet fit for any hungry hunter while preserving peace and dignity in the kitchen.

Get back from the hunt in time to clean your own game, and spare your wife the labor of cooking it, especially if she has invited a lot of relatives in to enjoy a sumptuous dinner of the wild game you have shot. Ten-to-one she'll tie the apron on you anyway and shove you into the kitchen. For some reason that surely must baffle hunters, most women just don't like to mess with wild game.

The best thing for you to do is just roll up your sleeves and invite a neighbor to lend a hand. Have fun, shock your wife, and impress those relatives. I've listed several recipes that are virtually foolproof. I've tried every one of them.

First, one important pre-cooking chore on rabbits, squirrels and some shot-up parts of venison:

Soak the game in salt, baking soda and water, working the meat with your hands to squeeze out blood. Using a small sharp knife, cut out deep red areas where shot caused excess bleeding. Pour out bloody water and refill. Repeat three times if necessary to let the water run clear. I can't tell you how much this will improve the taste of the finished product.

Quail

If you seek recognition on your street as a wild game gourmet, I'm sure you pluck your quail. To skin a quail is to stamp you as just plain lazy. Quail need the flavor stored in the skin. They are so tender they can be fried, baked, turned on a spit, or broiled. Just be careful that you don't overcook this delicate bird. As a rule, 1 ½ quail should satisfy a normal eater.

Cadiz Broiled Quail

Allowing 1½ birds per person, split quail down back and flatten out. Brush with melted butter, then salt and pepper and broil with breast down for 15 minutes, basting with chicken bouillon. Turn and baste until breasts are golden brown and tender. Serve with currant jelly.

Baked Quail

This is one way to keep quail moist while baking. The wet stuffing does the trick, so use it, even if you don't like stuffing.

8 quail
2 cups chicken bouillon
1 stalk chopped celery
1 chopped onion
2 cups cooked wild rice
1 teaspoon poultry seasoning
½ teaspoon thyme
salt and pepper
flour to dredge

Saute onions and celery. Add rice, thyme, salt and pepper, and enough water to keep rice moist. Stuff birds. Dredge in flour seasoned with salt, pepper and poultry seasoning. Brown in skillet. Place in baking pan, add one cup bouillon. Cover and bake at 350 degrees about one hour, until tender. Add rest of bouillon or water as necessary to maintain moisture. Remove cover and brown, if necessary. Will serve 4 to 6.

Lazy Man's Fried Quail

Quail is one game bird that's tender enough to fry as you would chicken. Split down the back. Salt and pepper and dredge in flour. Fry with breast down. Turn and complete cooking when breasts are nicely browned.

Pennyrile Smothered Quail

This was developed by Mack Sisk of Frankfort.

8 whole quail
flour to dredge, seasoned with black pepper, salt and celery seed
4 thinly sliced medium onions
1 can mushroom soup
½ pound sliced mushrooms
2 cups white wine or 1 cup apple cider and 1 cup orange juice
1 tablespoon rosemary
½ teaspoon tarragon
¼ teaspoon garlic salt
4 tablespoons cooking oil

Dredge quail in seasoned flour and brown in cooking oil. Place quail in baking dish or Dutch oven. Mix wine (or cider and orange juice), rosemary, tarragon, garlic salt and two thinly sliced onions with mushroom soup. Pour over quail.

Preheat oven to 450 degrees. Leave birds in oven five minutes, then turn oven to 325 degrees and bake for 20 minutes, basting often. Add water as needed. When tender, add sliced fresh mushrooms and two additional sliced onions. Serve when onions and mushrooms are tender. Serves six.

Mrs. Ruby's Stuffed Quail

Here is a real favorite everyone will like. In cleaning the birds, cut them down the back. Prepare any good chicken or turkey dressing, and overstuff each bird. Tie together with household string. Dredge in flour. Brown on both sides then place on rack in a Dutch oven with a little water. Cover and roast at 300 degrees until tender, adding a bit of water as needed. Cook approximately one hour.

Grouse

Here is a chunky bird highly prized in the woods and on the hunter's table but which requires expert handling in the kitchen. Its delicate texture and flavor can be lost easily by the use of strong seasoning.

Roast Grouse

All wild birds are dryer than their domestic counterparts, and the grouse is no exception. Here again the wet stuffing is a great help. This marvelous bird merits the kindliest attention.

4 grouse
½ cup chopped celery
½ cup chopped onions
½ cup chopped red cabbage
1 or 2 cups prepared stuffing
4 slices fat bacon
salt and pepper

Saute onions, celery and cabbage. Add stuffing and enough water to make wet dressing. Stuff birds and cover each with a strip of bacon. Roast covered in 375 degree oven until tender—about 50 minutes. Will serve four or more.

A popular variation: After stuffing the birds, brown each in a skillet, then wrap individually in foil. Bake up to two hours at 300 degrees. When done, the birds will have a tendency to fall apart, so be careful.

Grouse in Wine

Salt and pepper inside and out. Place in roaster with half cup of water. Roast up to 50 minutes in 375 degree oven until tender, adding water as needed to keep moist. Saute ½ cup chopped onions, add cup of chicken bouillon and cup of white wine. Add this to pot for last 15 minutes of cooking, basting a few times.

Pheasant

The old school of hunters-cooks, which is enthusiastic over bloody ducks, insists that to be at its best a pheasant must be hung, feathers and all, until it develops a "ripe" odor. If I did that, my wife wouldn't let me bring the bird into the house. The pheasant is a dry bird and needs special handling to preserve what little moisture it has. That's why I'll take this recipe over the others:

Ruby's Pheasant Halves

2 pheasants
1 cup chicken stock
bacon fat
salt and pepper

Split the pheasants in half. Rub with bacon fat, then salt and pepper and place with breasts up on heavy-duty foil. Turn up edges to form a dish to hold the juices. Add one-fourth cup of chicken stock for each half. Fold foil over and crimp tightly. Bake at 350 degrees until tender—about one hour and 20 minutes. Remove top foil and brown. Serves four.

Stuffed Pheasant

2 pheasants
2 tablespoons chopped onions
½ cup white wine
6 sliced, cooked chestnuts
6 slices country bacon
2 cups prepared stuffing

Saute onions in skillet. Add stuffing, wine, chestnuts and enough water to make it moist. Stuff both birds and wrap three slices of bacon around each. Roast at 375 degrees uncovered for about one hour, or until tender. Remove bacon 10 minutes before birds are done and brown nicely. To serve, cut each in half. Serve dressing separately. Serves four.

Dove

This little fellow has been abused so in the kitchen that it's a wonder it has anything to do with us. The dove is the smallest of Kentucky's game birds but is a wonderful treat on the table when prepared properly.

It is best to pluck rather than skin doves, but when you are long on birds and short on time, this poses a problem. On such occasions I have skinned mine, and once or twice I have kept only the breasts. This recipe is perfect for such situations:

Breasts of Dove

12 breasts of dove
3 cups chicken bouillon
salt and pepper
flour to dredge

Dredge breasts in flour seasoned with salt and pepper. Brown on both sides in Dutch oven. Add cup of chicken bouillon. Cover and cook at 300 degrees until tender—about 20 minutes. Add remainder of bouillon as needed. Turn occasionally.

Will fill four hungry hunters.

Doves With Garlic

There is just enough garlic in this to give the dish a distinctive lift:

12 doves
1 clove crushed garlic
1 chopped onion
1 small can tomatoes
Pinch of thyme
chopped parsley

Brown the doves in skillet. Place in a Dutch oven with garlic, and other ingredients. Cover and cook at 350 degrees about 20 minutes, until tender. Will satisfy four.

Ruby's Steamed Doves

I like this simple recipe. It combines the browning of the birds with a steam bath that brings them out a golden brown, yet moist and tender.

Dredge the birds in flour seasoned with salt and pepper. Fry in shallow fat until well browned all over. Add just enough water to create a bit of steam. Cover and let steam until tender—usually not more than 15 minutes. When tender, remove the lid and allow to brown a little more, being careful not to let doves dry out. Serve with cream gravy. Two birds should satisfy a normal eater.

Duck

How to cook a duck depends primarily on where you bagged it. If you came back with it from Stuttgart, Ark., or Ballard County, or Reelfoot, you are in luck. These ducks feed for the most part on grain and acorns and are delicious. A duck taken from some rivers or mud flats needs special treatment.

The acorn-fed duck may be baked like a chicken with oyster, mushroom, or chestnut stuffing. You shouldn't stuff the other ducks with anything, unless it is apples or sauerkraut to absorb some of the river taste.

I have always cooked my ducks long enough to get the legs tender. But many old-timers insist that if the duck isn't served bloody, it has been ruined by the cook. Ted Trueblood recommends cooking at 500 degrees for 20 mintues.

Reg Lowery's Duck

Reg Lowery of Princeton has a unique recipe for cooking duck that can't miss. He did all the duck cooking on several trips to Reelfoot with Smith Broadbent Jr. of Cadiz and several others and is considered an expert among duck chefs.

Lowery salts, peppers and wraps each duck and a handful of rice in foil. Then he wraps the ducks again in foil, and cooks them four hours in 250-degree oven. When done, he throws the rice away and serves the ducks. Delightful. The rice seems to absorb some of the wild taste, leaving the duck sweet and tender. Personally, I've never found too much wild taste in an acorn-fed duck, but I like Lowery's recipe.

Ruby's Roast Duck

Here is something fancy for your best neighbor: Clean two mallards thoroughly and wipe dry. Fill the cavities with chestnut stuffing (recipe below). Rub outside with bacon drippings, then salt and pepper. Arrange birds on heavy-duty foil. Bring foil over top and crimp securely, making sure the bottom piece of foil forms a pan to catch the juices. Add half cup of chicken broth for each duck. Bake at 350 for about one hour. Check for tenderness. Continue cooking until tender. Remove foil and brown.

Chestnut stuffing: Boil a pint of chestnuts until tender. Drain. Chop coarsely. Chop one onion and saute. Add a cup of country sausage, a cup of prepared poultry stuffing and a bit of water or chicken broth. Add chestnuts and cook five minutes to blend.

Bill Short's Wild Duck Cooked in Baker's Dough

Even fancier is this unusual recipe:

2 wild ducks
1 tablespoon garlic powder
1 coarsely chopped medium onion
1 teaspoon cracked pepper
¼ pound melted butter
2 chopped celery tops
6 to 8 cups flour
2 cups salt
1 ½ to 2 cups water

Butter duck cavities, sprinkle with garlic powder and pepper, and stuff with mixture of onions and celery tops. Butter ducks on all sides.

Mix flour and salt, then add water. Knead until dough is a consistency that will hold together and can be handled without sticking to bowl or hands. Mold dough around each duck to encase bird and conform to carcass shape. Punch three or four holes in top of dough to permit steam to escape.

Bake one hour, 15 minutes in 325-degree oven. Remove from oven and place ducks on solid surface. Break dough from ducks with a hammer or heavy mallet. Serve ducks with mixed wild rice.

If you want to really get fancy for company, after you have encased duck with dough, wrap a small juice can with baker's dough and place on head of duck to form a neck. Mound the dough on top of can to form the rounded head. Insert two wooden tongue compressors or several layers of foil side by side and cover with dough to form duck's bill.

On one occasion Mack Sisk painted the duck with water colors to resemble a mallard. What a conversation piece!

Ruby's Fail-Safe Duck

Place rack in Dutch oven. Fill with water up to, but not over, the rack. Rub two ducks with bacon drippings, then salt and pepper. Place ducks on rack, cover securely. Bake at 275 or a bit lower, checking every now and then to maintain water level and test birds for tenderness. Cooking time between 1 ½ and 2 ½ hours. When tender, remove ducks. Siphon off excess fat (if any). Mix pot liquor with flour and water for gravy. To serve, cut breasts in thin slices arrange on platter with skinned whole legs, ladle gravy over them.

Turner's Charbroiled Duck

Tom E. Turner of Madisonville offers this new way to enjoy mallards:

"With very sharp fillet knife, remove the breast fillets from the breastbone, leaving the skin attached to the fillet.

"On medium heat charcoal grill, place the skin side of the fillet down and cook until brown, sprinkling the top side of the fillet with a seasoned salt (Cavanders is excelent and can be bought in the Reelfoot Lake area. It may be found in some of the larger grocery stores, though I have not been able to locate any except around Reelfoot and Stutgart, Ark.). Frequently during the cooking of the duck, liberally brush melted butter on the top side.

"When the skin side is browned, then turn the fillet over and cook the opposite side until browned, continuing to apply melted butter liberally and seasoning.

"When both sides are brown, slice the fillet so that the inside can be cooked. I usually slice the fillet almost nearly through, leaving it attached at one small place so that I have only one piece instead of two. You will find that the cooking of the inside will take a very short period of time. On thin fillets, especially if one prefers the duck somewhat rare, the last step may not be necessary."

Coot

The lowly coot is not considered worth fooling with by many duck hunters, but I have served coot breasts to neighbors and received many compliments. Here is how:

Cut out the breasts, soak in salt and baking soda two or three times until no blood shows in the water. Set aside. Boil legs and backs until they fall apart, strain.

Dredge breasts in flour, salt and pepper. Brown all over in skillet. Transfer to Dutch oven, add one cup of strained liquid the legs boiled in. Cover and roast at 375 degrees until tender, adding liquid as needed. Make gravy from pan drippings, a cup of chicken broth, and touch of Kitchen Bouquet.

Goose

There have been more mistakes made by respected chefs in the cooking of geese than of all other wild game combined. And that's a shame, because you'll rarely find a more rewarding repast if you know what you're doing.

The Canada goose, which is the favorite of all who hunt in Ballard County, has fine, flavorful, dark, very lean meat—a marvelous treat at Christmas time.

Roast Wild Goose

The big point here is to keep the big bird moist all the way to the table.

1 wild goose
1 package cornbread stuffing
½ pound country sausage
1 tablespoon flour
1 cup chopped celery
1 cup chopped onions
1 cup chicken bouillon
pinches of thyme and sage
salt and pepper

If the bird looks old loosen it up by parboiling it 15 minutes. Saute onions, celery; cook sausage almost done. Mix with stuffing and water, and ladle into goose. Don't pack it. Roast covered at 325 degrees, first on one side and then the other. Baste frequently with chicken bouillon. After one hour check for tenderness. When tender to fork, uncover, turn breast up and brown. Remove goose and stir tablespoon of flour into pan scrapings. Add water and simmer until a smooth gravy forms. Test for salt and pepper. Should serve four if they aren't starving.

Ruby's Roast Goose

The ingredients are the same as for the above recipe.

Stuff the goose and place in heavy-duty aluminum foil, making sure the bottom half of the foil forms a pan to hold the juices. Add the bouillon. Salt and pepper the bird. Fold foil over goose and crimp tightly. After one hour of baking at 350 degrees, check for tenderness and moisture. If tender, roast uncovered until brown. If not, add water, re-cover, and continue cooking up to 2 ½ hours in all, checking for moisture and tenderness now and then.

Wild Turkey

The noblest and most wary of our American game birds is the wild turkey. It is prized above all other birds by Kentuckians in the mountains and the Purchase, the two areas where most turkeys are found.

The wild birds are much leaner than domestic turkeys and for this reason demand constant basting if not cooked in foil. Also, there is less waste and more solid meat than you'll find in the city cousin, hence, more servings per bird.

Kentucky Turkey

1 wild turkey
1 cup cooked, diced country ham
1 cup chopped onions
1 cup chopped celery
6 cups prepared stuffing
1 teaspoon poultry seasoning
salt and pepper

Saute the onions and celery until transparent. Add cooked ham, mix with stuffing and water to form wet dressing. Add salt and pepper to taste. Fill cavity and breast, skewer closed. Place turkey in roasting pan, rub with bacon fat or cooking oil. Sprinkle with salt, pepper and poultry seasoning. Roast on one side, then the other, covered, at 325 degrees for approximately three hours. When tender remove lid, turn breast side up and brown nicely.

Ruby's Turkey in Foil

1 wild turkey
½ pound (or more) hot country sausage
1 cup chopped onions
½ teaspoon thyme
½ cup melted bacon drippings
*1 to 2 packages of stuffing mix, depending
   on size of bird*
poultry seasoning
salt and pepper

Cook sausage until almost done. Add onions and thyme and cook until onions are transparent. Add prepared stuffing and mix thoroughly. Fill cavity and breast with dressing and skewer openings closed. Rub the turkey well with bacon drippings. Sprinkle with salt, pepper and poultry seasoning. Place turkey on foil so that, in crimping the foil, the bottom forms a pan to catch the juices.

Roast 15 minutes per pound at 325 degrees. Remove foil. Test for tenderness. If not brown enough, pour off pan drippings and continue roasting uncovered, basting frequently, until golden brown.

I like this recipe because wild turkey is so lean I find I have to use every means possible to preserve what little moisture there is.

Venison

If your deer was taken from Canada or the northern United States, it must be stripped of all fat, as the fat is not edible. Kentucky deer are much easier to prepare for cooking. But no matter where your deer was taken, it should be hung in a cool place for several days to age and tenderize. I have let mine hang in the garage for 10 days or more in near-freezing weather. If yours is a young deer, its steaks may be served rare. An older one must be cooked as you would a tough cut of beef. This recipe for venison pot roast makes even the toughest cut a delight:

Venison Pot Roast

4-pound venison rump
6 medium potatoes
6 medium onions
2 ribs celery
3 teaspoons instant beef bouillon crystals in water
6 carrots
cooking oil
salt and pepper

Marinate the venison in the refrigerator overnight (longer for older deer) in 2 cups oil, pinch of pickling spices and three cups of red wine, turning occasionally. Drain. Dredge venison in flour, seasoned with salt and pepper. Brown in oil in deep skillet. Add bouillon crystals and two cups of water. Cover and simmer over low heat for up to three hours until tender. Add water as needed. Drop in the vegetables and cook until they also are tender. Thicken the gravy and pour over meat when sliced and served. Serves up to six.

Venison Roast

1 5-pound venison roast	*1 tablespoon flour*
8 medium potatoes	*2 cups white wine*
8 medium onions	*salt and pepper*
8 carrots	
3 teaspoons beef bouillon crystals	

Marinate the venison over night in wine and a bit of cooking oil. Drain and dry. Sear well in skillet, place in deep roasting pot. Mix crystals with three cups water. Add to pot. Cover and cook at 300 degrees up to three hours, until tender. Remove venison. Add vegetables to pan juices, add water if necessary, and cook until tender, turning occasionally to brown up. Add flour and water to make plenty of gravy. Return venison to pot, add salt and pepper to taste. Reheat and serve. Will serve four to six.

Venison Steaks

Marinate 1¼ inch steaks of young deer three hours in mixture of chopped carrots, onions, pinch of thyme, salt and pepper, three cups of white wine and cup of olive oil.

Dry steaks and drop into sizzling skillet. Sear three minutes on each side, or until rare, or as you like it. Make gravy with pan scrapings.

Venison Liver And Bleu Cheese

Venison liver is a delicacy not to be overlooked, as most deer slayers will attest. If it has been treated with care from kill to kitchen, you can't beat it for a camp meal, any time of day.

Slice it thin and soak it in a solution of salt and baking soda, kneading it well to remove all trace of blood. Dry. Fry over a moderate fire five to ten minutes, depending on thickness. Set aside. Break eight eggs into bowl and add one cubic inch or more of bleu cheese, crumbled. Mix thoroughly and drop in oiled skillet. Work into omelet. Place liver on a warm serving dish and cover with the omelet. Serves four.

Barbecued Venison

Some cuts of old deer aren't much good for anything other than hamburger or barbecue. One of the best meals I ever served featured the latter. It has somewhat the flavor of mutton, which is superior to beef or pork barbecue, in my estimation.

Roast the venison at a low temperature in Dutch oven several hours until it is ready to fall apart. Slice and place in a skillet covered with your favorite barbecue sauce. Simmer until the sauce permeates the meat.

Hodgen's Venison

This suggestion for cooking venison came from a popular hunter-chef in Lebanon:

"I enjoyed your column on cooking wild game, as I dabble in it myself," W. R. Hodgen wrote. "I've got a row of herbs and spices more than a yard long. One is 'Italian Seasoning,' which you do not mention. I find it a great blessing for marinating and tenderizing venison. It contains oregano, thyme, marjoram, sage, rosemary and savory, all mixed together.

"I find that by thawing venison overnight and tenderizing it all day at room temperature and by basting it almost constantly on the grill with a butter and oil mix, I can almost always come up with a juicy, tender feed.

"I slice my venison in one-half to three-quarter inch slabs and fry like steaks."

Rabbit

Now here is truly the "bread of the woods," a delight forever if you handle it properly after the kill. A young rabbit that has been drawn and bled in the field is hard to surpass in delicate flavor and tenderness. Whatever you have done with chicken can be done with a young bunny. If your bunny is somewhat elderly, you can save it and one or two other tough ones for hasenpfeffer.

Fried Rabbit

2 rabbits
1 cup flour
½ teaspoon oregano
½ teaspoon thyme
salt and pepper

Cut up rabbits and dredge in flour seasoned with salt, pepper, thyme, oregano. Brown on hot fire. Reduce heat, cover and fry in about one inch of oil until fork tender—usually less than half an hour. Uncover and allow to perk up. Should serve six if they're not too hungry.

Mack Sisk's Pennyrile Smothered Rabbit

2 whole wild rabbits
1 pint fresh mushrooms
2 large sliced onions
½ teaspoon garlic powder
½ teaspoon black pepper
salt and pepper
2 garlic cloves
flour to dredge
1 pound hot country sausage
Marinade:
 3 cups vinegar
 bottle of red wine
 water to cover
 4 bay leaves

Clean rabbits thoroughly and leave whole. Soak in salt water for four hours. Combine marinade ingredients and place rabbit in crock or glass container. Marinate at least three days, turning several times each day. After third day remove from marinade, drain and pat dry. Strain marinade and reserve liquid. (If it is too bloody, start a new batch with one-third each of wine, vinegar and water.)

Lightly dredge each whole rabbit with flour, seasoned with salt and pepper. Lightly brown on all sides in a heavy iron skillet. Stuff rabbit with highly saged hot country sausage. Place stuffed rabbit in roasting pan and dust with flour. Pour reserved marinade over animal. Add sliced onions, garlic, garlic powder, black pepper and mushrooms. Bake at 350 degrees for nearly three hours, or until tender and rabbit is falling off the bone.

A suggestion: If you are having company who may not eat rabbit, when you start the final baking process, surround the stuffed rabbit with smoked Polish sausages cut in three-inch sections.

Place on a hot platter and serve. Serves six or more.

Baked Whole Rabbit

If you come home with an extra large and possibly an elderly rabbit, try baking it whole as Sisk does. First stuff it with any tasty prepared stuffing, then truss. Brush with bacon fat. Place in roasting pan and add a cup of water and cup of chicken broth or consomme. Bake at 325 one hour or so, basting frequently. Add water as needed. Serves four.

Ruby's Fail-Safe Rabbit

Rabbits of any age can be cooked this way without fail:

Place rack in Dutch oven. Fill with water up to, but not over the rack. Cut up rabbits, dredge in flour seasoned with salt and pepper, and brown nicely on both sides in a skillet. Place pieces on rack, stacked as high as necessary to accommodate them. Cover well and bake at 275 or even a bit lower, checking now and then to maintain water level and to test pieces for tenderness. Cooking time is one to two hours. When tender, remove to shallow baking dish and let crisp up in oven. Make gravy with Dutch oven drippings.

This method may be used on squirrels, also.

Mrs. Patterson's Hasenpfeffer

Nobody makes better hasenpfeffer than Wiz Patterson of Louisville, Bowling Green, Paducah and Lexington. (Her husband moved around a lot.) Here is her recipe, and I will swear by it.

Cut up three rabbits and place in a crock with half vinegar and half water to cover. Add a handful of pickling spices. Marinate two days, turning occasionally.

Wash, dry, salt and pepper, and dredge in flour. Brown rabbit well in cooking oil on both sides. Remove rabbit. Add three tablespoons of flour to three or four tablespoons of drippings in the skillet and add enough water to make ample gravy. Return the rabbit to the gravy. Add a small sack of pickling spices and simmer on top of the stove until tender, approximately one hour. Add sugar to taste—this is important. It is best to put the large pieces in the gravy first and hold the small legs until later so that all the meat will be tender at the same time. Serve with mashed potatoes to six hungry hunters.

Squirrel

This little resident of the woods has provided excellent food for the table since pioneer days and remains in good supply everywhere nut trees abound. Young ones may be fried like chicken, but the older ones are best as foundation for stew, or mulligan.

I include the heads in my mulligan because the tiny brain is a delicacy beyond compare. But because some people shriek when confronted by a hollow-eyed head staring back from the plate, it is best to crack the skull in the kitchen and save only the brain.

I was introduced to this squirrel mulligan by Ray Ashcraft of Elizabethtown, who got it from E.H. Black of that city:

6 squirrels	2½ pound chicken
6 roasting ears of corn	½ pound bacon chopped
1½ pints butterbeans	2 pods red pepper
1 pint diced potatoes	salt to taste
2 teaspoons cayenne pepper	

Place the squirrel and chicken in a two-gallon cooker and cover with water. Cook until the meat falls off the bones, removing scum as it forms, and adding water when necessary.

Remove the bones and add potatoes, bacon, butterbeans and corn (after removing from cob).

Boil 20 minutes, reduce heat to low. Stir enough to prevent sticking and allow to simmer, adding water as needed. Add two teaspoons of cayenne pepper. Also two pods of red pepper if you like it real hot.

Before removal from fire add Worcestershire sauce to taste, and thicken with flour if necessary.

Serve with toast strips.

As an added bit of elegance, you might save the squirrel heads and place them in the stew after the other meat has been cooked off the bones.

When done, serve one or two squirrel heads with each serving.

Squirrel in Gravy

Fry squirrels until tender as you would chicken. Remove and make brown gravy. Return squirrels and simmer until bones pull out freely. Salt and pepper to taste. Serve with mashed potatoes.

Brunswick Stew

If you have some squirrels or a rabbit that looks too tough for frying, try them in a stew. This recipe for marvelous Brunswick stew came from Gladys Ward, whose family served it to her, and who has served it to many large gatherings of friends. It is a large order, but it freezes well.

1 hen
2 pounds stew beef
1 large soup bone
2 pounds veal
2 squirrels
1 quart limas
1 pound okra
4 medium onions
1 tablespoon mustard
1 dozen ears corn
½ peck potatoes
1 cup tomato puree
1 bunch celery
1 large can tomatoes
½ pound butter
1 cup vinegar
1½ cups sugar
pinch cayenne pepper
salt and pepper to taste

Put meat in large pot with enough water to cover. Cook slowly until meat falls off bones. Meanwhile prepare vegetables. Dice celery, onions and okra. Remove meat and set aside. Add vegetables and butter to the broth. When tender, add meat, well chopped up. Stir constantly until of consistence of thick mush. Add cayenne and salt and pepper to taste. Cook five minutes more, and then dig in!

Varmint

A tradition as old as Kentucky and as identifiable with the commonwealth as Daniel Boone is a varmint dinner. But never in his wildest dreams did Daniel set before his family a feast of the variety and style whomped up by latter-day Epicurean pioneers like Martin Turner and Mack Sisk at the request of Kentucky governors and for the edification and enjoyment of members of the General Assembly.

Where else could anyone find a buffet bedecked with such zesty delicacies as tender, succulent and savory raccoon, unbelievably rich groundhog, spiced 'possum, gamey squirrel, uniquely delicate wild rabbit, plus tantalizing breasts of wild goose and mallard duck, not to mention such regal tidbits as breasts of dove and quail?

Gov. Earle Clements, a lifelong wild game gourmet, enjoyed the first of these annual bashes in 1948 when Judge Jim Cammack invited him to his Franklin County farm for a raccoon supper. A bit later Allan Trout, a revered columnist for *The Courier-Journal,* bought the judge's farm and enlarged the dinners to include other game. During this period all cooking was done by Turner, janitor at the Court of Appeals.

Then in 1951, after Gov. Lawrence Wetherby had taken office, Sisk, a chef with a flair for the unusual, took over the kitchen with Turner's help. Sisk moved the dinner to Dawson Springs as part of a national fox hunt. He even served a delicacy he insisted was roast skunk, but Wetherby quickly, and hopefully, identified it as muskrat.

Sisk, who is happiest when tempting the palates of his friends, does little hunting, but he insists that those who furnish the footin's do their jobs properly. With raccoons he is especially careful. He insists on only raccoons that haven't fought dogs before being bagged because "fear and fighting," he says, makes the meat strong and muscles tough. Sisk seasons them with salt and pepper and garlic and onions but says raccoons caught properly really don't need much doctoring. They are very clean game.

Groundhogs also eat clean food, such as grass, clover and corn. Sisk cuts down on garlic for that reason but uses a bit of vinegar along with salt, pepper and onions in his pot. In dressing a groundhog, be sure to remove the two red pea-sized musk glands—they can ruin the flavor—which are inside the upper front legs and to trim off excess fat. Age the meat in the refrigerator one or two days, then soak overnight in salt water to which you have added a tablespoon of baking soda. Do this with coons as well.

Stuffed Groundhog

Boil the varmint up to half an hour in water, salt and pepper. Remove and dry. Save water for dressing and basting. Make dressing of prepared stuffing (regular or Stove Top), salt and pepper, two chopped onions, two stalks of chopped celery. Add sufficient water to make it moist. Stuff varmint and place back-down in roasting pan. Cover and roast in 350 degree oven until tender, basting frequently and adding water as needed. Remove cover and brown when varmint is fork tender.

A wonderful gravy can be made with the pan scrapings after the fat is siphoned off. Add tablespoon of flour and add enough of water varmint was boiled in to make rich gravy. Add cup of beef bouillon and a dash of Kitchen Bouquet. Will feed four or more.

Garnett's Fried Varmint

Sam Garnett of Danville will pit this recipe for groundhog against all others:

Cut off all the fat possible. Place varmint in a pressure cooker and cook until almost done. Cut into serving pieces, dredge in flour, salt and pepper, and fry like chicken. Will serve a lot of folks, who'll call for more.

Varmint Barbecue

Raccoon and possum are at their best when barbecued. Try either one in this manner and hear the compliments.
1 young varmint
1 tablespoon garlic salt
1 tablespoon pepper
juice of two limes
your own barbecue sauce

Parboil varmint with pepper, garlic salt and lime juice, for 30 minutes. Cut in pieces and place in baking dish with barbecue sauce. Roast at 350 degrees until amost falling off bones. Time will depend on age of the varmint.

Bud's Varmint Burgoo

Tailgating, embraced so enthusiastically by football fans, fox hunters, dove hunters and some squirrel hunters, is the delightful practice of serving hot and tasty food and thirst quenching libation from the tailgate of a station wagon or in the comfort of a houseboat.

A man who knows much about instant nourishment for hungry hunters is Rowan W. "Bud" Waskom of Madisonville. He concocts what he calls instant burgoo on his spacious houseboat while his buddies are off hunting squirrels. He uses that newcomer to the culinary scene, the slow-cooking pot.

Waskom starts with whatever varmint or other meat is available—squirrel, groundhog, buffalo, venison or raccoon. He usually cooks the varmint in advance, then all he has to do aboard is place the meat in his slow-cooking pot and add a lot of seasoning and any canned vegetables that tickle his fancy—corn, tomatoes, okra, black-eyed peas, lima beans, green beans. In 10 minutes he is ready to serve hot burgoo to cold and hungry hunters as they return from the woods. I highly recommend this shortcut cooking to campers.

Camp Cooking

Take a Dutch oven and some heavy-duty foil on your next camping trip and you will eat better. Use the Dutch oven to fry, boil, bake or steam, as well as making instant burgoo with leftover squirrel, rabbit, venison or birds. Potatoes (jackets on), onions (peeled) and other fresh vegetables can be wrapped in foil with a bit of butter, and rolled into hot ashes of your fire. Wrap them twice, and remove the outer wrap before serving. Both are dirtproof and foolproof, and virtually eliminate dirty grease, which usually saturates most meals cooked over an open fire.

Leftovers

There never was a hunter who didn't find himself with more cooked venison, goose, duck, squirrel or rabbit than could be devoured in a single meal. What can be done with those delicious leftovers? Try barbecue.

Odds and ends of cooked venison make barbecue so good it might be mistaken for mutton. Slice it across the grain and simmer it in barbecue sauce for 10 to 15 minutes. Marvelous!

Any leftover rabbit (except hasenpfeffer) or squirrel should be cut cross-grain, covered with barbecue sauce, and allowed to steep 10 to 15 minutes.

As wonderful as Canada goose and mallard duck are when first served, they are a problem the next day when bits and pieces cling to the carcass. Chop all the remaining fowl into small pieces, cutting across the grain. Mix with barbecue sauce and simmer for about 10 minutes. It's so good you may plan on leftovers after every hunt.

Recipes for *Fish*

Kentuckians are blessed with future banquets swimming in the state's lakes, creeks, ponds and rivers. Not only can a fish make a splendid main course, but it also provides protein and minerals and very few calories. Most people think of a fish as a thing to fry, but cooks and anglers should not overlook baking and broiling the catches.

Most fish caught in and near Kentucky may be prepared and cooked alike. Just be sure to remember this general rule: Cook up to eight to ten minutes for each inch of thickness at the thickest part. Test as you go for flakiness and juiciness.

Black Bass

The black bass—largemouth, smallmouth and Kentucky—provides superior table fare when cooked one of three ways. The flesh is firm and white and tends to flake easily when properly prepared. Smaller bass should be fried, medium-sized fish are perfect for filleting and broiling, and the larger ones are ideal for baking, all with mouth-watering results. With bass, as with most fish, be careful not to overcook. Test for flakiness when in doubt.

Baked Bass in Wine

The late Sandy Wood served up this dish on a vacation trip to Florida. It was a great success.

1 four pound bass   *1 cup chopped celery*
1 bottle white wine   *1 stick of butter*
1 cup chopped onions
Pinches of tarragon and thyme
Paprika

Saute the onions and celery until transparent. Sprinkle bass with salt and pepper. Place sheet of foil in a baking dish, leaving enough of the foil on two sides to lift it by later. Add vegetables, seasoning, butter, and half the wine. Bake at 375 degrees, basting with pan liquid and wine as necessary. Test for flakiness after giving it eight minutes for each inch of thickness. When done, sprinkle with paprika, lift out by grasping foil on each side, and slide onto serving plate.

Broiled Fillet of Bass

2 two-pound bass   *2 cups fish broth*
paprika   *1 stick butter*
salt and pepper

Season fillets with salt and pepper. Place on buttered foil on broiler. Broil six inches from flame eight minutes for each inch of thickness. Ladle broth and melted butter as needed, and sprinkle with paprika just before removing from flame. To make the broth, boil the heads (minus the gills), backbones and tails for 20 minutes in water enough to cover. Season with salt and pepper. Will serve four hungry anglers.

Muskellunge

This magnificent fish deserves more attention as table fare than it usually receives. Muskie may be broiled as cross-cut steaks or as fillets, or baked. Because the muskie is a lean fish, it should be basted often with seasoned butter if it is broiled.

You might try this recipe for baked stuffed muskie:

Baked Stuffed Muskie

1 five-pound muskie
1 cup chopped celery
1 cup chopped onions
½ cup chopped green pepper
1 package prepared stuffing
salt and pepper

Saute onions, celery and pepper. Mix with stuffing and water to form a wet dressing. Stuff muskie and tie up. Bake covered at 375 degrees eight minutes for each inch of thickness. Test for flakiness. Remove when it turns flakey and is still juicy. Serves six.

Sauger and Walleye

The sauger and the walleye, members of the yellow perch family, have firm, white flesh and are excellent on the dinner table.

Most sauger caught in Kentucky average one pound. These may be pan-fried in the same manner as croppie or small catfish. My preference for both sauger and walleye, however, is deep-frying. Heat the oil to 375 degrees. Dredge the fish in a mixture of white cornmeal and flour amply seasoned with salt and pepper. Carefully lower each fish or part of fish into the oil. Cook up to 10 minutes for each inch of thickness. Deep-frying can be tricky. Just be sure the oil is not too hot, and avoid overcooking.

Rockfish

This newcomer to Kentucky waters poses something of a culinary problem because of its unusually large size. Several rockfish weighing 40 or more pounds have been taken from Herrington and Cumberland lakes and below the dam at Lake Barkley. There is only one way to handle the larger fish: Cut into steaks and freeze in half-gallon milk cartons covered with water until the fish is wanted for the table. The smaller ones can be baked or broiled as you would black bass. Or try the following:

Broiled Rockfish

If the rockfish is small enough, fillet it. Sprinkle with salt, pepper and paprika, and broil six inches from the flame eight to 10 minutes per inch of thickness, basting with melted butter.

If you have cut steaks, broil them as you would the fillets. If frozen, give them twice the time you would give thawed fish.

Baked Rockfish

One day in 1972 I decided to experiment with a five-pound rockfish. So little was known about the table qualities of this fish that I decided to bake this one just as I would a red snapper or a bass of the same size.

I baked it at 350 degrees in a sauce of tomatoes, onion and green pepper, allowing 10 minutes for each pound, or 40 to 50 minutes for that particular fish. I made a cradle of two thicknesses of heavy-duty aluminum foil and baked the fish in its juices and in the sauce. When done I lifted the whole fish out by grasping the tops of the foil in each hand. Then it was a simple matter to slide the fish onto a platter garnished with parsley, pepper rings and lemon wedges.

It was the consensus of all diners that the rockfish of this size, cooked in this manner, was superior even to a red snapper of like size.

Carp

T. S. Waller of Paducah once wrote, "I read in your column that you are a carp enthusiast. So am I. You said they are delicious if cooked right. I find them delicious cooked my way but would like to know your way."

I have several techniques, not counting the old one advocated by carp-haters: Bake carp in a cake of mud, crack open the mud, throw away the carp, and eat the mud.

Actually, a carp is very good eating. The main point is to clean thoroughly, making sure to remove the red veins running the length of the fish on both sides and to cut out the dorsal fin using a deep V cut. Also soak several hours in salt, baking soda and water.

If you have a big fellow, you can cut into steaks, crosswise like salmon steaks, fry with croppie or bass, and dare your friends to taste any difference. Or you can bake it like a red snapper in a sauce of butter, salt, pepper and white wine, or in a creole sauce of tomatoes and green peppers.

Ruby's Baked Carp

1 4-to-5 lb carp	*2 medium onions*
1 bottle white wine	*½ stick butter*
1 small can tomatoes	*salt and pepper*
1 cup chopped mushrooms	

Clean carp thoroughly and soak in salt and baking soda for two hours. Remove and dry. Saute onions until transparent. Put carp in baking dish with vegetables and cup of wine. Bake covered at 375 eight to 10 minutes for each inch of thickness, or until flakey. Baste with pan juices and additional wine as needed.

Baked Carp Fillets

Cut carp fillets into serving portions. Dredge in half flour and half white cornmeal, salt and plenty of pepper. Place on greased pan and bake up to 10 minutes for each inch of thickness. Turn once.

Rainbow Trout

I'm not as gung ho as some folks are about the taste of the small rainbows that are stocked in Kentucky on a put-and-take basis, but the larger ones are something else.

Try filleting them. Broil six inches from the flame in an oiled pan and baste with melted butter. Be very careful not to overcook. Sprinkle with salt, pepper, juice of a lemon and paprika. Wonderful!

The seven- and eight-inch rainbows stocked in small streams may be fried whole, or broiled whole, head and all, after cleaning. The flesh tends to get mushy, so be careful when removing from the pan.

Panfish and Croppie

I include croppie among the panfish because I cook all of them the same—cooked whole after cleaning and removing the head, tail and fins. The one exception is the larger, slab-size croppie, which has to be filleted.

These smaller fish should be fried (see catfish).

However, there are some anglers, like Davis "Zeke" Morgan of LaGrange, who fillet even the smallest sunfish. These tiny morsels tend to curl up, but go great with eggs at breakfast.

Catfish

Now here is a marvelous fish that rates with any I've cooked—the channel catfish. Skin the fish with the help of a pair of pliers. Soak in salt, baking soda and water for one or two hours. Cats up to eight inches may be fried whole in deep fat; larger ones should be cut into steaks or filleted.

In frying fish of any kind I recommend this procedure: Dry the fish on paper towels. Dip in mixture of milk and egg. Then dredge in well-seasoned mix of half flour and half cornmeal. Place pieces on rack or paper toweling and let stand at least half an hour, to give the coating time to set. You will find this will keep the coating from dropping off in the skillet.

Turtle

I learned these turtle tips from Dr. Herman Mahaffey, a Louisville surgeon who is a real turtle enthusiast.

When preparing to cook the turtle meat, he soaks it in water, salt and baking soda twice for a couple of hours each time to remove all traces of blood and any unusual game odor. Then he proceeds just as he would with fried chicken, except that he cooks it over a lower fire and for a longer time.

Some hunters prefer to soak the meat overnight in the salt, baking soda, and water solution, keeping it refrigerated all the while. Then, after browning, they pour off most of the cooking oil, put a lid on, and let the turtle cook slowly for an hour or so.

I prefer Mahaffey's way of frying without a lid. It keeps the meat crisp like chicken. The lid softens the crust.

Frog Legs

Now here is something extra special—delicate, tender, tasteful frog legs. Eating them is second only to the sport of floating down a placid stream catching them in the dark of the night. I use the whole frog except for the head when I pick up a jumbo; there is a lot of nibbling on those forelegs.

Fried Frog Legs

Tie the legs together at the ankles with household string or small rubber band to keep them from spreading apart in the skillet. Dip in salt, pepper and pancake flour. Fry in one inch of oil, turning once, until brown all over—from two to five minutes, depending on the temperature of the oil and size of the legs. Frogs are ruined easily by too hot oil and overcooking, so be especially careful with this marvelous dish. If you have an electric skillet set it at 350 and don't move it.

Three medium-sized pairs of frog legs should be ample for the average person.

Note—Don't worry about the rubber bands, they leave no taste. Just pull them off before serving.

Kentucky Fried Frog Legs

Roll legs in salted and peppered pancake flour, dip in milk, then roll in cracker crumbs. Fry in deep fat (not too hot) until brown all over—between two and five minutes. Remove frog legs and all but three or four tablespoons of oil. Brown three tablespoons of flour, add two cups of milk, and stir in pan scrapings until a rich gravy forms. Add salt and pepper to taste. Serve with the frog legs.

Crawfish

On a recent trip to Jacksonville, Fla., my old hunting and fishing buddy, Jack Gerber, purchased too many live shrimps for bait. We had about two pounds left over. "We can freeze 'em and use 'em later," I suggested.

"Not these!" said Gerber. "Any shrimp that can't catch me a supper becomes my supper!" After beheading them he tossed six or eight of them at a time into boiling water. After a few minutes he heaped all of the red morsels in the center of the table, and we and our wives attacked them, shucking as we went. They were as fresh as any I've eaten.

All of which reminds me of the days when crawfish were plentiful in the part of Beargrass Creek that flows through Louisville's Cherokee Park. As kids we gathered dozens of them. One mother on the block boiled the crawfish tails, and we ate them as fast as we could shuck them.

Hunting & Fishing in Southern Indiana

Hunting & Fishing in Southern Indiana

More Kentuckians are making annual pilgrimages to Santa Claus land, but not because of Christmas. This Santa Claus is a town in Southern Indiana, and visitors from Kentucky have found their luck with quail, rabbits and deer often is better in Southern Indiana than in their home range.

I have done most of my Hoosier rabbit chasing with Tom Dunlevy, of Jeffersonville, and enjoyed mixed results. My bird hunting has been centered around Jasper, where Alvin Ruxer has some of the best bird dogs that ever breathed.

Others have ventured far, and brought back many a quail, rabbit, pheasant and deer.

Looking over the situation in Southern Indiana with Ed Guljas, Dave Howell, Mike Oliver and Randy Showalter, Hoosier wildlife experts, I have found this:

Quail
The severe winters of 1977 and '78 greatly hurt the quail crop. The little fellows were 40 percent down in '77, and sank further in '78. It may take two to three years to recover.

Most of the areas where quail are found are privately owned. Permission to hunt usually may be had for the asking. As for which counties are best, it depends on local conditions. The birds are very well distributed throughout the southern section.

Pheasant
There are no huntable pheasants in Southern Indiana. But sportsmen enjoy put-and-take hunting at both the Crosley and Glendale fish and wildlife areas. Hunting is by permit only, and Guljas urges hunters to try during the week, rather than on weekends. Morning and afternoon hunts are usually permitted. The limit has been two pheasants of either sex, but this is subject to change, so be sure to check.

Rabbits
The rabbits came through the two awful winters with less of a loss than quail. They can be found in virtually all counties in Southern Indiana, but they are spotty. The rabbit season usually opens during the first week in November. But on all fish and wildlife management areas the opening date has been shoved up to Oct. 1, to allow hunters to harvest a portion of those cottontails usually lost to predators and cars. This was a popular move.

Grouse
The grouse came through the ice and snow with no loss. The hunting of this fine bird is restricted to certain areas, and visitors should read the limitations carefully when they receive their hunting regulations with their license.

Whitetail Deer
Much of Indiana's best deer hunting is found on military land at Atterbury, near Indianapolis, Crane near Bloomington, Jefferson Proving Grounds near North Vernon, and the Charlestown Ammunition Depot near Jeffersonville.

The Mogan Ridge area near Tell City is another popular spot.

Good hunting also is found in the Hoosier National Forest, Harrison—Crawford State Forest and the Pike State Forest.

Squirrel
The squirrels thrived despite the two bad winters because of bumper mast crops. Indications were that many older squirrels produced early litters in 1978, and another in mid-summer. Good hunting usually is found wherever there's a patch of nut

trees, on private land as well as the state-owned land. Hoosier farmers are a friendly lot, and usually will permit hunting when asked.

Ducks and Geese
Monroe Reservoir near Bloomington offers the best duck hunting, and Hovey Lake in Posey County, the hottest goose hunting. Dogwood Lake on the Glendale management area, Hardy Lake near Scottsburg, and Boggs Creek Reservoir near Loogootee also offer fair to good hunting. Also, good jump shooting frequently may be found on White River, the Muscatatuck and Blue rivers.

Wild Turkey
Turkey hunting in Indiana is reserved for Hoosiers only. During the hunt of 1977, 80 percent of the hunters heard at least one turkey, 40 percent saw a turkey and 10 percent bagged one. Turkey licenses are available only at Room 607, State Office Building, Indianapolis.

Record Buck Program
Any deer taken legally in Indiana is eligible for entry in the popular Hoosier Record Buck Program. Antler scoring is divided into two categories— typical and non-typical, and the scoring system is that used by the Boone and Crockett Club (see Boone and Crockett instructions in another section).

Any hunter in Southern Indiana having a rack that he thinks might qualify for recognition should contact one of these biologists: Dave Howell, Box 393 Winslow, 47598. Randy Showalter, R.R. 1, Box 234, Nashville, Ind., 47460, or Ed Guljas, R.R. 1, Comiskey, Ind. 47227.

The all-time record for a rack taken in Indiana boasted 190 2/8 points and was taken by Robert Dollar of VanBuren, Ind., in 1974.

Fishing
Southern Indiana has many fishable streams, lakes and farm ponds. Actually, most of the state's record catches have been made south of Indianapolis. For example, the biggest largemouth bass ever taken in the state was taken from Ferdinand Reservoir in Dubois County by Curt Reynolds of Ferdinand in 1968. It weighed 11 pounds, 1 ounce. The state record smallmouth came from a small stream in Rush County. It tipped the scale at six pounds, eight ounces and was pulled in by Jim Connerly of New

Marvin Dunaway and son Tracy, of Corydon fish at the dam on Big Indian Creek.

Alvin Ruxer of Jasper delights in the efforts of his Brittany spaniels.

Castle in 1970. Jim Vinyard of Boonville holds the state mark for muskie with a 12-pounder taken from Little Blue River in Crawford County in 1965. A tremendous croppie weighing four pounds, seven ounces came from a farm pond in Posey County to set a new record in 1965. The fish was taken by Mary Ann Leigh of Evansville. State record redear, rock bass, blue catfish, flathead catfish, drum, bowfin and paddlefish also came from the southern part of the state. (A list of record catches in Indiana is on page 134).

Feeling the need to reduce its population of bluegill in lakes it owns or leases, the state of Indiana adopted a 14-inch minimum size limit on largemouth black bass several years ago. This has discouraged many bass anglers, including those in major tournaments, and has increased the number seeking such other underwater species as croppie, bluegill, walleye, smallmouth bass, white and yellow bass, trout and catfish.

Most state-owned and controlled lakes are small, and electric trolling motors only are allowed. The largest lake, of course, is Monroe Lake, where outboards of all sizes are permitted. This lake covers 10,000 acres.

Other interesting lakes in Southern Indiana include: Elk Creek near Salem, which is producing a surprising number of 14-inch and longer bass; Hardy Lake near Austin, which is well stocked with walleye as well as other popular species; Versailles Lake near Versailles, known for its big bluegills; Deam Lake in Clark County, a very popular 340-acre lake; Cypress Lake near Seymour, a big bass lake; Grouse Ridge Lake near Ogilville, which also has good camping sites; Clark State Forest lakes near Henryville (Oak Lake is the best of the four); Brush Creek near North Vernon, noted for its bluegill; Strave Hollow Lake near Vallonia, another great bluegill lake; Ferdinand Lake near Ferdinand; Indian Lake near St. Croix; New Shakamak Lake near Jasonville; West Boggs Creek near Loogootee, a relatively new lake just reaching its prime; Dogwood Lake near Glendale, which has lots of stickups.

The most popular streams include the Blue River in Washington, Harrison and Crawford counties. Other worthwhile streams are Salt Creek, a good, wadable, smallmouth bass stream that runs through Monroe and Lawrence counties, and Indian Creek in Green, Lawrence and Martin counties.

Indiana Sport Fishing Seasons and Limits

Kind of Fish	Open Season	Daily Catch Limit	Minimum Size
Bluegill	All year	None	None
Yellow Bass	All year	None	None
Redear, Croppie, Rock Bass	All year	25—singly or in aggregate	None
Smallmouth Bass	All year	6—singly or in aggregate	None
Kentucky Bass	All year	6—singly or in aggregate	None
Largemouth Bass	All year	6—singly or in aggregate	14 inches if taken from lake, pond, or impoundment owned by Department of Fish and Wildlife
White Bass	All year	12	None
Rockfish	All year	2	None
Walleye, Sauger	All year	6—singly or in aggregate	None
Muskellunge	All year from Brookville Reservoir, Whitewater River and tributary streams. All other waters closed to muskellunge fishing.	1	30 inches
Northern Pike	All year	3	20 inches
Yellow Perch	All year	None	None
Catfish: In Streams	All year	None	10 inches
In Lakes and Reservoirs	All year	10	10 inches
Bullheads	All year	None	None
Trout (Brook, Brown and Rainbow): In Streams	Last Saturday in April through Oct. 31	10—singly or in aggregate	7 inches
In Inland Lakes	All year	10	7 inches
Salmon, Rainbow or Brown Trout, Lake Trout and Striped Bass in Lake Michigan	All year	5—singly or in aggregate	10 inches
Non-Game Fish	All year	None	None
Frogs (requires a hunting license)	June 15-April 30	25	None

The possession limit on all game fish and frogs is two days' legal catch. The fishing seasons and limits may be changed at any time by the Indiana Department of Fish and Wildlife.

Indiana Licenses & Permits

Resident

Hunting, Fishing and Trapping	$5.25
Hunting and Trapping	3.25
Fishing	3.50
Trout-Salmon Stamp	2.25
Deer Hunting—Archery	5.75
Shotgun	5.75
Muzzle-loading Rifle	5.75
Turkey Hunting	5.25
Waterfowl Stamp	5.00

Non-Resident

Hunting and Fishing	25.25
Annual Fishing	7.50
Annual Hunting	20.25
Annual Trapping	25.25
14-Day Fishing	3.25
Trout-Salmon Stamp	2.25
5-Day Hunting	5.25
Deer Hunting—Archery	30.75
Shotgun	30.75
Muzzle-loading Rifle	30.75
Waterfowl Stamp	5.00

Most licenses may be purchased from county clerks or at the Division of Fish and Wildlife, 607 State Office Building, Indianapolis, Ind.

Indiana Record Catches

Species	Weight	Where Caught	County	Angler	Year
Largemouth bass	11 lb. 11 oz.	Ferdinand Reservoir	Dubois	Curt Reynolds, Ferdinand	1968
Bluegill	3 lb. 4 oz.	Pond	Greene	Harold L. Catey, New Castle	1972
White bass	4 lb. 3 oz.	Lake Freeman	Carroll	James Wagner, Lafayette	1965
Smallmouth bass	6 lb. 8 oz.	Stream	Rush	Jim Connerly, New Castle	1970
Northern pike	26 lb. 8 oz.	Lake	LaGrange	Wayne Lewis, LaGrange	1972
Crappie	4 lb. 7 oz.	Pond	Posey	Mary Ann Leigh, Evansville	1965
Walleye	14 lb. 4 oz.	River	Lake	Leon Richart, Waldron	1974
Sauger	5 lb.	Wabash River	Tippecanoe	N. L. Merrifield, Indianapolis	1964
Redear	3 lb. 10 oz.	Lake	Brown	R. Peckham, Nashville	1974
Yellow perch	2 lb. 1 oz.	L. Crooked Lake	Whitley	George Nagel, Ft. Wayne	1974
Muskellunge	12 lb.	Little Blue River	Crawford	Jim Vinyard, Boonville	1965
Steelhead	20 lb. 11 oz.	Lake Michigan	LaPorte	Dan Bowen, Hammond	1972
Coho	20 lb. 12 oz.	Lake Michigan	LaPorte	John Beutner, Michigan City	1972
Rainbow trout	10 lb. 2.5 oz.	Lake Gage	Steuben	Sonny Bashore, Paulding, Ohio	1973
Brown trout	16 lb. 10 oz.	Lake Michigan	Lake	Jack E. Phillps, Gary	1975
Brook trout	3 lb. 15 oz.	Lake Gage	Steuben	Sonny Bashore, Paulding, Ohio	1973
Channel catfish	27 lb.	Tippecanoe River		Chester Keith, Rushville	1970
Blue catfish	57 lb.	Lake	Clark	Raymon Ries, New Albany	1975
Flathead catfish*	79 lb. 8 oz.	White River	Lawrence	Glen T. Simpson, Indianapolis	1966
Bullhead	3 lb. 13 oz.	Pond	Delaware	Fred J. Stewart, Muncie	1970
Freshwater drum (White perch)	30 lb.	White River	Martin	Garland Fellers, Loogootee	1963
Carp	38 lb. 1 oz.	Lake	Lake	Frank J. Drost, Hammond	1967
Rock bass	3 lb.	Sugar Creek	Hancock	David Thomas, Indianapolis	1969
Bowfin (Dogfish)	13 lb. 8 oz.	Stream	Greene	Jim Spice-J. Holtsclaw, Bloomfield	1971
Spotted bass	5 lb. 1.5 oz.	Lake	Howard	John William Pio, Kokomo	1975
Chinook	37 lb. 4 oz.	Lake Michigan	LaPorte	Terry Snyder, Michigan City	1974
Lake trout	21 lb.	Lake Michigan	LaPorte	Terry Snyder, Michigan City	1974
Paddlefish	62 lb.	Farm Pond	Ripley	Timothy Christman, Osgood	1975
Buffalo*	47 lb. 2 oz.	Lake Tippecanoe	Tippecanoe	David Hulley, Marion	1975
Yellow Bass*	2 lb. 4 oz.	Lake Monroe	Monroe	Don Stalker, Bedford	1977
Rockfish	9 lbs.	Brookville Lake	Franklin	Riley Allen, Brookville	1978

*World Record

(This list official as of Jan. 1, 1976)

Information Centers

For further information on hunting and fishing in Southern Indiana contact one of these sources:

DEPARTMENT OF NATURAL RESOURCES
ENFORCEMENT DIVISION
606 State Office Building
Indianapolis, Indiana 46204
Phone: (317) 633-5254

Randy Showalter, who has charge of southcentral Indiana, with headquarters in Brown County. Phone (812) 988-7856

Ed Guljas, southeasern area with headquarters at Crosley Wildlife Area. Phone 812-873-6633.

Dave Howell, southwestern area with headquarters at the Patoka Fish and Wildlife Area. Phone 812-789-2724.

Public Access Sites to Indiana Lakes and Streams

Name of Site	County	Acres of Water Made Available	Location of Site
Vincennes	Knox	Wabash	city of Vincennes
Spencer	Owen	West Fork	near Spencer
Anderson	Perry	Anderson River	near Troy
Lawrenceport	Lawrence	East Fork-White River	2 miles northeast of Lawrenceport
Bedford	Lawrence	East Fork-White River	two miles south of Bedford on U.S. 50
Jasper-Patoka River	Dubois	Patoka River	U.S. 164, southern edge of Jasper
Batesville Reservoir	Ripley	200	east of Batesville
Shelbyville	Shelby	Big Blue River	city of Shelbyville
Ohio River	Harrison	Ohio River	Harrison State Forest
Brownstown	Jackson	East Fork-White River	2 miles west on U.S. 50
Seymour	Jackson	East Fork-White River	¼ mile west of Rockford off U.S. 31A
Atterbury-Sugar Creek #1	Johnson	Sugar Creek	Atterbury Fish and Wildlife Area
Atterbury-Sugar Creek #2	Johnson	Sugar Creek	Atterbury Fish and Wildlife Area
South Lake	Sullivan	8	½ mile west of Pleasantville in Greene-Sullivan State Forest
Downing	Sullivan	12	2 miles south of Ind. 64 in Greene-Sullivan State Forest
Pond No. 1	Sullivan	3	2 ½ miles south of Dugger
No. 26 Reservoir	Sullivan	50	3 ½ miles south of Ind. 64
White-Muscatatuck	Washington	White-Muscatatuck	Millport
Millport	Washington	Muscatatuck	Millport
Merom	Sullivan	Wabash	city of Merom
Tell City	Perry	Ohio River	city of Tell City
Troy	Perry	Ohio River	city of Troy
Dogtown Ferry	Posey	Wabash River	8 miles northwest of Mt. Vernon
New Harmony	Posey	Wabash River	city of New Harmony
Azalia Bridge	Bartholomew	East Fork-White River	Azalia Bridge
Columbus	Bartholomew	East Fork-White River	city of Columbus
Mill Rice Park	Bartholomew	East Fork-White River	city of Columbus
Lowell Bridge	Bartholomew	Driftwood River	south of New Bridge
Laughery Creek	Dearborn	Laughery Creek	Old Ford Road
Elnora	Daviess	West Fork-White River	5 miles northwest of Elnora
Portersville Bridge	Daviess	East Fork-White River	1 mile northeast of Portersville
Worthington	Greene	West Fork-White River	2 miles east of Washington Road

Appendix

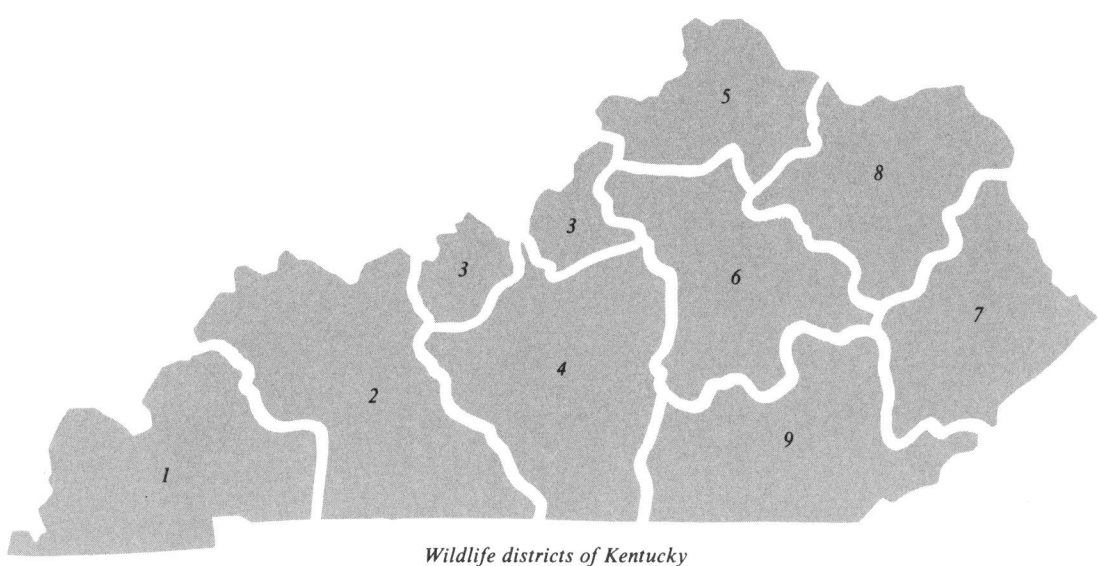

Wildlife districts of Kentucky

Kentucky Fish and Wildlife Resources Commission

All hunting and fishing in Kentucky, all game management, fisheries, and law enforcement connected with fishing and hunting are administered by the Kentucky Fish and Wildlife Commission through the Department of Fish and Wildlife Resources.

The commission is made up of one representative from each of the nine wildlife districts. Sportsmen in each district choose five nominees for the post, and the governor of the Commonwealth names one of the five to serve on the commission.

The commission is financed by the sale of hunting and fishing licenses and an annual allotment from the federal government as the state's share of excise taxes on sporting guns, ammunition, fishing rods, reels, boxes, and related supplies.

Suggested individuals to call if information is desired on the workings of the commission are Dr. Robert Webb of Grayson, Joe Fay Britt of Madisonville, and Dr. James Salato of Columbia.

Kentucky Department of Fish and Wildlife Resources

The Department of Fish and Wildlife Resources is building a new headquarters building on the Game Farm, Frankfort. Hunters or fishermen who have any questions should call the appropriate office at the following numbers:

Commissioner ....Carl E. Kays
Phone 564-3400

Assistant Commissioner .... Don McCormick
Phone 564-3400

Game Management
Director ....Joe Bruna
Assistant Director ....Jim S. Durell
Assistant Director ....Bill Graves
Phone 564-4406

Fisheries
Director ....Charles C. Bowers, Jr.
Assistant Director ....Pete Pfeiffer
Assistant Director ....Jim Charles
Phone 564-3596

Law Enforcement
Director ....R. W. Garrison
Phone 564-3176

Engineering
Director ....Don Hayes
Phone 564-4762

Fiscal Control
Director ....Harold Wallace
Phone 564-4224

Public Relations
Director ....Hope D. Carleton
Assistant Director ....Martha Jane Harrod
Phone 564-4336

Conservation Education
Director ....Bill Bell
Assistant Director ....Kelly Hubbard
Phone 564-4762

Regional Directors
David Loveless ....Benton
Wayne Riley ....Bowling Green
Hugh Crump ....Louisville
Kenneth Merideth ....Bonnieville
Paul Oliver ....Dry Ridge
George Roberts ....Lexington
Tommy Cantrell ....Van Lear
James R. Lyons ....Frenchburg
William H. Buchanan ....Barbourville

(All telephone numbers are area code 502.)

Carl E. Kays, Commissioner, Kentucky Department of Fish and Wildlife Resources

The League of Kentucky Sportsmen

The League of Kentucky Sportsmen has a membership of 30,000 or more and is the legislative watchdog for all sportsmen in the state. It is governed by a president, secretary/treasurer, and nine directors representing the league's nine districts.

While the officers and directors change regularly, there always will be several present and past officers ready to answer any questions. Among them are Al Blum of Murray, Redmon Payne of Franklin, Roy Haddix of Lexington, and Joe Coomes, Owensboro, 1978 president.

Each year the League honors one member as Sportsman of the Year for his outstanding work for conservation and sportsmanship. Those sportsmen who have received this honor are:

John Osborne	1978	Russell Springs
Willie Rienemann	1977	Fort Mitchell
Lemon Rogers	1976	Lebanon
Burnis Skipworth	1975	Glasgow
Reid Love	1974	Vanceberg
R. P. Countzler	1973	Greenville
Dr. James Salato	1972	Columbia
Warren C. Rosbottom	1971	Louisville
Louie B. Nunn	1970	Frankfort
Earl Ruby	1969	Louisville
Flenor M. Heath	1968	Somerset
Edward T. Breathitt	1967	Hopkinsville
Miller A. Welch	1966	Lexington
Dr. Robert C. Webb	1965	Grayson
Dr. C. L. Allen	1964	Martin
R. Lester Mullins	1963	Williamstown
Clyde W. Hubbard	1962	Louisville
Edgar W. Ernst	1961	Louisville
Dr. F. R. Scroggin	1960	Dry Ridge
Fred Nunn	1959	Emdonton
Dr. Joe Hill	1958	Lebanon
John E. Murphy	1957	Covington
Arthur S. Curtis	1956	West Paducah
J. C. Poyner	1955	Lewisburg
J. M. Smith	1954	Franklin
Lawrence W. Weatherby	1953	Frankfort
Dennie Gooch	1952	Somerset
Burt L. Monroe	1951	Anchorage
Al Blum	1950	Murray

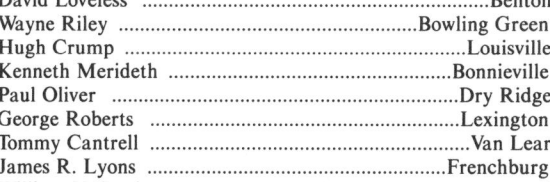

Al Blum, president emeritus of the League of Kentucky Sportsmen.

Open Season

Because of constant changes in length of our hunting seasons, we can list only the usual starting times.

The squirrel season usually opens on the third Saturday in August, the dove season on September 1, and the rabbit, quail and grouse seasons on the third Thursday in November.

Kentucky Game and Fish Licenses

License	1978 Res.	1978 Non-Res.	1979 Res.	1979 Non-Res.
Statewide fishing	$ 5.00	$10.00	$ 6.50	$12.00
Combined hunting and fishing	9.00		12.00	
Non-resident hunting		27.50		35.00
Non-resident fishing		10.00		14.00
Non-resident 15-day fishing		4.00		5.50
Non-resident 3-day fishing		2.50		4.00
Non-resident 3-day small game		10.00		12.50
Trout Stamp	2.25		3.00	
Ohio River Fishing (Residents of Indiana, Ohio and Illinois only)		5.00		6.50

All persons are required to procure the proper license to fish ponds, lakes, and streams except persons 16 years of age or under and persons 65 years of age or older. In addition, a resident of Kentucky who owns Kentucky farmland, his wife, and dependent children may take fish from waters on his land without a license. A tenant and his family also may fish from Kentucky ponds located on farms on which they work.

Kentucky Bag Limits

Although bag limits are subject to annual change by the Department of Fish and Wildlife Resources, these bag limits were enforced during the 1978 season.

Species	Daily Bag Limit	Possession Limit
Squirrel	6	12
Rabbit	6	12
Quail	10	20
Grouse	4	8
Deer	1	1
Doves	12	24
Woodcock	5	10
Geese	5	5
Ducks	point system	point system
Frogs	15	30
Raccoon		
Night		
Training Season	none may be taken	none may be taken
Shake-out Season	1 per hunter; 3 per party	
Gun Season	1 per hunter; 3 per party	
Opossum		
Night		
Training Season	none may be taken	none may be taken
Shake-out Season	no limit	
Gun Season	no limit	

Kentucky Fish Creel and Size Limits

Species	Daily Limit	Poss. Limit	Size Limit
Black bass	10	20	12"
Rockbass	15	30	none
Walleye	10	20	15"
Sauger	10	20	none
Muskellunge	5	10	30"
Northern Pike	5	10	none
Chain pickerel	5	10	none
White or yellow bass	60	60	none
Rockfish	5	5	15"
Croppie	60	60	none
Trout	8	8	none
Frogs	15	30	none

Fish are measured from the longest jaw to the longest tail fin. Fish that are below the keeper size must be returned immediately to the water in the best possible physical condition.

Because limits are subject to annual change, the angler should check current limits each season.

Kentucky Public Hunting Areas

There are 46 public hunting areas that are owned by various agencies of the state and federal government and two that are privately owned. This guide is designed to give specific directions to these places to hunt, most of which are not shown on standard highway maps.

Although statewide hunting regulations generally apply, the hunter should check for special regulations through the Department of Public Relations, Department of Fish and Wildlife Resources, Frankfort, Kentucky 40601.

The Department of Fish and Wildlife Resources, which prepared this guide to Kentucky's public hunting areas, and other agencies, carry out extensive wildlife management practices on many of the areas listed. Still, because of heavy hunting pressure, public hunting areas may be inferior to good privately owned lands. So while public hunting areas are useful to hunters who do not have access to suitable private land, hunters should look first to private lands, always remembering to secure permission from the landowner before hunting.

Eastern Kentucky

Beaver Creek (15,000 acres): McCreary and Pulaski counties, one mile north of Greenwood off U.S. 27 to Bauer A Road; gravel rough through center.

Beech Creek (1,260 acres): Clay County, 4.5 miles northeast of Manchester on Beech Creek and Littleton Roads; no roads within area.

Buckhorn Lake (2,580 acres): Portions of lake shoreline, Perry County, Ky. 15 and Ky. 28 west from Hazard, Ky. 257 north from Hyden; two old roads follow lake shore.

Cranks Creek (1,288 acres): Harlan County, 15 miles southeast of Harlan on Stone Mountain Road (off U.S. 421); jeep trail through area.

Dale Hollow (3,000 acres): Cumberland and Clinton counties, along shoreline of Dale Hollow Lake; access by several state and county roads and by boat.

Daniel Boone National Forest (618,341 acres): From Tennessee line in McCreary County north to Fleming and Lewis counties. Many U.S., state, and county roads lead into and cross area; also Forest Service roads and marked hiking trails in many sections.

Dewey Lake (8,650 acres): Portions of lake shoreline, Floyd County, six miles east of Prstonsburg on Ky. 194.

Fishtrap Lake (10,000 acres): Portions of lake shoreline, Pike County, south of Pikeville on U.S. 460, Ky. 1789 to dam area, Ky. 1499 to upper end of lake.

Grayson Lake (7,350 acres): Portions of lake shoreline, Carter and Elliott counties, seven miles south of Grayson, can be reached by Ky. 7, Ky. 409, Ky. 1496, and by boat.

Jefferson National Forest (961 acres): Two portions extend into Kentucky—845 acres in Letcher County on Ky. 932 and 116 acres in Pike County, which can be reached by trail by Vanover Hollow from Ky. 197.

Kentenia State Forest (3,624 acres): Harlan County, take U.S. 421, 3.5 miles north from intersection with U.S. 119 to trail 1679 (Little Shepherd Trail) which runs through center of area.

Kentucky Ridge State Forest (11,600 acres): Bell County, five miles southwest of Pineville on Ky. 190; fire trails provide limited access to interior of area.

Mead Forest (6,600 acres): Lewis County, 15 miles south of Vanceburg, reached by gravel roads off either Ky. 377 or Ky. 1068; dirt road through area passable by car in dry weather.

Olympia State Forest (780 acres): Bath County, reached by unimproved road southeast from Olympia Springs (between Olympia and Sudith on Ky. 36).

Pine Mountain (5,018 acres): Letcher County, take Little Shepherd Trail, five miles southwest of Whitesburg off U.S. 119, travel 10 miles west to Letcher-Harlan County line.

Pioneer Weapons Hunting Area (7,300 acres): Bath and Menifee counties, five miles south of Salt Lick, reached by Forest Service Road 129 or by boat on Cave Run Lake; access to center of area by Forest Service Road 918 (Tater Knob Road).

Sterns (10,000 acres): McCreary County, west from Stearns on U.S. 92 then south on Rock Creek Road to either Koger Hollow Road or Peters Mountain Road.

Tygarts State Forest (800 acres): Carter County, west of and adjacent to Carter Caves State Park off Ky. 182; county road on west edge of area; also accessible by short hike from state park.

Central Kentucky

Barren Lake (5,200 acres): Barren and Allen counties, access from U.S. 31E and Ky. 87, Ky. 98, Ky. 100, and Ky. 252; also access by lake.

Central Kentucky (1,323 acres): Madison County, nine miles southeast of Richmond, from U.S. 421 take Bearwallon Road at Kingston; gravel road through center.

Curtis Gates Lloyd (1,179 acres): Grant County, one-half mile southeast of Crittenden; dirt roads provide access to all portions.

Fort Knox (80,000 acres): Hardin and Bullitt counties, 30 miles south of Louisville on U.S. 31W, take U.S. 60 to Grahampton Outdoor Recreational Center, where all users of the area must check in at Hunt Control Headquarters, Building 9210.

Glen Dean (284 acres): Breckinridge County, approximately 3.5 miles south of Glen Dean on Glen Dean Road and Rock Lick Creek.

Green River (14,625 acres): Taylor and Adair counties, 10 miles south of Campbellsville along shoreline of Green River Lake.

John A. Kleber (1,088 acres): Owen County, on Ky. 368 (Cedar Road) between U.S. 127 and Ky. 227.

Knob State Forest (4,000 acres): Nelson County, on Ky. 733 off U.S. 62 between Bardstown and Elizabethtown.

Lake Cumberland (23,000 acres): Along shoreline of Lake Cumberland in Pulaski, Russell, Wayne, and Clinton counties; numerous access points.

Mullins (267 acres): Kenton County, one mile north of Crittenden Bordering I-75; access to all portions by dirt roads.

Nolin Lake (6,500 acres): Portions of lake shoreline, Grayson, Edmonson, and Hart counties; can be reached by Ky. 88, Ky. 1214, Ky. 694, and Ky. 728 with many secondary roads leading to within a short distance of lake.

Rough River (2,999 acres): Portions of lake shoreline, Breckinridge and Grayson counties; access by Ky. 737, Ky. 259, Ky. 108, and Ky. 79, and by boat.

Twin Eagle (166 acres): Owen County, four miles northeast of Perry Park on Ky. 355; adequate roads and trails within area.

Yellowbank (4,055 acres): Breckinridge County, 40 miles north of Hardinsburg on Ky. 259, near Ohio River and Meade County line.

Western Kentucky

Ballard County (8,373 acres): Ballard County, 35 miles west of Paducah; from U.S. 60 take Ky. 358 at LaCenter, turn left on Ky. 1105 for 3.8 miles then right on Ky. 473 to Headquarters Building; several roads within area.

Lake Barkley (2,400 acres): Trigg, Lyon, and Livingston counties; public lands consist primarily of islands in Barkley Lake.

Fort Campbell (34,000 acres): Christian and Trigg counties, 15 miles south of Hopkinsville on U.S. 41A.

L. B. Davison (150 acres): Ohio County, between Dundee and Hartford on Davidson State Road (off Ky. 878).

Higginson-Henry (5,420 acres): Union County, two miles east of Morganfield on Ky. 56.

Jones-Keeney (1,604 acres): Caldwell County, between Princeton and Dawson Springs on U.S. 62.

Kentucky Lake (3,274 acres): Calloway, Marshall, and Lyon counties. Public areas consist of mudflats, islands, and lowlands at back of bays and a narrow strip along much of lake shoreline.

Land Between the Lakes (100,000 acres): Trigg and Lyon counties, between Kentucky Lake and Lake Barkley; access by Ky. 453 (The Trace) and Ky. 80; many secondary roads and trails within area.

Peal (1,821 acres): Ballard County. Tract No. One located four miles west of Barlow on Ky. 118; Tract No. Two located one mile west of Wickliffe on U.S. 60.

Pennyrile Forest (15,200 acres): Christian County, eight miles south of Dawson Springs; many roads and trails within area, some paved.

Reelfoot Lake (2,040 acres): Fulton County, on Ky. 94 west of Hickman; adequate trails within area.

Sloughs (3,016 acres): Henderson County. This area composed of three separate units: Sauerheber Refuge, 5.5 miles northwest of Geneva on Ky. 268; Jenny Hole, turn left off Ky. 136 one-half mile northwest of Smith Mills onto Burbank Road, follow signs from junction with Gray-Aldridge Road; Ash Flats, Mason Landing Road northeast from Hebbardsville, follow signs to area.

Tradewater (728 acres): Hopkins County, one mile south of Dawson Springs on Ky. 109; access points on both sides of road one-half mile south of Tradewater River Bridge.

West Kentucky (6,896 acres): McCracken County, 12 miles west of Paducah on Ky. 358; 50 miles of roads within area.

West Kentucky 4-H Camp (125 acres): Hopkins County, one mile north of Dawson Springs off Ky. 109.

Winford (237 acres): Carlisle County, six miles northwest of Bardwell on U.S. 62.

Commercial Waterfowl Hunting Preserves *As of July, 1978*

Kirby Davenport, Wickliffe, 28 or more hunters. (335-3968)

Larry Drummond, Barlow, 36 or more hunters. (665-5877)

Dale Perry (Sandridge), LaCenter, 15 hunters. (502) 224-2249

William F. Agnew, Barlow, 30 hunters. (334-3242)

Joe W. Carroll (Ashford's), LaCenter, 24 to 26 hunters. (442-6678)

Harvey J. Rice, Barlow, 32 hunters. (334-3997)

Archie Renfrow, LaCenter, eight hunters. (665-5951)

Hugh Renfrow, Barlow, 28 hunters. (334-3990)

Jerry Renfrow, Barlow, 20 hunters. (334-3990)

Harry Renfrow, Barlow, 20 hunters. (334-3990)

Ivan Renfrow, Barlow, 28 hunters. (334-3995)

Tommy Wilson, Oscar, 15 hunters. (224-2249)

Neal Piper, Barlow, 20 hunters. (665-5286)

Martin Flournoy, Barlow, 20 hunters. (224-2488)

Arthur Azar, Wickliffe, 12 hunters. (443-4594)

Joe Frazier, Wickliffe, 16 hunters. (335-3958)

*All telephone numbers are in area code 502.

Kentucky Shooting Preserves *as of July, 1978*

Kentucky hunters were blessed with 10 commercial hunting preserves where they may sharpen their shooting eye for the seasons to follow. Most of the preserves offer quail, some offer quail and pheasants, and some have quail, pheasants, and chukars.

The chukar partridge is a relatively new game bird in America, having been brought here from Asia. It is dove-colored with dark bar markings along the sides. Its legs and feet are red. The chukar grows to about the size of a spring chicken and is a marvelous table delicacy.

The pheasant also came from Asia. The highly colorful male has a green-black head and a white ring around its neck, giving it the name ring-necked pheasant. The female is gray-white-brown and has a speckled appearance. The adult pheasant will weigh two pounds or more. Because of its extremely long tail, the cock will look much bigger when he is in flight. When properly cooked, pheasant is a delight.

Neither bird can be raised in the wild in Kentucky, but they both are popular at the commercial hunting preserves. The pheasant is inclined to run, which makes a point sometimes impossible. On the other hand, the chukar will sit so tight you may have to kick him out to get him in the air.

The charges at the shooting preserves vary, but most offer healthy, full-grown birds. Some of the preserves provide dogs and others suggest that you bring your own dog and let him improve while you are doing the same.

Here are the preserves and their owners, as of January, 1978:

RED HILL, Owensboro. Mary Moran. 1-502-275-4764. Pheasant $5 each. Quail 10 for $23. Dogs and guides, if desired.

ROBERTSON COUNTY, Brooksville. Glen Hester. 1-606-724-5655. Pheasants 3 for $30. Chukars 5 for $30. Quail 8 for $30. Dogs and guides if desired.

WOODFORD COUNTY, Versailles. Jesse Jones. 1-606-873-8834. Pheasants $6, quail $3. Dogs and guides if desired.

SPORTSMEN'S PARADISE, Wurtland. Doyle Bonzo. 1-606-836-5434. Pheasants $7, Chukars $4, Quail $2.50. Dogs and guides if desired.

CLINTON. Willis R. Hilliard, Clinton. 1-502-653-6275. Pheasants $6, Chukars $4, quail $2.50, plus $10 gun charge. Guide goes with. Dogs available if desired.

LAKE MALONE, Dunmor. Kermit Driskill. 1-502-755-4739. Pheasants 3 for $20, quail 8 for $20. Guide if desired.

WHISTLING QUAIL, Bagdad. Fred Duncan. 1-747-8786. Chukars $4, quail $2, plus $5 gun charge. Guide available.

MCCLELLAN'S, Central City. Charles McClellan. 1-502-338-6645. Quail 12 for $25. No dogs or guide.

ARMSTRONG'S, Shelbyville. Murray Armstrong. Pheasants 3 for $35. Quail 6 for $35. Dogs and guides available.

FLEMING COUNTY, Flemingsburg. Ben Arnold. Quail $3. Dogs and guides available.

Prices subject to change.

Kentucky Deer Hunting Regulations

Certain Public hunting areas have special regulations in regards to deer hunting, and sportsmen should be aware of these restrictions before the opening of the season.

Area and Location	Advance Registration	Miscellaneous
West Kentucky Wildlife Management Area (McCracken County)	None required but all hunters must check in and out at check station on area.	All tracts designated by the letter "A" are closed to hunting.
Land Between the Lakes (Trigg and Lyon counties)	Required for gunhunts. Write Land Between the Lakes, Golden Pond, Kentucky, 42231 for application blanks and complete regulations.	This area has special regulations for hunting deer and most other species. Write for complete information.
Pioneer Weapons Area (Bath and Menifee counties)	None required.	Muzzle-loading shotguns must be loaded with No. Two or larger buckshot. Crossbows may be used.
Fort Campbell Military Reservation (Christian and Trigg counties)	Required for daily hunts and for all weekends. Telephone (502) 798- 3293 or 798-2413 for further information or for reservations.	No hunting on Monday or Tuesday unless holiday, in which case hunting will be allowed. Bows must be at least 35 pounds pull. Broadhead points must be between ½ and ⅞ inches for single or double head blades or not more than three inches in circumference for three or more blades. Minimum weight for all points is 100 grains.
Fort Knox (Hardin, Bullitt, and Meade counties)	Required for both bow and gun hunts. Separate application required for each hunt.	Write Fort Knox Conservation and Beautification Committee, P.O. Box 1052, Fort Knox, Kentucky 40121.
Higginson—Henry Wildlife Management Area (Union County)	Required for gun hunt. Mail request for application to: Manager Higginson-Henry Wildlife Management Area, Route 5, Morganfield, Kentucky 42437.	All hunters must check in and out daily at check station. Permits to those successful in drawing for gun hunt will be mailed. Unsuccessful applications will not be notified.
Bluegrass Army Depot (Madison County)	Required for all hunts. Write: Chairman, Wildlife Management Subcommittee, Building S-14, Lexington Bluegrass Army Depot, Lexington, Kentucky 40507 for details.	Postcard application must include: name and address of hunter (one per card), age, and telephone number. More than one card from an individual will disqualify that applicant. A $10 fee will be charged, payable only after hunter is notified of his selection and specific hunting date.
Ballard County Wildlife Management Area (Ballard County)	Advance registration is required.	Mailing address is Ballard County Wildlife Management Area, Rt. 1, Box 100, LaCenter, Ky. 42056

Speciality Sportsmen's Clubs in Kentucky

There is a variety of specialty clubs — coon clubs, fox hunting clubs, among others — that are associated with the League of Kentucky Sportsmen. Those that were recognized by the League as of May, 1978, and the persons who can be contacted for more information are:

Coon Clubs

Pennyrile—Bill Ford, Pilot Rock Road, Hopkinsville, 42240.
Hickman County—Neil Mathis, Clinton, 42031.
Burna—Ralph Harein, Burna, 42078.
Twin Lakes—Grant Black, Hardin, 42048.
Trigg County—Earl Thomas, Cadiz, 42211.
Allen County—Tom Shelton, Adolphus, 42120.
Daviess County—Ronald Evans, Calhoun, 42327.
Henderson—William Garrett, Old Green River Road, Henderson, 42420.
Hopkins County—Phillip Nash, Lewisburg, 42256.
Muhlenberg County—Sherman Harris, Central City, 42330.
Ohio County—Remus Hudson, Hartford, 42347.
Uniontown—Rick Moore, Waverly, 42462.
Warren County—James Montgomery, Rockfield, 42274.
Bullitt County—Larry Hardin, Route 4, Taylorsville, 40071.
Shelby County—David Steppe, 4413 Brookhaven Avenue, Louisville, 40220.
Spencer County—Bonnie Bryant, Mt. Eden, 40046.
Dry Fork—Patricia Gentry, Route 6, Glasgow, 42141.
North Central—Mike Gentry, Radcliffe, 40141.
Lincoln Trail—Lewis Gugginsburg, New Haven, 40051.
Monroe County—Nelda Thomas, Mt. Herman, 42157.
Metcalfe County—Tony Perkins, Route 2, Edmonton, 42129.
Jackson County—Pershing Hayes, Tyner, 40486.
Harlan County—Tipton Baker, Cawood, 40815.
Knox County—Ernest Tuggle Jr., Heidrick, 40949.
Laurel County—Kenneth Gray, Route 6, London, 41741.
Owsley County—Earl McIntosh, Booneville, 41314.
Long Hollow—W.F. Adams, Route 3, Somerset, 42501.
Lake Cumberland—Obie Smith, Monticello, 42633.
Cumberland River—Lester Shelley, Route 3, Williamsburg, 40769.

Foxhunting Clubs

Kentucky State Foxhunters Association—Jimmy Richardson, Owingsville, 40360, or Virginia Ann Rose, 3473, Milam Lane, Lexington, 40507.
Green River Foxhunters—Jerry Snell, Caneyville, 42721, or Lareca Fleenor, Hartford, 42347.
Twin Lakes Foxhunters—Coy Meredith, Anneta, 42710.
Lincoln Foxhunters—Ralph Chelf, Magnolia, 42765.
Pendleton and Grant County Foxhunters—Herb Huffman, Berry, 41003.
Blue Ribbon Foxhunters—Barbara Stephens, Catlettsburg, 41129.
Beauty Ridge Foxhunters—Vernon Ensor, South Shore, 41175.
Double Gate Foxhunters—Virgil Gibbs, Mount Sterling, 40353.
Gateway Foxhunters—George Williams, Mount Sterling, 40353.
Clay County Foxhunters—Stanley Jackson, Manchester, 40962.
Jackson County Foxhunters—Buford Combs, Maulden, 40449.
Knox County Foxhunters—Ernest Tuggle Jr., Heidrick, 40949.
Kentucky and Tennessee Foxhunters—John Kidd, Revelo, 42638.
Eastern Kentucky Foxhunting Ass'n—Neal Million, Richmond.
Central Kentucky Foxhunting Ass'n—Parley Richardson, Owensville.
Western Kentucky Foxhunters Ass'n—James Utterback, Madisonville.
Nat'l Trigg Foxhunters Ass'n—Kenneth Love, Glasgow.
Tri-State Foxhunters Ass'n—Otis Noe, Rising Sun, Ind.
Kentucky-Tennessee Foxhunters Ass'n—Leamon Kidd, Pine Knot.

Kentucky Chapter National Wild Turkey Federation

Contact David Hale, Gracey, 42232, or Robert Smith, Route 4, Cadiz, 42211.
Washington County—Watson Shewmaker, Route 3, Springfield, 40069.
Campbell County—Carl Shell, Butler, 41006.
Sun Valley—Harlon Steffen, Alexandria, 41001.
Northern Kentucky—Mary Crase, Verona, 41092.
Harrison County—Larry Whitaker, Route 6, Paris, 40361.
Central Kentucky—Robert Feeback, 704 Byrd Avenue, Winchester, 40391.
Estill County—T.J. Brinegar, Route 1, Lancaster, 40444.
Dix River—Dale Lancaster, Route 3, Stanford, 40484.
Fishing Creek—Earlin Cress, Eubank, 42567.
Madison County—Virgil Isaacs, 212 Irvine View, Richmond, 40475.
Silver Creek—Ed Hembree, Berea, 40403.
Blue Grass—James Pridemore, 1233 Keeneland Court, Lexington, 40507.
Breathitt County—Walter Baker, Houston, 41336.
Elliott County—Willard Knipp, Webbville, 41180.
Lawrence County—Enoch O'Brien, Route 2, Catlettsburg, 41129.
Boone Fork—Steve Sparks, McRoberts, 41835.
Cumberland Mountain—Roy Lee McCarty, Ashcamp, 41512.
Shelby Valley—Dempsey Smallwood, Myra, 41549.
Bath County—Edith Bradley, Route 1, Owingsville, 40360.
Eastern Kentucky—Isaac Moore, Catlettsburg, 41129.
Carter County—Phillip Bush, Grayson, 41143.
Northeastern Kentucky—Lennon Spears, Flatwoods, 41139.
Montgomery County—Joe Parker, Route 1, Jeffersonville, Indiana 47130.
Clay County—Stanley Jackson, Manchester, 41062.

Kentucky Falconers Association

Contact Denny Wynn, 5605 Mt. Washington Road, Louisville, 40229.

Bowhunters Clubs

Kentucky Bowhunters Association—Marvin Almon, executive secretary, 1429 Longfield Avenue, Louisville, 40215.
Balocky Bow Club—Wayne Sanders, Kevil, 42053.
Chief Paduke Bow Club—Bunny Cooper, 329 S. 21st St., Paducah, 42001.
Midway Archery—Debbie Mitchell, Princeton, 42445.
Christian County Archery—Sharon Durham, 117 Adams, Hopkinsville, 42240.
Hardin Bowhunters—Kathy Darnell, Benton, 42025.
Indian Hill Archery—T.J. O'Hearn, 2456 Mayfair, Owensboro, 42301.
Fallow Field Archery—Glenda Mays, Earlington, 42410.
Franklin-Simpson Archery—Wayne Mayhew, Franklin, 42134.
Chickasaw Archery—Sue Hayden, 6900 Cozy Court, Louisville, 40228.
Pleasant Valley Archery—Linda Lee Hill, Providence, 42450.
Iroquois Bowhunters—Brenda Young, 3662 Dena Road, Louisville, 40216.
Jefferson County Indian Bowhunters—Dennis Spaulding, 6208 Upper Hunters Trace, Louisville, 40216.
Waverly Archers—William E. Painter, 2325 Manchester Road, Louisville, 40205.
Wilderness Bowhunters—Don Cornett, Route 3, Crestwood, 40014.
Green River Archery—Donald Neat, 104 Floyd, Campbellsville, 42718.
Marion County Bowhunters—Jackie Crouch, Lebanon, 40033.
Boone County Bowhunters—Ted Perkinson, 68 Blue Ridge Drive, Fort Mitchell, 41017.
Buck Skin Bowhunters—Everett Harrison, Alexandria, 41001.
Campbell County Bowhunters—Everett Harrison, Alexandria, 41001.
Pioneer Archery—Alma Jones, 15 Harris Drive, Winchester, 40391.
Kentucky Bowhunters, Madison Unit—Darrell Slone, Berea, 40403.
Powell County Archery—Rex Hall, Clay City, 40312.
Greenbo Archery—Carl Delaney, Catlettsburg, 41129.
Trophy Hunters Archery—Arvil Arrington, Grayson, 41143.
Kyowva Valley Bowhunters—Ed Williams, Flatwoods, 41139.

Kentucky Silver Muskie Club

Contact Ed Thompson, WAVE TV and Radio, Floyd and Broadway, Louisville, 40202.

Kentucky Brittany Club

Contact James O'Brien, 805 English Station Road, Anchorage, 40223.

Eastern Kentucky Deer Club

Contact Ronald Combs, Hyden, 41749.

Pioneer Weapons Clubs

Hopewell Frontiersmen—Ed Ratcliff, Main Street, Millersburg, 41348.
Kentucky Rx Long Rifles—John Jayne, Morehead, 41351.

Beagle Clubs

Three Rivers—Charles Hook, 330 Pepper Lane, Paducah, 42001.
Trigg County—Tom Dixon, Route 3, Cadiz, 42211.
Owensboro—Ruth Henderson, Route 3, Owensboro, 42301.
Southwestern Kentucky—Lester Walker, 744 Greenlawn, Bowling Green, 42101.
Bluegrass—Fred Brohman, 909 Vine St., Louisville, 40204.
Shelbyville—Kenneth Moore, Route 7, Frankfort, 40601.
Rolling Fork—Robert J. Hill, 404 Trica, Elizabethtown, 42701.
Honey Bee—Marl Lucas, 114 Knollwood, Highland Heights, 41076.
Briar Hollow—Bill Herzog, 2313 Center, Covington, 41015.
Ohio Valley—Dave Trauth, 118 Ridgewood, Alexandria, 41001.
Elkhorn—Coffman Glass, Route 3, Georgetown, 40324.
Scenic—Waldo Tarter, Cains Store, 42520.

Field Trial Clubs

Calloway County Field Trial Club—Jerry Lancaster, Dexter, 40236.
Mayfield Field Trial Association—Guy Sullivan, Route 4, Mayfield, 4206.
West Kentucky Field Trial Club—Arthur Curtis, Route 2, West Paducah, 42086.
Green River Amateur Field Trial Club—John Green, Utica, 42376.
Central Kentucky Field Trial Club—Faye Racke, Alexandria, 41001.

Mid-Kentucky Kennel Club

Contact Amos Ennis, Route 2, Hodgenville, 42748.

Northern Kentucky Pointer and Setter Club

Contact Mrs. Robert Highland, Morning View, 41063.

Kentucky Trap and Skeet Clubs

When the seasons on quail, grouse, and rabbits open in November, hunters in increasing numbers flock to trap and skeet ranges throughout the state to sharpen their shooting eyes.

In Kentucky and Southern Indiana there are five trap ranges, seven skeet ranges, and one club with both trap and skeet. All are open to the public at virtually no cost other than for ammunition and targets. Jefferson Gun Club on Old South Park Road near Louisville is the club with both trap and skeet.

The trap clubs are:
Central Kentucky Gun Club, Berea. (606-986-4130)
Bowling Green Trap Club, Bowling Green. (502-842-4388)
Fern Creek Sportsman's Club, Fern Creek. (502-239-7100)
Evansville Gun Club, Evansville, Indiana. (812-867-3121)
Floyd Knobs Gun Club, Floyd Knobs, Indiana. (812-267-1346)

The skeet clubs are:
Ashland Gun Club, Ashland.
Boyd County Skeet Club, Ashland.
Calvert City Gun Club, Calvert City. (502-395-5676)
Chief Paduke Gun Club, Paducah. (502-488-3248)
Eagle Skeet Club, Fort Campbell. (502-798-7397)
Gold Vault Skeet Association, Fort Knox. (502-624-2952)
Jackson Purchase Gun Club, Murray. (502-489-2567)
Jefferson Gun Club, Louisville. (502-957-4661)

Kentucky Lakes

Many Kentuckians have changed from stream fishermen to lake anglers in the last two generations, due to the construction of 15 major impoundments. The U.S. Army Corps of Engineers has built 13 lakes, Tennessee Valley Authority has built Kentucky Lake, and Kentucky Utilities has built Lake Herrington.

These 15 man-made lakes, covering more than 190,000 acres, abound in largemouth, Kentucky, and smallmouth bass, white bass, bluegill, channel catfish, muskie, rockfish, and rainbow trout.

In addition to these major impoundments, there are 41 Kentucky public fishing lakes that have been stocked by the Division of Fisheries with bass, bluegill, and channel catfish. A few have even been stocked with rainbow trout.

The following is a rundown of the major lakes as prepared by the Department of Fish and Wildlife Resources:

Lake Barkley: Western Kentucky. 57,920 surface acres, with 45,600 in Kentucky and the remainder in Tennessee. 1,004 miles of shoreline, extending 118 miles from the dam on the lower Cumberland River. Fisheries similar to Kentucky Lake (to which it is connected by a canal) with good bass, croppie, bluegill, and white bass. Rather shallow, with a great deal of structure. Fair numbers of rockfish and catfish taken below the dam. Created in 1966 by Corps of Engineers.

Barren River Lake: Southcentral Kentucky. 10,050 surface acres; 140 miles of shoreline; 33 miles long. One of the best for largemouth black bass and croppie, also good for bluegill, white bass, and some walleye. Rockfish stocked 1974-75. Created in 1964 by a Corps dam on Barren River.

Buckhorn Lake: Eastern Kentucky. 1,200 surface acres of water; 65 miles of shoreline; 21 miles long. One of the best bass lakes. Also croppie, bluegill, and catfish. Created in 1960 by the Corps with the impounding of the Middle Fork of Kentucky River.

Cave Run Lake: Eastern Kentucky. 8,270 surface acres; 166 miles of shoreline; 48 miles long. Rapidly developing population of black bass, bluegill, croppie, and catfish and best bet for muskie. Created in 1973 when Licking River was impounded by the Corps. (Located immediately below the dam is the Department of Fish and Wildlife Resources' new Minor Clark Hatchery.)

Lake Cumberland: Southcentral Kentucky. 50,250 surface acres, the largest impoundment lying completely within Kentucky boundaries; 1,255 miles of shoreline extending 101 miles upstream from the dam on the Cumberland River. Good for largemouth black bass, white bass, and croppie. Fair trout fishing in the lake, excellent in the tailwaters where the 14-pound, six-ounce state record rainbow was taken in 1972. Other records: 21-pound, eight-ounce walleye, 1958; 72-pound spoonbill catfish, 1957; and sturgeon, 36 pounds, eight ounces, 1954. Impounded by the Corps in 1950.

Dale Hollow Lake: Southcentral Kentucky. 27,700 surface acres of water with 4,300 within Kentucky, the remainder in Tennessee; 61 miles long; 620 miles of shoreline. Good populations of both large and smallmouth bass, white bass, croppie, and bluegill. The world record smallmouth—11 pounds, 15 ounces—was taken out of Dale Hollow in 1955. Created in 1943 when Tennessee's Obey River was dammed by the Corps.

Dewey Lake: Eastern Kentucky. 1,150 surface acres of water; 52 miles of shoreline; extends 18.5 miles upstream from the dam on John's Creek. Good largemouth black bass, bluegill, croppie, and catfish. Some white bass. Muskie stocked in 1957. Impounded by the Corps in 1951.

Fishtrap Lake: Eastern Kentucky. 1,131 surface acres; shoreline, 43 miles; 16.5 miles long. White bass, croppie, and largemouth black bass. A Corps project, created in 1968 with impoundment of the Big Sandy River.

Grayson Lake: Eastern Kentucky. 1,500 surface acres; shoreline 60 miles; 22 miles long. Good population of largemouth black bass, croppie, and bluegill. A scenic mountain lake with interesting bank structure. Muskie and walleye have been stocked but the harvest so far is spotty. Created in 1968 by a Corps impoundment of Little Sandy River.

Green River Lake: Southcentral Kentucky. 8,360 surface acres; 147 miles of shoreline; length, 25 miles. Consistent good strings of fish, especially black bass, croppie, and bluegill. Created 1969 by Corps dam on Green River.

Lake Herrington: Central Kentucky. 1,860 surface acres of water; extends 35 miles upstream from the dam on Dix River; 165 miles of shoreline. Good population of white bass, largemouth black bass, croppie, and a good developing fishery for rockfish. The 44-pound, four-ounce state record rockfish was taken here in 1970. Created in the mid-1920s by KU.

Kentucky Lake: Western Kentucky. 158,300 surface acres of water, with 48,100 in Kentucky, the remainder in Tennessee; 184 miles long; 2,380 miles of shoreline. Best known for spring croppie run but also very good for largemouth black bass and white bass. Large population of sauger which are seldom fished for; rockfish and catfish below the dam on the Tennessee River. State record fish taken from the lake are: six-pound, one-ounce sauger, 1972; freshwater drum (white perch), 31 pounds, 1956; 100-pound blue catfish, from the tailwaters, 1970; and five-pound white bass, 1943, which ties with a five-pounder taken from Herrington in 1957. Created by TVA in 1944.

Laurel River Lake: Eastern Kentucky. 5,600 surface acres; shoreline, approximately 200 miles; length, 19.2 miles. Rapidly growing population of largemouth and smallmouth bass, croppie, walleye, and rainbow trout. The deepest lake in the state, and one of the more scenic ones, Laurel was created in 1973 by the Corps with a dam on Laurel River.

Nolin Lake: Westcentral Kentucky. 5,795 surface acres; 172 miles of shoreline; 39 miles long. Noted as good producer of bass, croppie, and bluegill, and white bass in spring. Created in 1963 by a Corps dam on Nolin River.

Rough River Lake: Westcentral Kentucky. 4,830 surface acres of water; some 220 miles of shoreline; 35 miles long. Good lake for bass, croppie, and white bass, especially in spring. One of the largest populations of walleye, ranging up to 26 inches in size, and little walleye fishing pressure. Created in 1961 with the impounding of Rough River by the Corps.

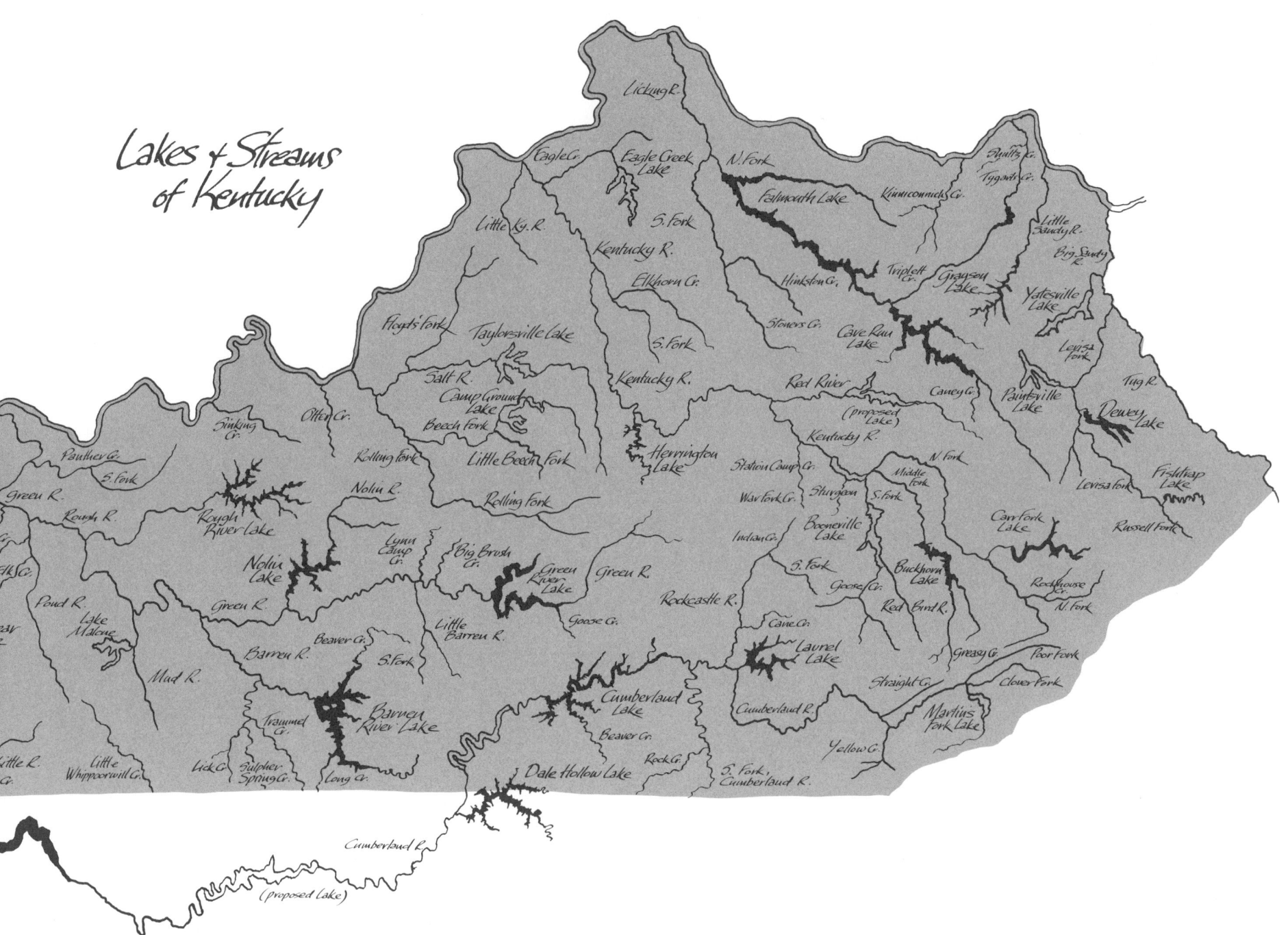

Lakes & Streams of Kentucky

The 42 Kentucky public fishing lakes that cover a total of 6,625 acres are:

Lake	(Acres)	County	Ownership	Nearest Town
Beaver	170	Nelson	Fish & Wildlife	Lawrenceburg
Bert Combs*	25	Clay	Fish & Wildlife	Manchester
Boltz	96	Grant	Fish & Wildlife	Dry Ridge
Bullock Pen	142	Grant	Fish & Wildlife	Crittenden
Carpenter	68	Daviess	Fish & Wildlife	Owensboro
Carter Caves	37	Carter	Fish & Wildlife	Olive Hill
Corinth	83	Grant	Fish & Wildlife	Corinth
Elmer Davis	140	Owen	Fish & Wildlife	Owenton
Game Farm Lakes	3 & 7	Franklin	Fish & Wildlife	Frankfort
Greenbo	192	Greenup	Fish & Wildlife	Ashland
Guist Creek	304	Shelby	Fish & Wildlife	Shelbyville
Kincaid	196	Pendleton	Fish & Wildlife	Falmouth
Kingfisher (New)	22	Daviess	Fish & Wildlife	Owensboro
Kingfisher (Old)	14	Daviess	Fish & Wildlife	Owensboro
Malone	692	Muhlenberg-Todd & Logan	Fish & Wildlife	Dunmor
Marion County	32	Marion	Fish & Wildlife	Lebanon
Martin County	5	Martin	Fish & Wildlife	Inez
McNeely	53	Jefferson	Fish & Wildlife	Louisville
Shanty Hollow	106	Warren	Fish & Wildlife	Bowling Green
Shelby	23	Ballard	Fish & Wildlife	La Center
Spurlington	33	Taylor	Fish & Wildlife	Campbellsville
Turner	50	Ballard	Fish & Wildlife	La Center
Washburn	26	Ohio	Fish & Wildlife	Hartford
Briggs	25	Logan	Fish & Wildlife	Russellville
Bardstown City	200	Nelson	Bardstown	Bardstown
Beshear	712	Caldwell-Christian	Fish & Wildlife (Operation deeded to city of Dawson Springs)	Dawson Springs
Campton	27	Wolfe	Campton	Campton
Chenoa	32	Bell	Parks Department	Pineville
Dennie Gooch	5	Pulaski	Pulaski County	Somerset
Fish Pond	45	Letcher	Letcher County	Jenkins
Herb Smith	260	Harlan	Harlan County	Harlan
Jericho	145	Henry	Little Ky. River	New Castle
Kingdom Come*	3	Harlan	Parks Department	Cumberland
Linville	370	Rockcastle	Mt. Vernon Water District	Mt. Vernon
Max Blyth	90	Christian	Hopkinsville	Hopkinsville
Mill Creek*	30	Wolfe	Parks Department	Slade
Pan Bowl	74	Breathitt	Finance Department	Jackson
Wilgreen	225	Madison	Madison County	Richmond
Williamstown	305	Grant	Williamstown	Williamstown
Willisburg	146	Washington	Willisburg	Willisburg
Woods Creek*	700	Laurel	Laurel County	London

*stocked with rainbow trout

Barren River Lake

to Haywood
to Glasgow
to Tracy

31·E
252

87
921
98

31·E

Beaver Creek ramp

Austin

Browns Ford ramp

Lucas

252

The Narrows ramp

87
State Park ramp

Austin ramp

255
Rocky Hill

to State route 80 & U.S. 68

Walnut Creek ramp

Maynard

671

Bailey Point ramp

517

31·E

Finney
State Park

Peninsula Site ramp

1855

98

Oak Forest

252
Cedar Springs

252

31·E

Barren River

1533

to Scottsville

to Scottsville

to Bowling Green 101 & I·65

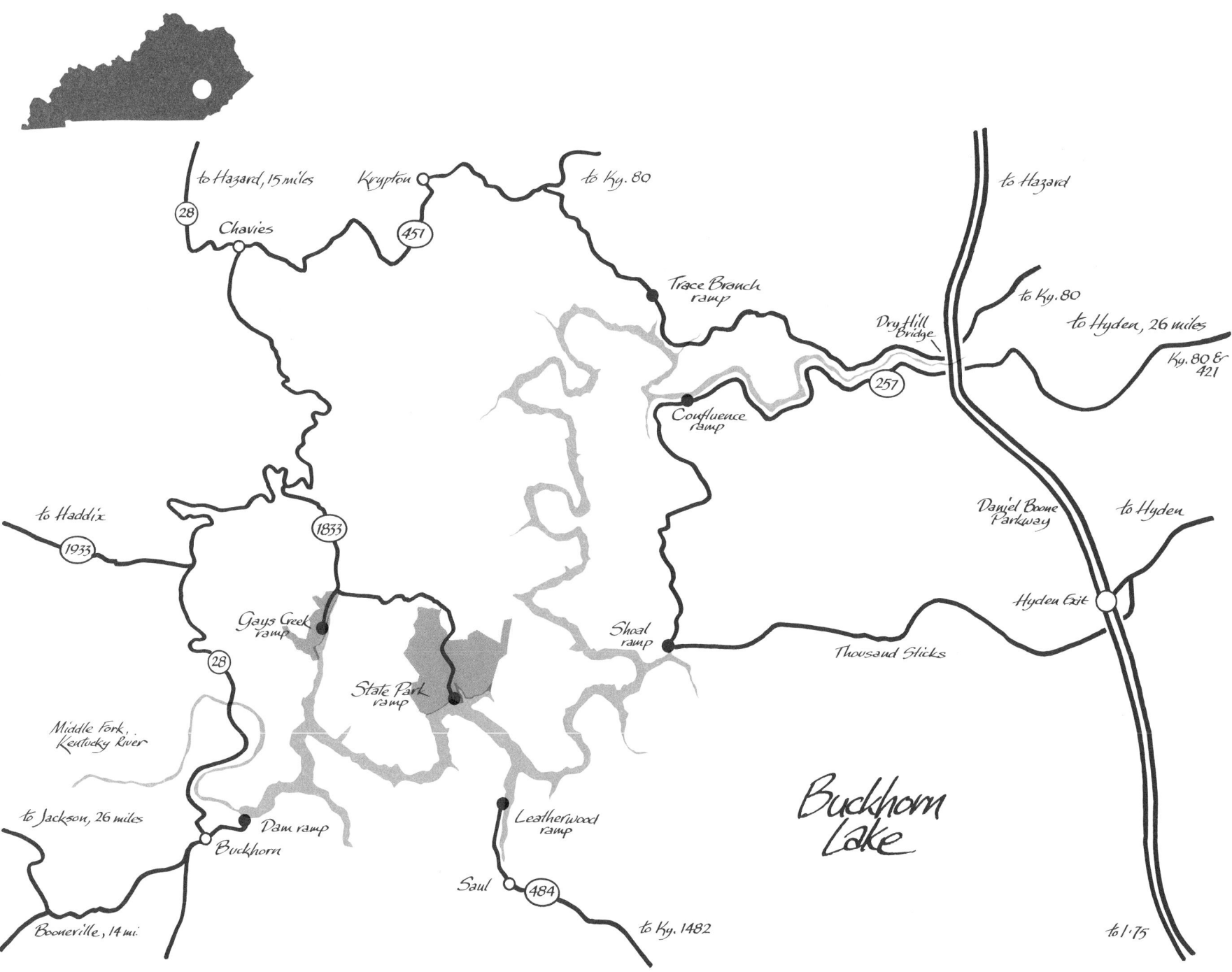

to Hazard, 15 miles

Krypton

to Ky. 80

28 Chavies

451

Trace Branch ramp

to Hazard

Dry Hill Bridge

to Ky. 80

to Hyden, 26 miles

257

Ky. 80 & 421

Confluence ramp

to Haddix

1933

1833

Daniel Boone Parkway

to Hyden

Gays Creek ramp

Shoal ramp

Hyden Exit

28

State Park ramp

Thousand Sticks

Middle Fork, Kentucky River

Buckhorn Lake

to Jackson, 26 miles

Dam ramp

Leatherwood ramp

Buckhorn

Booneville, 14 mi.

Saul

484

to Ky. 1482

to I-75

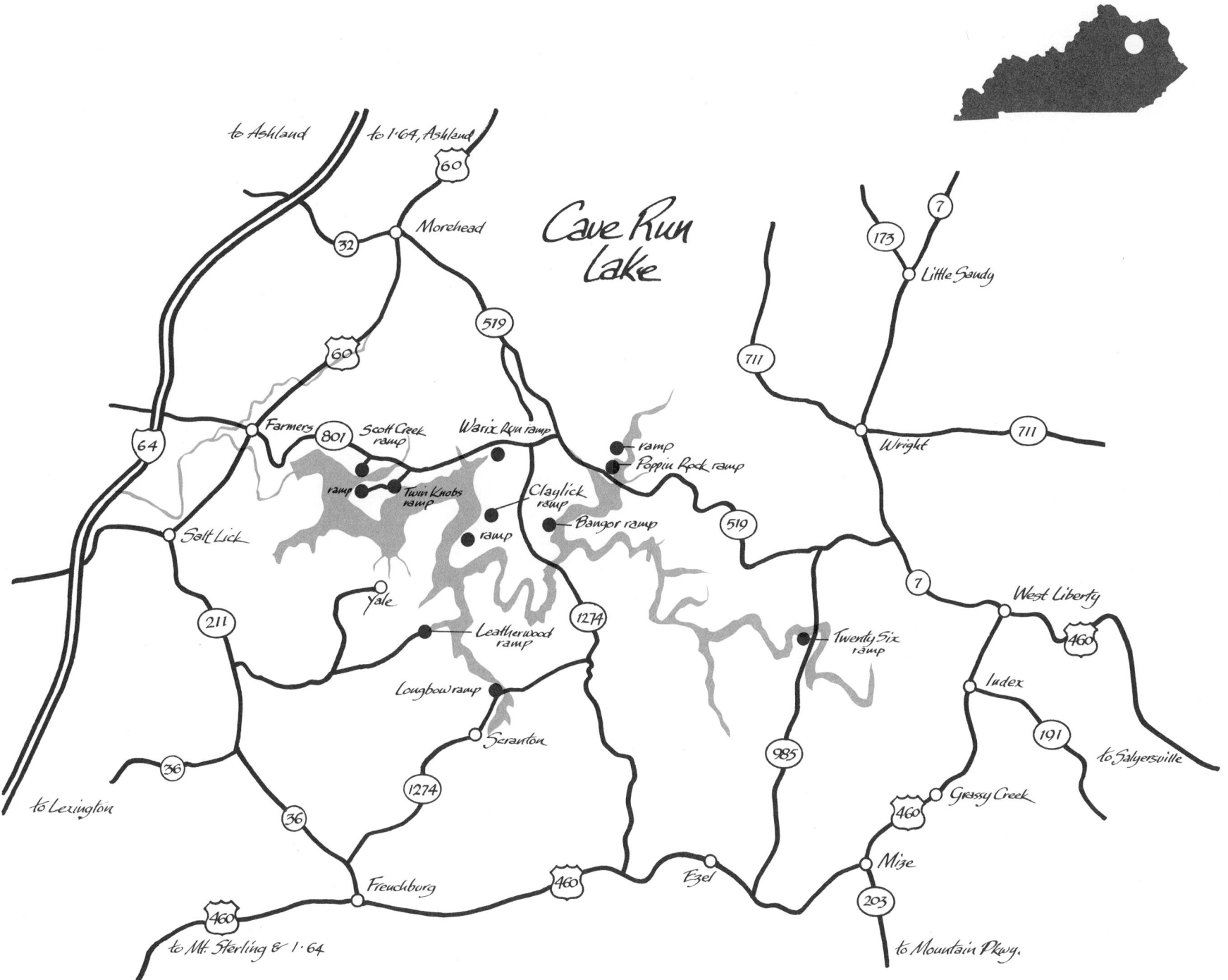

Cave Run Lake

to Ashland
to I·64, Ashland
60
32
Morehead
60
519
64
Farmers
801
Scott Creek ramp
Warix Run ramp
ramp
Poppin Rock ramp
Salt Lick
ramp
Twin Knobs ramp
Claylick ramp
Bangor ramp
519
211
Yale
ramp
Leatherwood ramp
1274
Longbow ramp
Scranton
36
1274
to Lexington
36
Frenchburg
460
to Mt. Sterling & I·64
460
Ezel
203
to Mountain Pkwy.
173
7
Little Sandy
711
Wright
711
West Liberty
7
460
Index
191
to Salyersville
Twenty Six ramp
985
460
Grassy Creek
Mize

149

Lake Cumberland

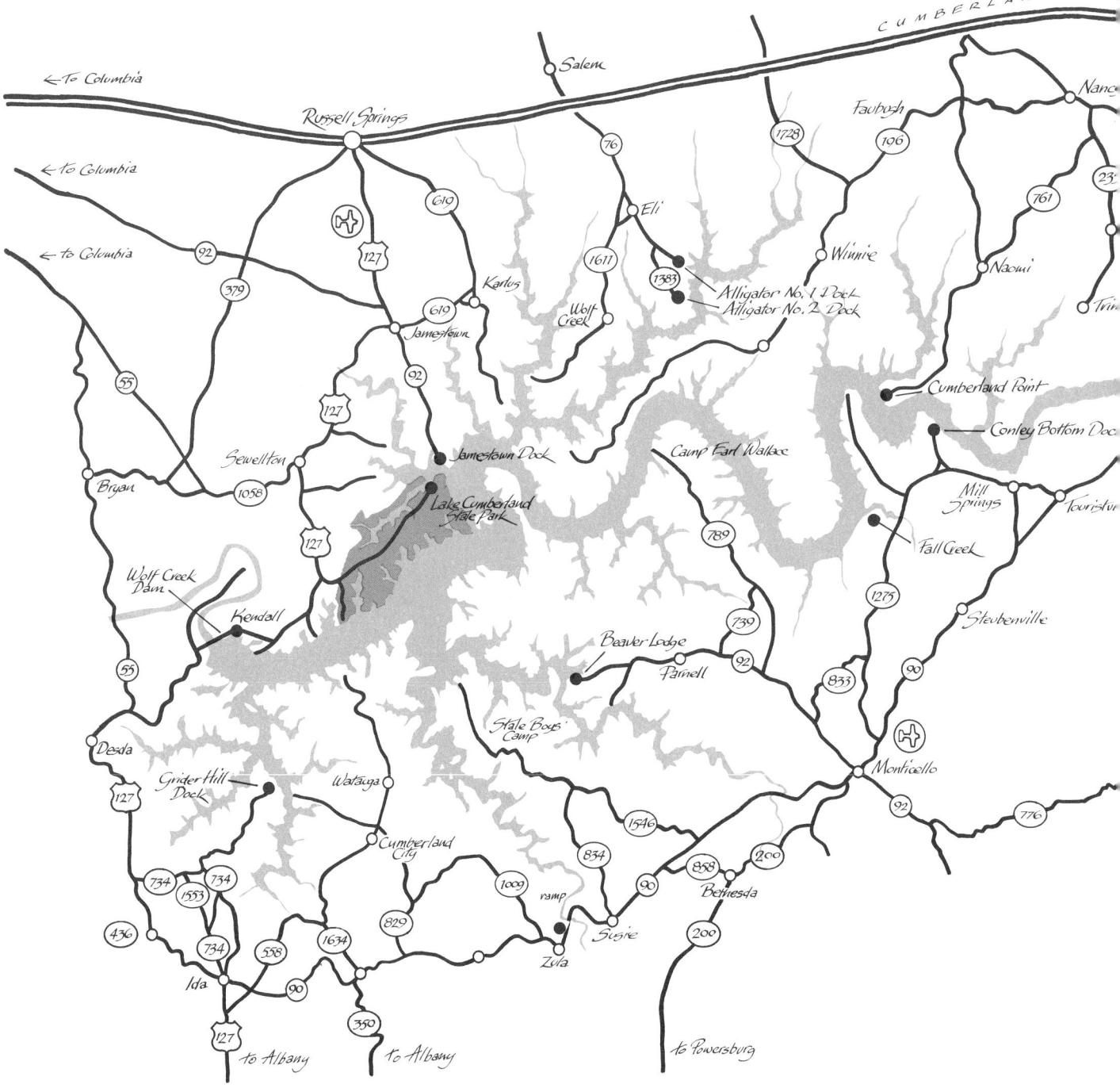

to London
and I·75 →

80

Somerset

Woodmont

80

769

192

Grade

Dykes

Fishing
Creek

to I·75 →

Ford Dock

Elihu

Alcalde

Meece

Mt. Victory

Bee Rock ramp

192

1247

Buck
Creek

Waitsboro
Ferry

Haynes

90

Burnside
Marina

Cave Creek

Rockcastle
Dock

General
Burnside
State Park

Frazer

Omega

Laurel Dock

Quinton

27

Beaver Creek
Game Refuge

Sawyer
ramp

to I·75

Kidder

Echo
Point

Sawyer

896

Delta

Gregory

Cumberland
Falls State Park

90

90

Parkers
Lake

27

1035

Wiborg

Alum Ford
ramp

Yahoo
Falls

700

to Whitely City

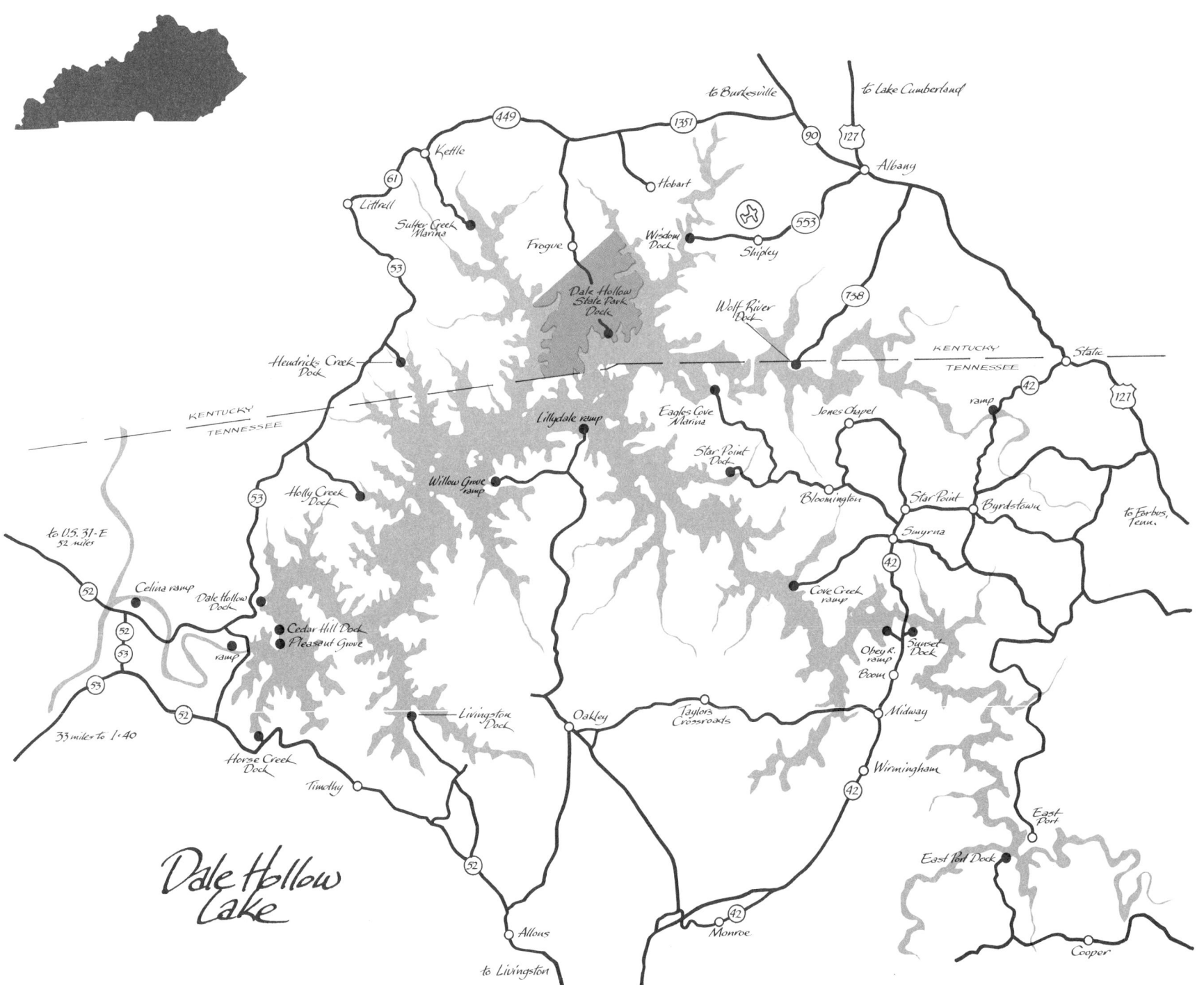

to Burkesville
to Lake Cumberland

449
1351
90
127
Albany

Kettle

61
Littrell

Hobart

Sulfer Creek Marina
Frogue
Wisdom Dock
Shipley
553

53

Dale Hollow State Park Dock
Wolf River Dock

738

KENTUCKY
Hendricks Creek Dock
TENNESSEE
Static

KENTUCKY
TENNESSEE

Eagles Cove Marina
Jones Chapel
ramp
42
127

Lillydale ramp

53
Holly Creek Dock
Willow Grove ramp
Star Point Dock
Bloomington
Star Point
Byrdstown
to Forbus, Tenn.

to U.S. 31-E
52 miles

52
Celina ramp
Dale Hollow Dock

Smyrna
42

52
53
ramp
Cedar Hill Dock
Pleasant Grove

Cove Creek ramp
Obey R. ramp
Sunset Dock

53
Boom
Midway

33 miles to I-40

52
Livingston Dock
Oakley
Taylors Crossroads

Horse Creek Dock
Timothy

Wirminingham
42

East Port

Dale Hollow Lake

52
East Port Dock

Allous
42
Monroe
Cooper

to Livingston

152

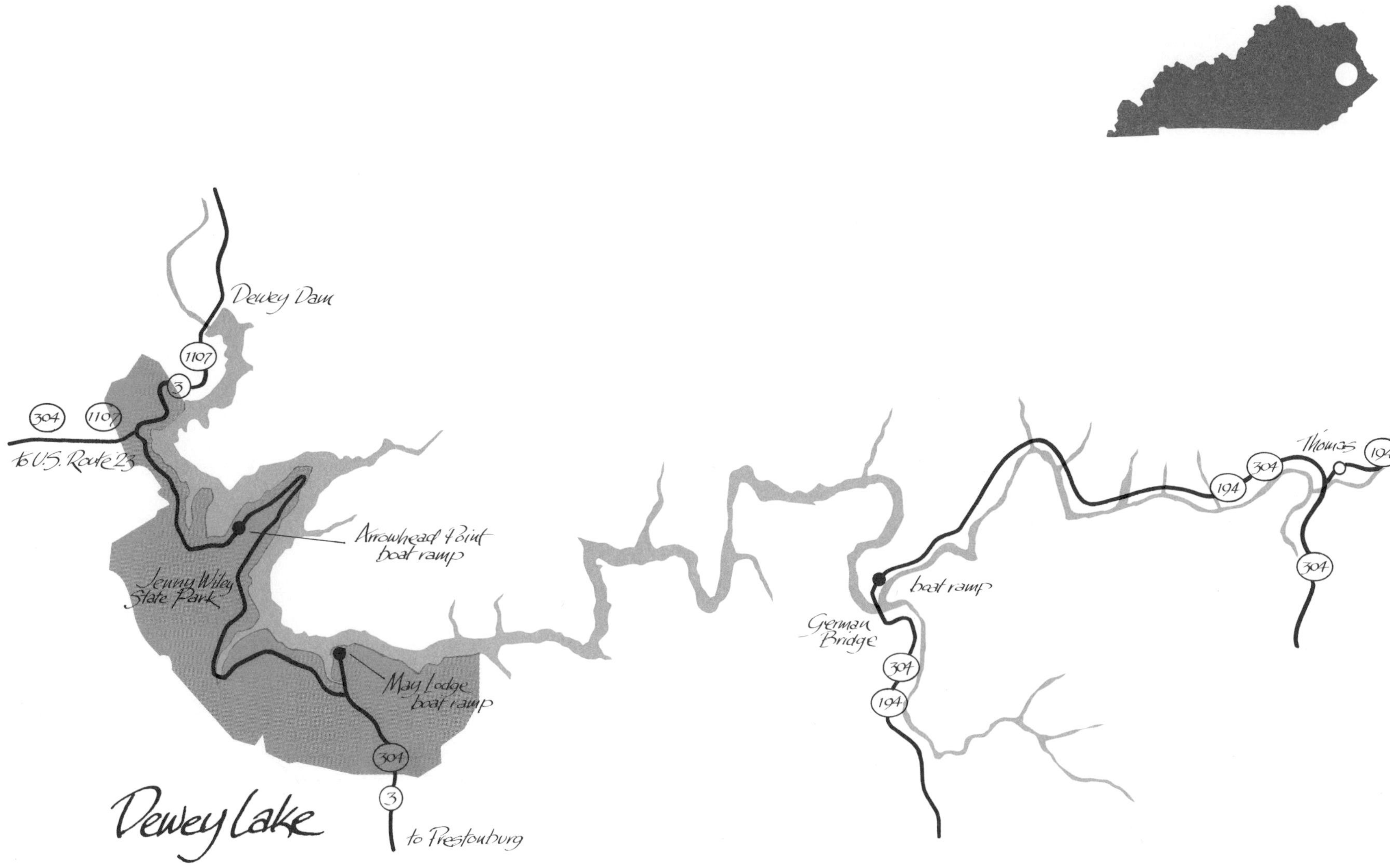

Dewey Dam

1107

3

304 1107

to U.S. Route 23

Arrowhead Point
boat ramp

Jenny Wiley
State Park

May Lodge
boat ramp

304

3

Dewey Lake

to Prestonburg

German
Bridge

boat ramp

304

194

194 304

Thomas

194

194

304

304

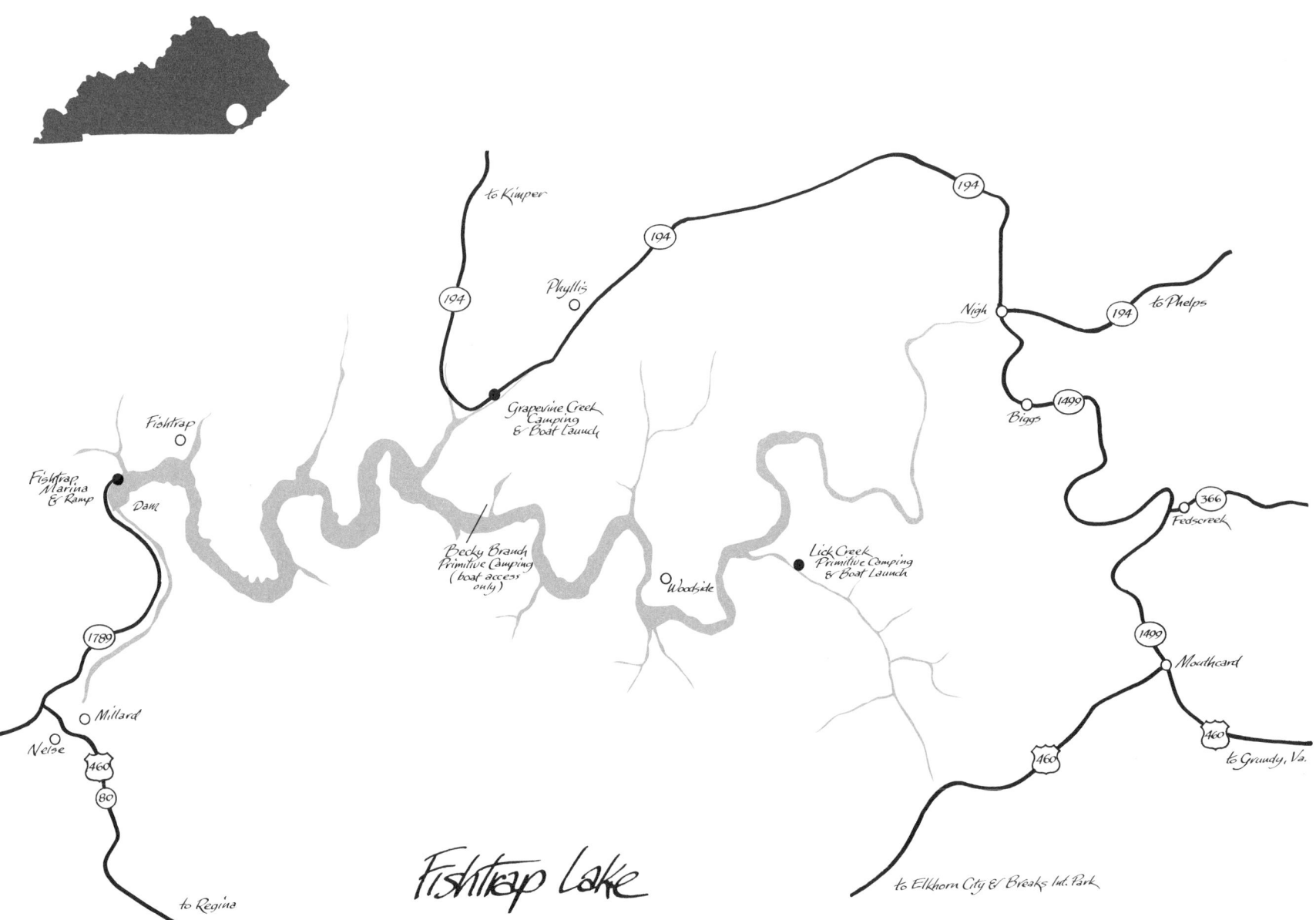

to Kimper

194

194

Phyllis

194

Nigh

194 to Phelps

1499

Biggs

Fishtrap

Grapevine Creek
Camping
& Boat Launch

Fishtrap
Marina
& Ramp

Dam

366

Fedscreek

Becky Branch
Primitive Camping
(boat access
only)

Woodside

Lick Creek
Primitive Camping
& Boat Launch

1789

1499

Mouthcard

Millard

Nelse

460

460

80

460

to Grundy, Va.

Fishtrap Lake

to Elkhorn City & Breaks Ind. Park

to Regina

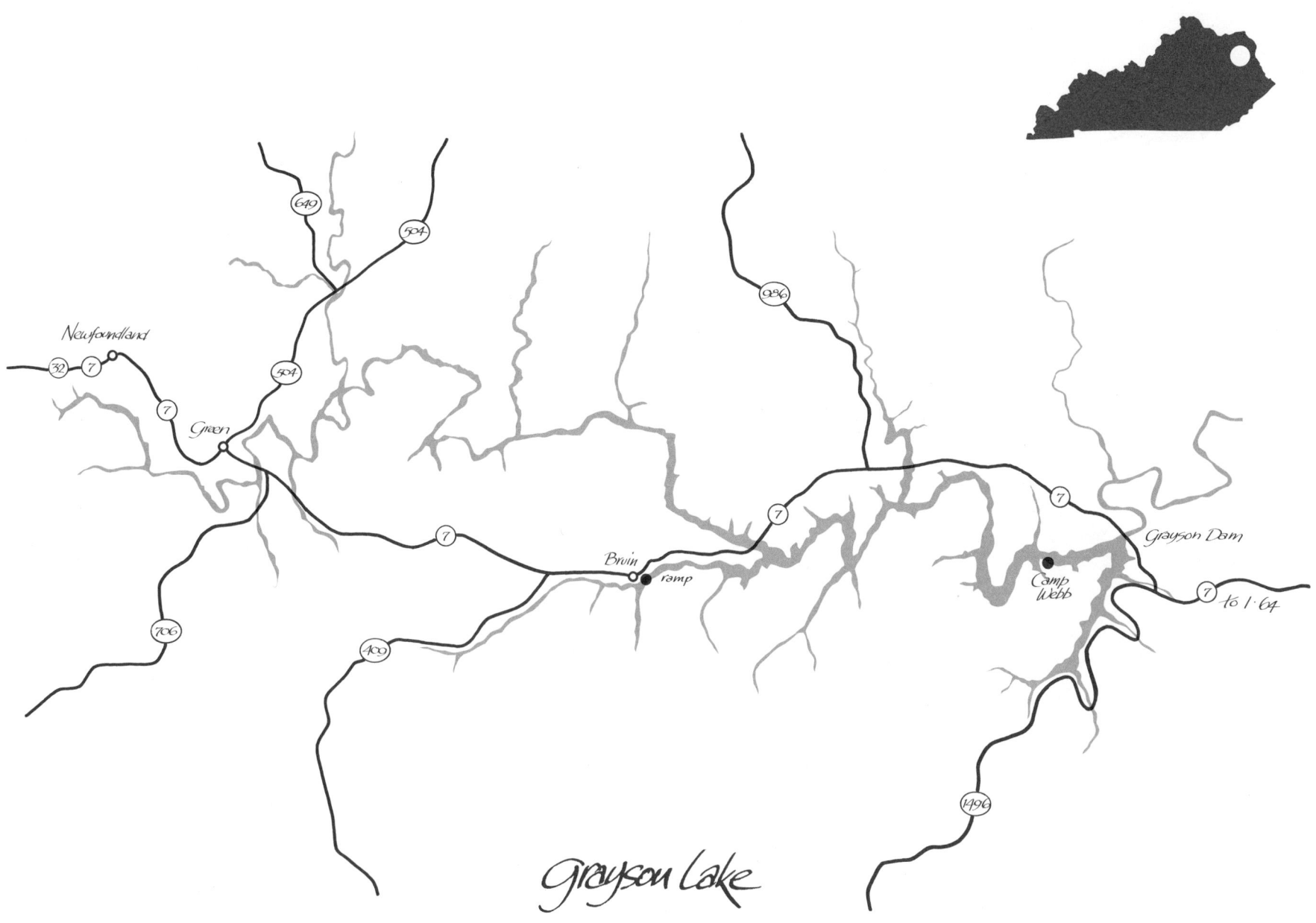

Newfoundland

Green

Bruin ramp

Camp Webb

Grayson Dam

to I-64

graysou Lake

649
504
504
936
32
7
7
7
7
7
7
706
400
1496

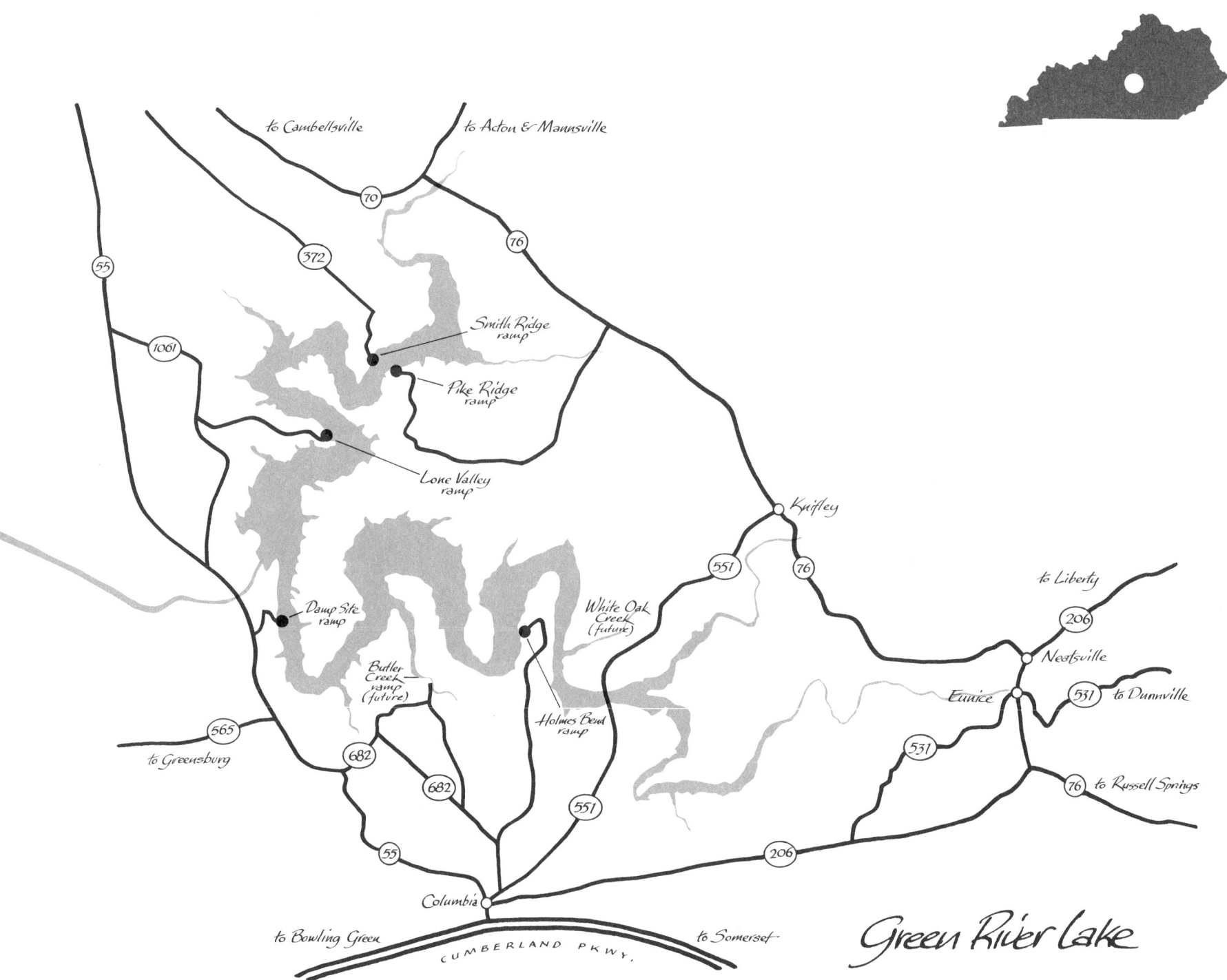

to Cambellsville
to Acton & Mannsville
70
76
55
372
1061
Smith Ridge ramp
Pike Ridge ramp
Lone Valley ramp
Knifley
551
76
to Liberty
206
Dam Site ramp
White Oak Creek (future)
Neatsville
Butler Creek ramp (future)
Eunice
531
to Dunnville
565
Holmes Bend ramp
to Greensburg
682
682
531
76
to Russell Springs
55
551
206
Columbia
to Bowling Green
CUMBERLAND PKWY.
to Somerset
Green River Lake

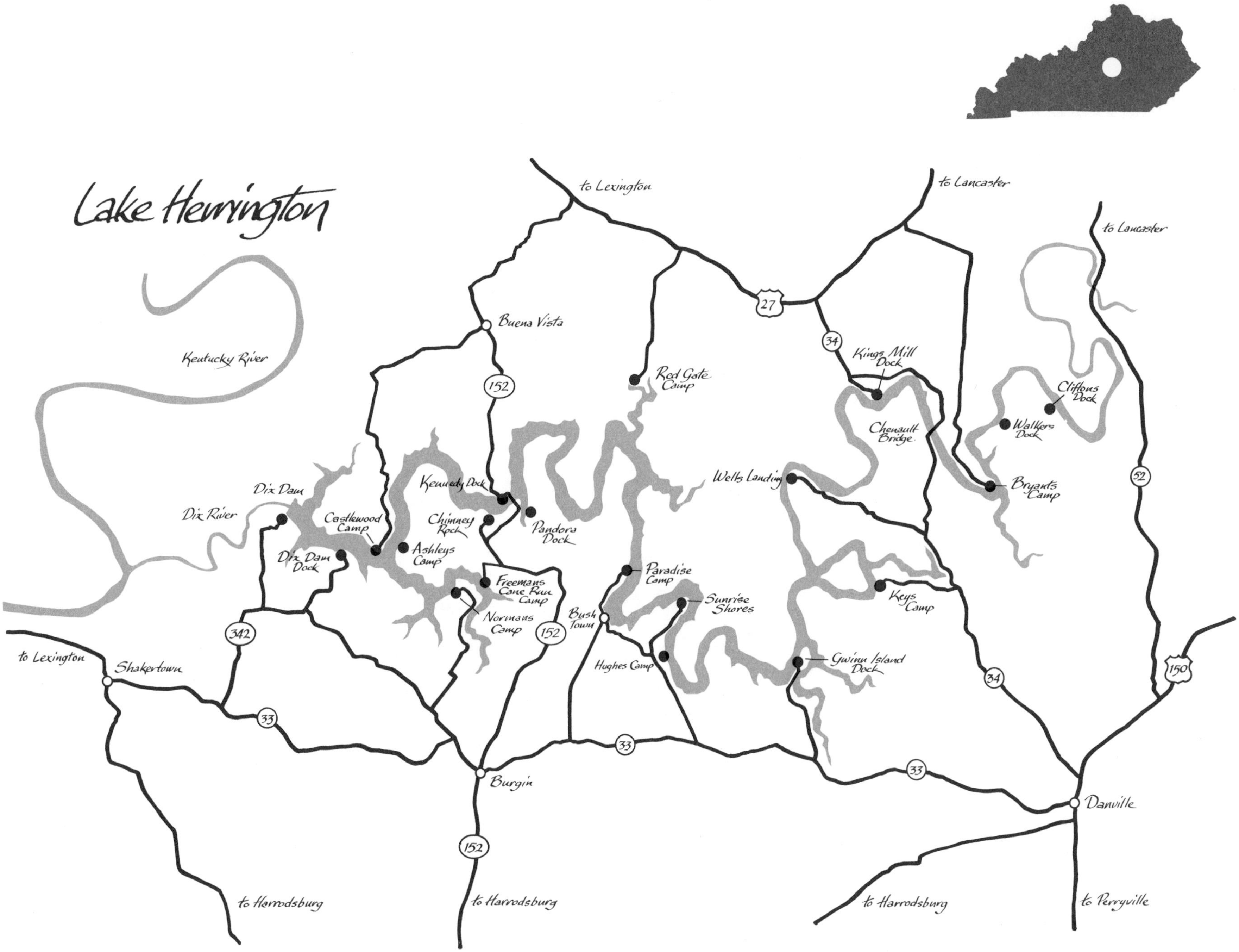

Lake Herrington

Kentucky River

Dix Dam

Dix River

Dix Dam

Castlewood Camp

Dix Dam Dock

Ashleys Camp

Chimney Rock

Kennedy Dock

Pandora Dock

Freemans Cane Run Camp

Normans Camp

Bush Town

Buena Vista

Red Gate Camp

to Lexington

to Lancaster

to Lancaster

Kings Mill Dock

Chenault Bridge

Cliftons Dock

Walkers Dock

Bryants Camp

Wells Landing

Paradise Camp

Sunrise Shores

Hughes Camp

Keys Camp

Gwinn Island Dock

Shakertown

to Lexington

Burgin

Danville

to Harrodsburg

to Harrodsburg

to Harrodsburg

to Perryville

27

34

52

152

342

152

33

33

152

33

34

150

Kentucky Lake &
Barkley Lake

to Princeton & 139
To 139
To Cadiz & 139

Little River

Lake Barkley State Park

Hurricane Creek
Rivers End

Western Kentucky Pkwy.

Eddy Cr. Port
Dryden's Cr.
Cannon Spring
Rock Castle
Port Pryer Point

Devil's Elbow
Calhoun Hill

Eddyville

ramp
ramp
ramp
ramp
ramp

Kuttawa Harbor
ramp
ramp

LAND   BETWEEN   THE   LAKES

Poplar Creek
Leisure Cruise Marina
Buzzard Rock

Boyd's Landing
ramp

453

ramp

Eureka
Barkley Dam
ramp

Cedar Point Res.
Kenlake State Park

Cumberland River
Dam Site
ramp

Lake City

Kentucky Dam Boat Basin

ramps

Kentucky Dam

Tennessee River

Kentucky Dam Marina

Port Ken-Bar
Grand Rivers
ramp

Moors Resort
ramp

ramp
King Creek
Big Bear
Millers Res.
Malcom Creek

Bee Spring Lodge
Will Vera Village
Spot in the Sun
Cozy Cove
Hickory Hill
962
Shawnee Bay

Town & Country Resort
Gordon's
ramp

Sportsmans Lodge

Cedar Knobs Resort

Pirates Cove
ramp

Hico
1346

Fairdealing
136A

ramp

Briensburg

Purchase Parkway, S.W.
to Mayfield

to 139

to Cadiz

To 79 & Clarksville, Tenn.

164

139

120

79

164

Linton

Bumpus Mills

Lick Creek ramp

Tobacco Port

ramp

KENTUCKY

TENNESSEE

Saline Creek

Bumpus Mills Marina

ramp

ramp

Dover

Dover ramp

Hickman Creek ramp

ramp

ramp

49

R E C R E A T I O N   A R E A

79

ramp

ramp

KENTUCKY

TENNESSEE

Paradise Dock

Little Oaks

781 Boat Dock

Standing Rock Creek Dock

Lynnhurst Resort

ramp

ramp

ramp

Hamlin

ramp

732

Irwin Cobb Res.

ramp

ramp

ramp

ramp

Lakeview Cottages

Cypress Springs Resort

ramp

ramp

ramp

ramp

Cypress Bay Resort

Shamrod Resort

ramp

Riverdale Cott.

Paris Landing Harbor

ramp

732

ramp

ramp

444

Wildcat Creek Dock

Blood River Dock

121

(Tennessee 119)

ramp

ramp

280

New Concord

ramp

79 Hide-a-Way

Oak Haven Lodge

ramp

Pine Point Dock

ramp

ramp

732

Pottertown

Buchanaus Dock

121

KENTUCKY

TENNESSEE

79

to Murray

to Murray

to Paris, Tenn.

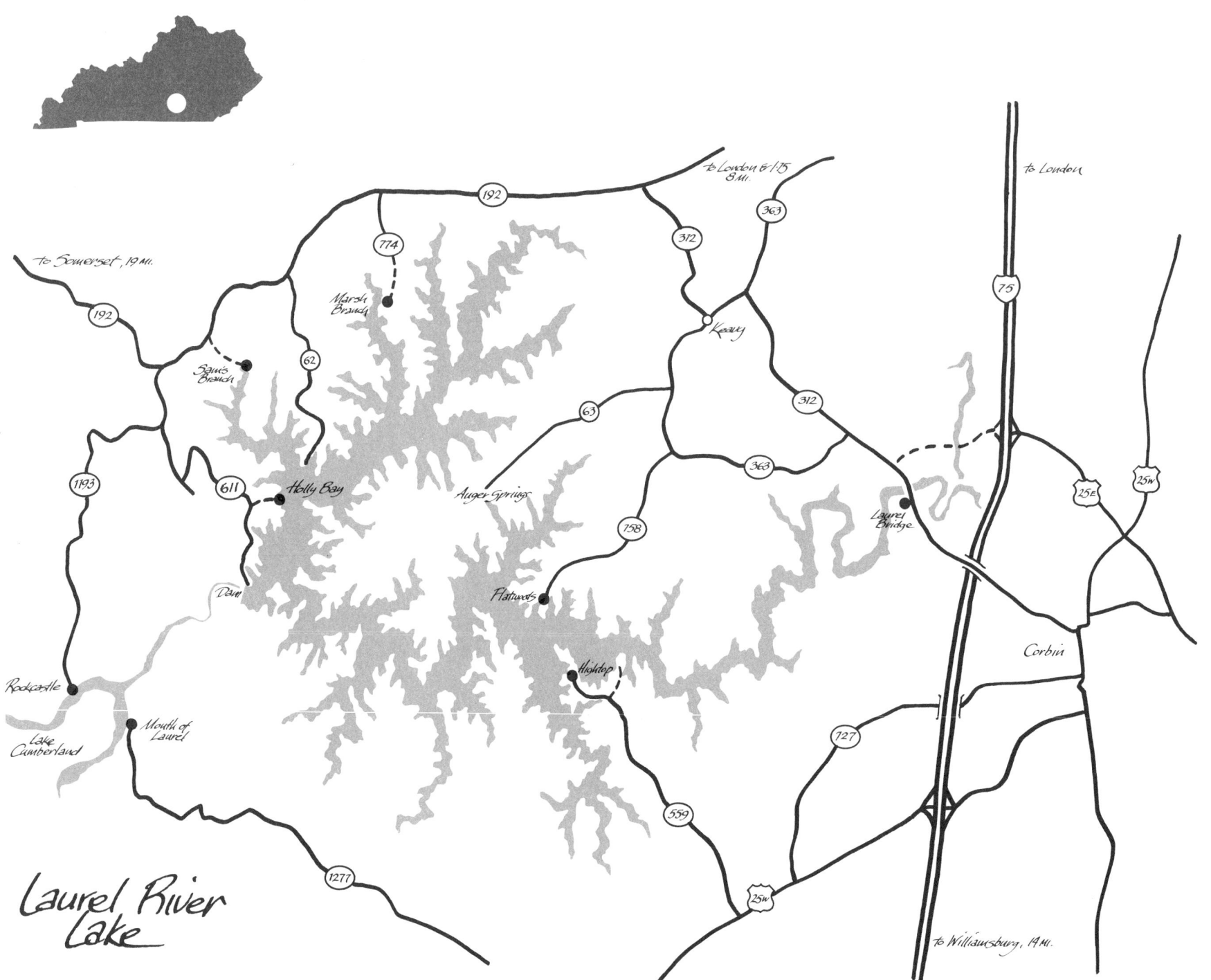

to London & I 75
8 MI.

192

to London

363

774

312

75

to Somerset, 19 MI.

192

Marsh
Branch

62

Keavy

192

Sam's
Branch

63

312

611

Holly Bay

363

Auger Springs

Laurel
Bridge

25E

25W

1193

158

Dam

Flatwoods

Corbin

Rockcastle

Hightop

Mouth of
Laurel

Lake
Cumberland

127

559

1277

25W

Laurel River
Lake

to Williamsburg, 19 MI.

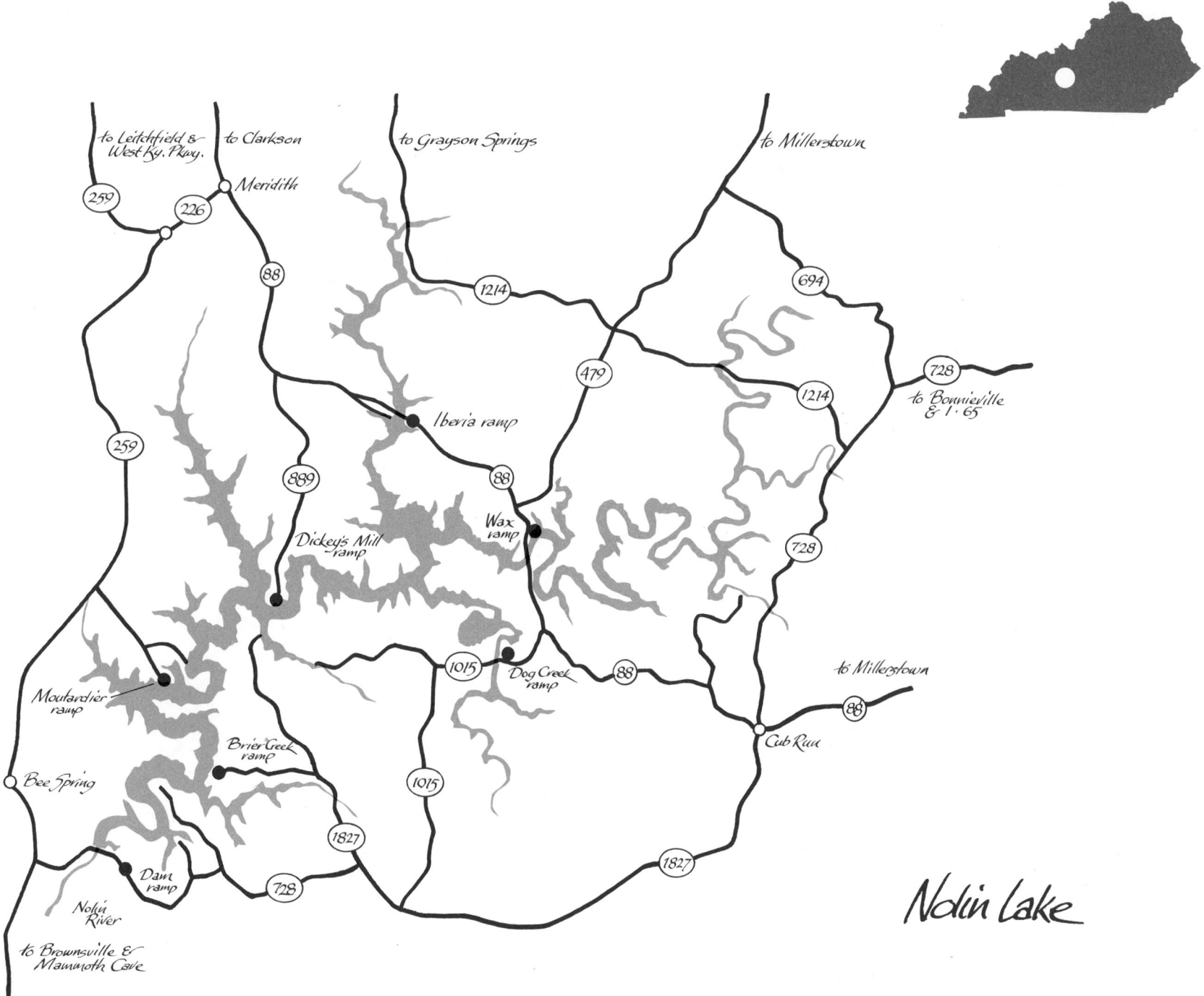

to Leitchfield &
West Ky. Pkwy.

to Clarkson

to Grayson Springs

to Millerstown

259

226

Meridith

88

1214

694

259

889

479

728

to Bonnieville
& I-65

Iberia ramp

88

259

Dickey's Mill
ramp

Wax
ramp

1214

1015

Dog Creek
ramp

728

Moutardier
ramp

Brier Creek
ramp

88

to Millerstown

Bee Spring

1015

Cub Run

88

1827

Dam
ramp

728

1827

Nolin
River

Nolin Lake

to Brownsville &
Mammoth Cave

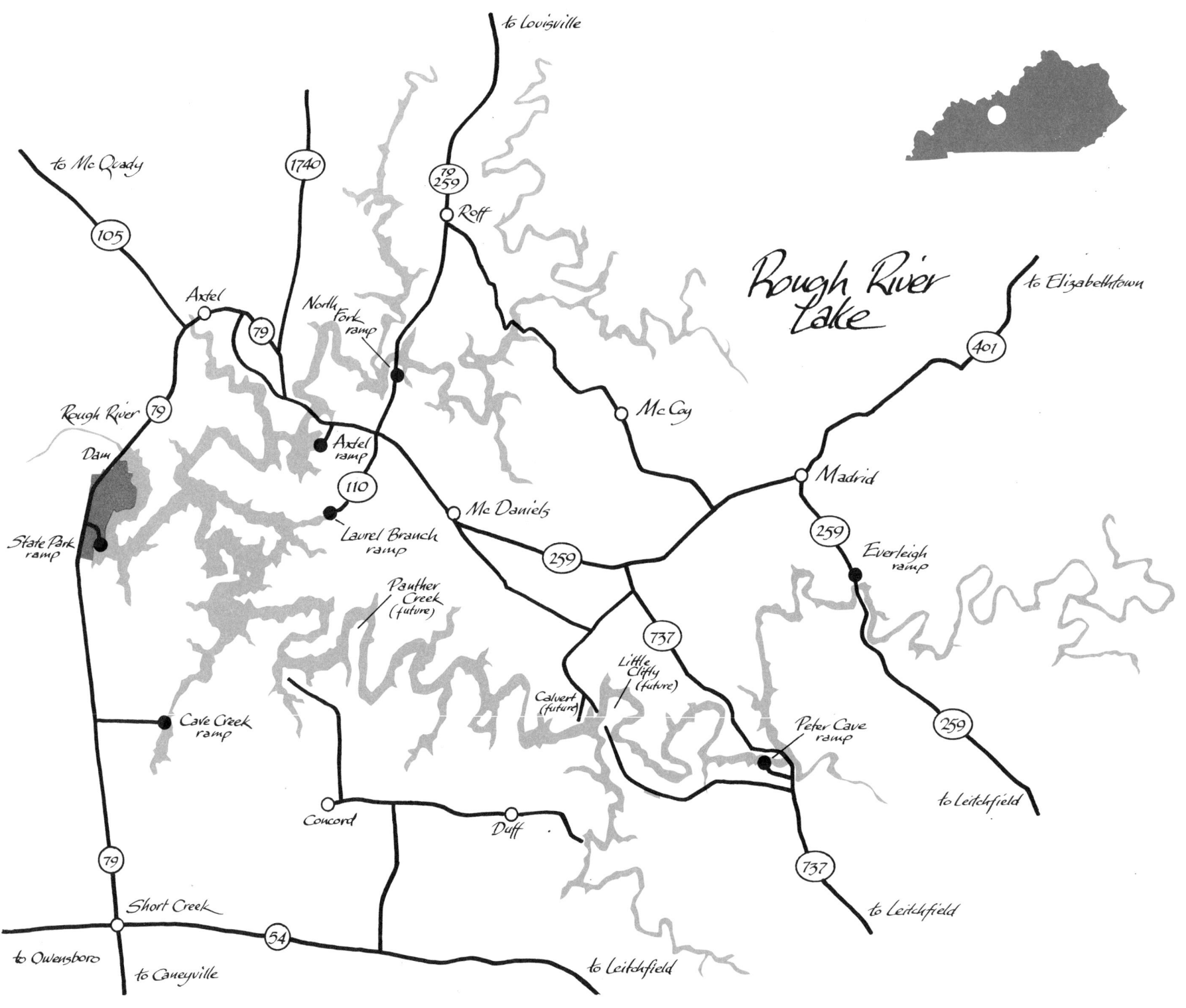

to Louisville

to McQuady

(1740)

(105)

(79/259)

Roff

Rough River
Lake

to Elizabethtown

(401)

Axtel

(79)

North Fork
ramp

McCoy

Rough River

(79)

Dam

Axtel
ramp

(110)

McDaniels

Madrid

(259)

Laurel Branch
ramp

(259)

Everleigh
ramp

State Park
ramp

Panther
Creek
(future)

(259)

(737)

Little
Cliffy
(future)

Calvert
(future)

Cave Creek
ramp

Peter Cave
ramp

(259)

to Leitchfield

Concord

Duff

(737)

(79)

Short Creek

to Leitchfield

(54)

to Owensboro

to Caneyville

to Leitchfield

Kentucky Record Catches

As of June, 1978, the following record fish were recorded fishes taken from Kentucky waters by rod and reel:

Name of Fish	Caught By	Date	Location	Weight
Alligator Gar *(Open)*				
Bluegill	W. S. Wolley, Campbellsville, Ky.	5/30/55	Buchanon Pond, Taylor Co., Ky.	3 lbs., 6 oz.
Blue Catfish	J. E. Copeland, Benton, Ky.	8/21/70	Tennessee River Below Ky. Dam	100 lbs.
Buffalo	P. Childers, Frankfort, Ky.	7/69	Kentucky River	32 lbs.
Bullhead Catfish	Phillip A. Huffer, Bowling Green	6/24/76	Farm Pond	4 lbs., 6 oz.
Bowfin	Steve A. Vantreese, Paducah, Ky.	6/24/77	Priester Lake, McCracken Co.	7 lbs., 10 oz.
Carp	Ricky Vance, Paris, Ky.	3/13/71	South Fork Licking River	54 lbs., 14 oz.
Channel Catfish	Fred Cornett, Lexington, Ky.	4/7/73	Beaver Lake, Anderson Co., Ky.	15 lbs., 6 oz.
Chain Pickerel	Steve Wunderle, Caterville, Ill.	10/19/74	Clear Lake, Ballard Co.	3 lbs., 2½ oz.
Flathead Catfish	Esker Carroll	6/56	Green River	97 lbs.
Freshwater Drum	Ernest E. Morgan, Henderson, Ky.	4/25/76	Tennessee River	37 lbs.
Gar—Long nosed, Short nosed, Spotted	Kelsie Travis, Jr. Paducah, Ky.	8/8/56	Ohio River	40 lbs.
Kentucky Bass	A. E. Sellers, Louisville, Ky.	6/70	Nelson Co., Ky.	7 lbs., 10 oz.
Largemouth Bass	Delbert Grizzle, Flatwoods, Ky.	8/3/66	Greenbo Lake, Greenup Co., Ky.	13 lbs., 8 oz.
Muskellunge	Portor Hash	3/6/78	Dale Hollow	43 lbs.
Rainbow Trout	Jim Mattingly, Somerset, Ky.	9/10/72	Cumberland River below Wolfe Creek Dam	14 lbs., 6 oz.
Rock Bass	H. S. White, Cadiz, Ky.	5/26/75	Casey Creek, Trigg Co.	1 lb., 10. oz.
Rockfish	James Fugate, Burlington & Ronald Warner, Burgin, Ky.	7/19/70	Herrington Lake	44 lbs., 4 oz.
Sturgeon	Barney Frazier, Corbin, Ky.	10/3/54	Lake Cumberland	36 lbs., 8 oz.
Smallmouth Bass (WORLD RECORD)	David L. Hayes Leitchfield, Ky.	7/11/55	Dale Hollow Lake	11 lbs., 15 oz.
Sauger	Wm. H. Price, Murfreesboro, Tenn.	7/26/72	Kentucky Lake	6 lbs., 1 oz.
Shellcracker	R. C. Masters, Louisville, Ky.	5/30/64		2 lbs., 5 oz.
Spoonbill	Ralph Pierce, Parksville, Ky.	3/6/57	Lake Cumberland	72 lbs.
Walleye	Abe Black, Shaker Heights, O.	10/1/58	Lake Cumberland	21 lbs., 8 oz.
Warmouth	Robt. Hayes, Hustonville, Ky.	4/28/74	Dix River	1 lb.
White Croppie Black Croppie	David C. Crowe Madisonville, Ky.	4/16/69	Lake Pewee	4 lbs., 3 oz.
White Bass	Tie Between: Lorne Eli, Dawson Springs & B.B. Hardin, Mt. Eden, Ky.	7/11/43 6/3/57	Kentucky Lake Lake Herrington	5 lbs.
Yellow Bass *(Open)*				

Kentucky Bass Association

Persons interested in the association might contact Jim Crowell, 1020 Fincastle Road, Lexington, 40582, or Richard Young, Alexandria, 41001.
Kentucky B.A.S.S. Federation
For information contact Burley Stevens, Jr.
2720 Jackson St., Ashland, 41101.
The member clubs of K.B.A. and K.B.F. follow:

Eastern Section

Ashland Oil Employees
Bass Club
% Dick Walters
Catlettsburg, Ky. 41101

Berea Bass Busters
% Robert G. Cotter
Berea, Kentucky 40403

Bluegrass Christian Bass Assoc.
% Steve Martin
Nicholasville, Kentucky 40356

Central Kentucky Bass Club
% Jim Crowell
Lexington, Kentucky 40505

Cumberland Valley Bassmasters
% Jerry Howard
London, Kentucky 40741

Happy Hookers
% Larry Stamper
Grayson, Ky. 41143

Kay-y Bass Club
% Carl Anderson
Danville, Kentucky 40422

National Mines Bassmasters
% Chris Erwin
Ashland, Ky. 41101

Rockcastle County Bass Club
% Ronnie McClure
Mt. Vernon, Kentucky 40456

Rockwell Bass Club
% Jimmy Sparks
Lexington, Kentucky 40502

Salt Lick Anglers of Bass
% Jack Frizzell
Salt Lick, Ky. 40371

Tackle Buster Bass Club
% Ted Crowell
Lawrenceburg, Kentucky 40342

Wayne County Bass Club
% Rick Burnett
Monticello, Kentucky 42633

Woodford County Bass Club
% Gordon Edington
Lawrenceburg, Kentucky 40342

Bourbon County Bass Club
% James T. Berry
Paris, Kentucky 40361

Bass Busters of Northern Ky.
% Gerald Shell
Covington, Kentucky 41015

Capital City Bass Club
% Frank Manns
Frankfort, Kentucky 40601

Tri-County Bass Club
Corbin, Kentucky

Richmond Bass Club
% David R. Lawson
Richmond, Kentucky 40475

Herrington Lake Bass Club
% Bobby Sparks
Lexington, Kentucky 40505

Lake Cumberland Bass Club
% Jim Rutherford
Ferguson, Kentucky 42533

Limestone Bassmasters
% Ed Curtis
Maysville, Kentucky 41056

Montgomery County Bass Club
% Doug Parkhurst
Mt. Sterling, Kentucky 40353

Northern Ky. Bass Anglers
% Richard Young
Alexnadria, Kentucky 41001

Rebel Bass Club of Nicholasville
% Cecil Dillard
Wilmore, Kentucky 40390

Red River Gorge Bass Club
% Mike Tipton
Mt. Sterling, Kentucky 40353

Golden Rod Bassmasters
% Dr. Jim Rich
Covington, Kentucky 41015

Frankfort Bassmasters
Frankfort, Kentucky 40601

Dirty Dozen Bass Club
% Ace Forney
Lexington, Kentucky 40503

Thoroughbred Bass Club
% Austin Carter, Jr.
Lexington, Kentucky 40503

Somerset Bass Club
% Clay Spears
Somerset, Kentucky

Ashland Oil Bass Club
% Ronald L. Sublett
Ashland, Kentucky 41101

Salt Lick Anglers of Bass
% Elmer Klaber
Owingsville, Kentucky 40360

Pinnacle-View Bass Club
% C.C. Mickey
Middlesboro, Kentucky 40965

Pike County Bass Anglers
% Danny L. Akers
Pikeville, Kentucky 41501

National Mine Bassmasters
% Bernie W. Moore
Ashland, Kentucky 41101

Louisa Bassmasters
% Mike Sullivan
Louisa, Kentucky

Hillbilly Bassmasters
% James T. Riffe
Ashland, Kentucky 41101

Highland Basscasters
% Bill Salyer
Paintsville, Kentucky 41240

Grayson Lunker Hunters
% Joe M. Brammell
Grayson, Kentucky 41143

Corbin Bassmasters
% Mike Harbin
Corbin, Kentucky 40701

Central Section

Castaway Bass Club
% Ray Mitchell
Louisville, Kentucky 40229

Derby City Bassmasters
% Bill Lyninger
Louisville, Kentucky 40228

Derbytown Lunker Hunters B.C.
% Jerry McGee
Louisville, Kentucky 40291

Dixie Bassmasters
% Stanley Sharp
Louisville, Kentucky 40216

East End Bass Club
% Phil Bettis

Louisville, Kentucky 40212

Green River Bassmasters
% Michael Walker
Campbellsville, Kentucky 42718

Jefferson County Bassmasters
% Ludy Gaunt
Pleasure Ridge Park, Kentucky 40258

Kentuckiana Bass Busters
% Miles Townsend
Clarksville, Ind. 47130

Louisville Lunker Hunters
% Mike Sipes
Louisville, Kentucky 40206

Louisville Line Bass Club
% George C. Thompson
Louisville, Kentucky 40218

Bass Hunters of Louisville, Inc.
% Shakey Summers
Louisville, Kentucky 40272

Pleasure Valley Bass Club
% Arls E. Barton
Pleasure Ridge, Kentucky 40258

Radcliff Bassmasters
% Mike Marcum
Elizabethtown, Kentucky 42701

River City Bass Club
% Sonny Wilson
Louisville, Kentucky 40216

Shelby County Bassmasters
% Harold Nichols
Shelbyville, Kentucky 40065

Southern Bassmasters of Ky.
% Roger Fegett
Scottsville, Ky. 42164

Three Rivers Bassmasters
% Bill Poppet
Carollton, Kentucky 41008

Louisville Bassmasters
% Mark Millner
Louisville, Kentucky 40223

Willow Lake Bass Club
% Leo Ziegler
Louisville, Kentucky 40204

Barren Bassmasters
% James Denton
Glasgow, Kentucky 42141

Bucketmouth Brigade
% Dave Kik
Prospect, Kentucky 40059

Bluegrass Bass Busters
% S.W. Greaves
Louisville, Kentucky 40214

Southern Bassmasters of Ky.
% Vernon Tabor, Jr.
Scottsville, Kentucky 42164

Cedar Creek Bass Anglers
% Ronnie Brown
Louisville, Kentucky 40229

Bass Bandits Bassmasters
% E.L. Jackson
Mt. Washington, Kentucky 40047

Bardstown Bassmasters
% Jim B. Bunce
Bardstown, Kentucky 40004

Bassmasters LTD
% Dawson Cook
Louisville, Kentucky 40219

Bowling Green Bass Club
% Halious Isbell
Bowling Green, Kentucky 42101

Western Section

Madisonville Anglers Club
% Larry Sisk
Madisonville, Kentucky 42431

Producing Bassmasters
% Joe Duffy
Bowling Green, Kentucky 42101

Poor Boys Bassmasters of FTCA
% Neil Hains
Oak Grove, Kentucky 42262

Hoptown Basscasters Inc.
% H. Sol Fritz
Hopkinsville, Kentucky 42240

FMC Boombusters
% Don Crousore
Smith Grove, Kentucky 42171

Allen County Bass Club
% Notley Cummings
Scottsville, Kentucky 42164

Barkley Lake Bass Club
Princeton, Kentucky 42445

Cadiz Bass Club
% Harold Knight
Cadiz, Kentucky 42211

Franklin Simpson Bass Club
% Billy Reid
Franklin, Kentucky 42134

Logan County Bass Club
% Bobby Taylor
Russellville, Kentucky 42276

Madisonville Bass Club
% Mickey DeMoss
Hanson, Kentucky 42413

Mayfield Bass Club
% Joe Kimbel
Mayfield, Kentucky 32066

Murray Bass Club
% Jerry McConnell
Murray, Kentucky 42071

Owensboro Bass Club
% Willis Snyder
Owensboro, Kentucky 42301

Warren County Bass Club
% Clifton Smith
Bowling Green, Kentucky 42101

Hancock County Bassmasters
% James L. Grantland
Hawesville, Kentucky 42348

Paducah Bass Club
% Greg Nichols
Paducah, Kentucky 42001

Henderson Bass Club
% William W. Hobson
Henderson, Kentucky 42420

Big M. Bass Club
% Ray Price Big
Greenville, Kentucky 43245

Davis County Bass Club
% Joe McKay
Owensboro, Kentucky 42301

Ken Bar Bass Club
% Jim Sermersheim
Evansville, Ind. 47711

Louisville Bass Club Association

For information contact Jim Barnes, a member of the Derbytown Lunker Hunters, and 1978 president of the association. Reach him at 1314 Lyndon Lane, Louisville, Ky. 40222.

Acknowledgements

My sincerest thanks to Hope Carleton, knowledgeable director of public relations for the Kentucky Department of Fish and Wildlife Resources. Hope checked my facts and fancies all the way.

Also my thanks to Vic Dunaway, his *Complete Book of Baits, Rigs, and Tackle,* which I highly recommend, and the *Florida Sportsman.*

And to these outdoor authorities, whose books are tops in their fields and have afforded me many wonderful hours of reading:

Ray P. Holland, *Bird Dogs.* A. S. Barnes, publisher.

Lee Wulff, *The Sportsman's Companion.* Harper & Row, publisher.

H. G. Tapply, *The Sportsman's Notebook.* Holt, Rinehart & Winston, publisher.

Frank Woolner, *Grouse and Grouse Hunting.* Crown Publishers, publisher.

Shirley E. Woods Jr., *Gunning for Upland Game Birds and Wildfowl.* Winchester Press, publisher.

Vlad Evanoff, *Modern Fishing Tackle.* A. S. Barnes, publisher.

William M. Clay, *The Fishes of Kentucky.* Kentucky Department of Fish and Wildlife Resources, publisher.

Ted Trueblood, *Hunting Treasury.* David McKay Co., New York.

Photo Credits

Page	8.	Karl Maslowski
Page	11.	Gean Baron
Page	13.	CJ&T staff photo
Page	16.	Earl Ruby
Page	17.	Left, David Sutherland
		Right, Charles Darneal
Page	19.	Joe Tom Erwin
Page	21.	Joe Tom Erwin
Page	23.	Joe Tom Erwin
Page	28.	Top left, Earl Ruby
		Top right, Cort Best
Page	34.	Tom V. Miller, Jr.
Page	35.	Earl Ruby
Page	36.	Earl Ruby
Page	37.	Earl Ruby
Page	39.	W. Klosterman
Page	40.	Left, Earl Ruby
		Right, Earl Ruby
		Top right, Jim Strader
Page	41.	State of Kentucky
Page	44.	Cort Best
Page	47.	Left, Bryce Combs
		Right, Earl Ruby
Page	51.	Billy Davis
Page	53.	Top, Buck Taylor
		Bottom, James N. Keen
Page	54.	Bottom, James N. Keen
Page	60.	Karl Maslowski
Page	65.	State of Kentucky
Page	68.	Tennessee Valley Authority
Page	75.	Top, Joe Tom Erwin
		Bottom, James N. Keen
Pages 80-81.		Tom Patterson
Page	84.	Left, James N. Keen
		Right, James Schwartz
Page	95.	Top, George Bailey
		Bottom, Earl Ruby
Page	99.	Gean Baron
Page	112	Norman Trigg
Page	131.	Billy Davis
Page	132.	Top, Cort Best
		Bottom, Joe Tom Erwin
Page	151.	Top, State of Kentucky
		Bottom, Joe Tom Erwin

Appreciation

With special thanks to the following individuals and organizations for allowing their photographs to be used as reference for certain illustrations:

Dr. E. R. Degginger, Convent, N.J.
Douglas Faulkner, Summit, N.J.
Farrell Grehan, New York, N.Y.
George H. Harrison, Hubertus, Wisc.
Ronald Klataske, Manhattan, Kansas
Leonard Lee Rue, III, Blairtown, N.J.
John Skene, W. Lafayette, Ind.
Robert Strindberg, FPSA, Weatogue, Conn.
Suzanne Troy, Northbridge, Australia
William J. Weber, Marshall, N.C.
Cornell University Press, Ithaca, N.Y.
J. B. Lippincott Company, New York, N.Y.